The Rise and Decline of the American Cut Nail Industry

Recent Titles in
Contributions in Economics and Economic History

The Organization of Arab Petroleum Exporting Countries:
History, Policies, and Prospects
Mary Ann Tétreault

Soviet Economy Today: With Guidelines for the Economic and Social Development of the USSR for 1981-1985 and for the Period Ending in 1990
Novosti Press Agency Publishing House, Moscow

The Era of the Joy Line: A Saga of Steamboating on Long Island Sound
Edwin L. Dunbaugh

The Role of Economic Advisers in Developing Countries
Lauchlin Currie

Perkins/Budd: Railway Statesmen of the Burlington
Richard C. Overton

The European Community and Latin America: A Case Study in Global Role Expansion
A. Glenn Mower, Jr.

Economics and Policymaking: The Tragic Illusion
Eugene J. Meehan

A Portrait Cast in Steel: Buckeye International and Columbus Ohio, 1881-1980
Mansel G. Blackford

The Strategic Petroleum Reserve: Planning, Implementation, and Analysis
David Leo Weimer

United States Oil Policy and Diplomacy: A Twentieth Century Overview
Edward W. Chester

The Emergence of Giant Enterprise, 1860-1914:
American Commercial Enterprise and Extractive Industries
David O. Whitten

The Marshall Plan Revisited: The European Recovery Program in Economic Perspective
Imanuel Wexler

The Rise and Decline of the American Cut Nail Industry

A Study of the Interrelationships of Technology, Business Organization, and Management Techniques

AMOS J. LOVEDAY, JR.

Contributions in Economics and Economic History, Number 53

GREENWOOD PRESS
Westport, Connecticut • London, England

Library of Congress Cataloging in Publication Data

Loveday, Amos J.
The rise and decline of the American cut nail industry.
(Contributions in economics and economic history,
ISSN 0084-9235 ; no. 53)
Bibliography: p.
Includes index.
1. Nail industry—United States—History. 1. Title.
II. Series.
HD9529.N323U64 1984 338.4'7621884'0973 83-5542
ISBN 0-313-23918-5 (lib. bdg.)

Library of Congress Catalog Card Number: 83-5542
ISBN: 0-313-23918-5
ISSN: 0084-9235

First published in 1983

Greenwood Press
A division of Congressional Information Service, Inc.
88 Post Road West
Westport, Connecticut 06881

Printed in the United States of America

10 9 8 7 6 5 4 3 2 1

Mary Jean, Amy, and "the Colonel"

Contents

Illustrations

Acknowledgments

I would like to express my gratitude to several people whose assistance has been invaluable. Mr. Jay Gaynor initially called my attention to the nail manufacturers in and around Wheeling and along with Mr. Don Hutslar and Mr. John Barsotti generously shared notes and nail specimens collected over the past few years.

I am especially indebted to Dr. John C. Burnham, Dr. Merritt Roe Smith, Dr. Mansel Blackford, and Dr. Julia Bonham for their encouragement, numerous suggestions, and excellent constructive criticism. Along with Mr. William G. Keener, Dr. Burnham directed my attention to business practices when the technology failed to offer an explanation of Wheeling's prominence.

I also wish to thank Mrs. Saundra Ball and Ms. Linda Nowalk, who typed several drafts of the manuscript, Mr. Bernie Stockwell, who helped prepare the illustrations, and Mr. Christopher S. Duckworth and Mr. Don F. Wittekind, who prepared the photographs.

Finally, I wish to express my gratitude to the Ohio Historical Society for its support during the two years the research and writing required, and especially the Wheeling-Pittsburgh Steel Corporation for allowing me to use the records of several firms that formed the present company.

Introduction

In the vaults of an important American corporation, Wheeling Steel, are carefully preserved a series of records of enterprises that were, in the nineteenth century, the ancestors of that company. These were major plants in the cut nail industry, and what remains of minutes of the boards of directors, account books, and other documents provides fresh and vivid glimpses into the dynamics of the interaction between technology and business. The story, filled in with the help of other sources, shows how historical forces operated through American inventors, entrepreneurs, and managers who tried to master circumstances.

The narrative focuses on the rise and fall of the cut nail industry, but it is a narrative with many ramifications. Nailmaking provides significant and instructive variations on the familiar themes of the shift from owner-mechanic to impersonal corporation and from skilled worker to production line help, and the ways in which technological change interacted with geography, economics, organizational skill, and leadership. But events in the history of the cut nail are of particular importance because they show what happened when a new technology confronted the social structures of an already established technology just as business structures were taking on a more contemporary form. These events raise questions as to the dynamics of obsolescence as well as innovation, particularly as they involved the business management practices that grew up to match the technology.

Both cut nail technology and associated business techniques reached their highest development in a small segment of the Upper Ohio Valley between Wheeling, West Virginia, and Steubenville, Ohio, and these firms became known among nail makers as the Wheeling industry.

The local setting affected the story, as it would any story. But the setting included also the national nail and iron industries. Within the national as well as the local setting, the Wheeling plants represented the ultimate development of the cut nail industry, and as a result the American nail industry can be understood by focusing on the plants of the Upper Ohio Valley. The local specifics reveal the historical factors at work and, in fact, by the second half of the century nail makers in other parts of the country were merely responding passively to events in Wheeling. Although comparatively small, nail manufacturing was important to the American economy throughout the nineteenth century. It consumed a significant portion of the output (up to 15 percent) of the iron industry and, particularly in the early part of the century, was symbolic of American mechanical genius.

Most contemporary observers and many later commentators viewed the industry largely in technological terms, focusing on the mechanical innovations that revolutionized nail manufacturing during the first third of the century. This story of a new manufacturing technology is a compelling one. The technology was completely American in origin, the product of late eighteenth- and early nineteenth-century New England inventors who were intent on mechanizing one of the most labor-intensive of the crafts. The link between this technology and new architectural styles and building techniques also illustrates the impact of advances in one area upon the course of development in other sectors of the economy.

As significant as the new technology was, it is not the intent of this study to dwell primarily upon its origin or refinement. To do so would add little to what is already known of the industry and the process of technological innovation in general. The purpose, rather, is to treat technology as one of several forces that combined to shape the course of development of the industry during the nineteenth century. Such an approach permits the examination of the complexities of growth and decline as well as innovation and obsolescence, themes central to the history of the process of industrialization. While there is no claim that the lessons learned from the nail industry can (or should) be generalized or uncritically transferred to other settings, the history of cut nail manufacturing confirms some and calls into question other observations that have been made about such widely recognized occurrences as vertical integration, cost accounting, and the rise of professional management.

Essentially, the history of nail manufacturing illustrates how technology and markets interacted in varying ways to shape the structure, organizational patterns, and management systems of an entire industry, as well as individual production units within that industry. During the first half of the nineteenth century, a large and expanding market that resulted from the country's extensive reliance on wood construction exerted considerable pressure on the industry to increase the volume of production while maintaining a price sufficiently low to ensure that nails could compete effectively with other methods of joining. The industry met this challenge during the first third of the century by introducing and perfecting machines that both increased volume and reduced costs through materials and labor savings.

As the machines were introduced, the industry underwent two very basic changes. First, machines that functioned best when grouped around power sources encouraged centralization of production into factories, thus eliminating the cottage industry that had flourished throughout much of the eighteenth and early nineteenth centuries. By the 1840s, commerical nail manufacturing was largely a factory enterprise confined to no more than 150 units that accounted for over 85 percent of the nation's nail output. Second, the raw materials requirements of the new nail factories began to relate nailmaking more closely to other stages of the iron manufacturing process (such as puddling and rolling). Nail manufacturers began to locate near iron-making facilities and, in a few instances, built their own puddling and rolling mills along with nail factories. Thus the first faltering steps toward integration were taken.

Both the market, which was constantly in advance of supply, and the technology, geared primarily toward volume increase, tended to emphasize structures and management techniques that maximized output. Profitability in the industry depended not so much on the ability to compete with lower prices as on the capability to satisfy the insatiable demand for nails. Until after the mid-century, there was little attention to cost efficiency or to organizational features and management strategies that had cost efficiency as a primary objective.

The typical nail factory was operated by a partnership, usually dominated by mechanics, who literally left their machines to participate in business meetings with a managing partner who saw to the ordering of materials and the sale of the final product. These mechanics understood the technology and were well equipped to organize the various components so as to increase the rate of output and even the output per worker. As long as the market was strong and technological improvements provided a means of increasing production, this system of management functioned well.

During the 1850s, the favorable market began to show signs of weakening. Production capacity approached demand levels, and the lack of significant technological improvements after 1840 led to a leveling off of price reductions. The Civil War intervened briefly, but by the late 1860s the implications of excessive manufacturing capacity and the emergence of regional markets that drew nail makers into direct competition with each other began to have a noticeable impact on the entire industry. For the first time, the ingredients for success lay not in expanding volume but in efficiency that could be translated into competitive advantage. The technology, structure, and management systems that had served so adequately earlier in the century were ill equipped for the new conditions that placed such a premium on competition.

Across the industry, manufacturers responded by turning their attention to strategies intended to circumvent market forces. Initially, the major manufacturers in both the East and the West attempted to organize for the purpose of establishing prices and limiting production. This approach, which found considerable support throughout the rest of the century, was a failure during the 1860s and only partially successful during the 1870s and 1880s. Technological innovation, which continued to facilitate production, could not be controlled by existing management systems, and organizational structures did not provide the flexibility to deal with market forces.

As a result, manufacturers who chose to rely on trying to control market forces either failed, were forced to diversify into other products, or had to rely on the uncertain profits of local markets and temporary rises in regional demand.

A second, and smaller, group of manufacturers, located in and around Wheeling, chose to respond to the adverse market differently. Like their counterparts in the other sections of the country, they concluded that salvation lay in market control. But instead of attempting to regulate the supply and price of nails, the Wheeling manufacturers concentrated on controlling the costs that went into the manufacturing process. They devised two related strategies to reduce costs. First, they focused attention on supply markets, particularly pig iron and kegs, attempting to minimize the input cost. Second, and at least partially as an outgrowth of the first, they began to concentrate on reducing internal processing costs.

These nail producers recognized the high-volume technology and, instead of limiting, actually relied upon it more heavily than before. But most importantly, they related cost to volume, making the former a function of the latter. As the production of the Wheeling firms rose, the cost (and the price) declined, and an increasingly larger share of the market came to the Wheeling manufacturers.

Just as the favorable market and high-volume technology had influenced the organization of the industry during the first half of the century, so the new conditions led to changes during the postwar period. Most notably, the attempt to achieve savings in the procurement and cost of pig iron forced firms to integrate back into blast furnace operations. By the early 1870s, all of the Wheeling firms had become multi-unit enterprises that controlled the flow of materials from ore to finished nail. In the process of acquiring blast furnaces, however, the old partnerships had to be replaced by modern corporations capable of raising the capital needed for the expansion. This brought a new leadership (made up largely of merchants, bankers, and entrepreneurs) to replace the mechanics who had been the guiding force of the industry during the preceding decades.

The coordination requirements inherent in the operation of multi-unit structures, the nontechnical backgrounds of the new owners, and the emphasis on cost containment led to basic changes in management goals and the systems for decision making. Most notably, management specialization began to evolve. Top management, supported by a cadre of clerks, became increasingly more responsible for transactional and inter-unit coordination decisions, while the mechanics who had formerly been so important were confined to intra-unit decisions related primarily to the technical processes.

Because of top managers' interest in the transactions, they quickly extended the cost containment concern expressed in inter-unit decisions to all facets of daily operations. Just as quickly, top managers also extended cost efficiency considerations to changes in methods of operation and in technology. By the early 1870s, efficiency of operation rather than volume alone became the central consideration in all decisions. Effective application of the cost containment strategies was markedly aided by the development of a cost accounting system during the late 1860s. This system, which became increasingly more sophisticated, not only had the capability to identify and isolate types of expenses at various stages of production but also allowed comparisons of categories either among competing firms or over recording periods of the same firms.

In short order, the cost containment strategy of the Wheeling firms placed them in a position to direct, if not control, the nail market and, therefore, to have considerable influence upon the entire industry. Because the strategy at once drove prices down and increased the volume of production, it tended to ensure that supply, at least in the western markets, was equal to, if not slightly in excess of, demand. This condition, of course, forced competitors to adopt measures to produce nails more cheaply or go out of business.

One form of adaptation, taken by firms mostly in the East, was a reduction of wages to offset Wheeling's advantage in efficiency. By the 1880s, the eastern manufacturers paid workmen fully one-third less, and the western nail mills paid 20 percent less, than the Wheeling firms. Other nail manufacturers, largely offshoots of the Wheeling mills, had taken up totally or in part the cost containment philosophy developed at Wheeling.

By the early 1880s, the two groups of mills had narrowed the advantage Wheeling enjoyed and had begun to meet and occasionally undercut Wheeling prices. As in the early 1860s, an upsurge in demand temporarily masked the competitive conditions but when, in 1883, demand receded, the industry was faced with an overabundance of production capacity of relatively equal efficiency.

The Wheeling manufacturers again turned to the supply markets, this time seeking to reduce labor expenses, first through negotiated reductions and later by replacing entire classes of workmen by substituting Bessemer steel nail plate for wrought iron nail plate. In the process, the Wheeling manufacturers substantially renovated the structure of their firms and, again, the entire industry.

Bessemer converters were expensive and capable of producing more steel than a single nail factory could consume. Both conditions suggested the possibility that existing firms might combine their resources in jointly constructed steel works. One group of firms took this path and eventually combined all operations into a horizontally integrated structure. A second group undertook individually the construction and operation of Bessemer plants and, because of the excess steel production, diversified into other product lines.

Quite aside from the internal implications, Bessemers were significant because they greatly reduced cost and, therefore, price. Manufacturers outside Wheeling had either to meet the Wheeling price or face the unpleasant prospect of being driven to the wall. In this context, Wheeling manufacturers took control of the Western Nail Association, the trade association for the western nail manufacturers, and began to establish pricing and wage policies for the entire industry.

In 1884, the Wheeling manufacturers, through the Western Nail Association, decided to extend their cost control policies further by reducing the wages of nailers. This resulted in a lengthy strike, which the manufacturers won. But during this strike, the "wire nail" (a relatively new type of nail made from steel wire at considerably lower cost than the cut nail) gained a significant share of the market.

Once established, the superior cost advantages of the wire nail made it difficult for the cut nail to compete. Moreover, since the manufacturing processes were significantly different, cut nail manufacturers found it expensive to shift to the new product. This was particularly true for the Wheeling manufacturers, who had invested so heavily in the Bessemers that they did not have the resources that would allow conversion to wire nail production.

During the 1890s, they struggled to maintain some semblance of profitability from their nail factories but concentrated most of their efforts on finding other products for their rolling mills. After the McKinley Tariff made tin plate manufacturing profitable, the Wheeling firms converted their faltering nail factories to this product and again found profits, at least temporarily.

Within the broader story outlined above are many lesser themes that are quite instructive. Most notably, the role and changing character of management suggests that the craftsman-entrepreneur may have been more complicated than heretofore suspected. Certainly the mechanics at Wheeling showed surprising astuteness in their ability to both diagnose the new market conditions and formulate new management techniques. It appears, for example, that the cost accounting system noted above was designed during the late 1850s or early 1860s by a group of these craftsmen-entrepreneurs at the LaBelle Company and later refined by the new managers who took over in the wake of the reorganizations of the late 1860s.

The nail industry system of cost accounting is one of the earliest examples of industrial cost accounting yet discovered. But most importantly, this system, by the late 1860s, had been expanded to include ratios of finished product to raw materials, a critical step in the evolution of cost-efficient management strategy. Moreover, the system quickly came to possess a diagnostic feature that permitted precise comparison with past performances and with current price performances of competitors. By the late 1870s, the cost accounting system was also beginning to assume importance as a planning tool that allowed management to project the economic impact of changing one or more components of the manufacturing process.

Another related theme that appears in the context of the nail industry is the rise of the professional manager--the product, not the originator, of the changes in structure and management philosophy noted above. Certainly, the craftsmen-entrepreneurs of the late 1850s do not qualify as examples of professional managers; nor do the bankers and businessmen who took over the mills after the Civil War fully meet the criteria. It was only after the mill clerks and secretaries rose in response to the needs of the accounting system that persons who may be described as truly professional came onto the scene.

The role of the merchant in establishing a cost philosophy and in bridging the gap between the craftsman-entrepreneur and the professional manager appears to have been crucial. A significant number of individuals who had been wholesale or retail merchants were in the class of boards of directors that took over in the late 1860s. At least impressionistically, there is a relationship between the merchants' attention to the margin between purchase cost and the competitive selling price and the industrialists' emphasis on low cost. This relationship goes well beyond the nail industry and calls to mind the early backgrounds of such notable figures as John D. Rockefeller, Cyrus Field, and Marcus Hanna who, like the Wheeling figures, began their careers or had sustantial experience in merchant houses. Since there are no records from the earlier businesses, or personal papers that illuminate the connection, the precise role of the early experience of the Wheeling men cannot be easily evaluated.

After the machines were introduced several specialized groups of workmen appeared. The nailer, the feeder, the puddler, and several other specialties provided central skills that were regarded as the foundation of the industry until the 1870s. The complex relationship between management and the "crafts" offers some insight into both the evolution of craft unions and management-labor relations. The role of management techniques, such as cost accounting, in reshaping these relationships during the 1870s and 1880s is particularly interesting.

Finally, the local history of the Wheeling area illustrates how a variety of decisions and attributes affect industrial development. Boosterism expressed primarily in the competition with Pittsburgh for mail routes, railroads, and leadership in nailmaking provided a background for the growth of the Upper Ohio Valley nail industry. Although not a definitive factor, local pride certainly played a small but noticeable role in the rise of the industry and served as the spice in a multicourse serving of claims and counterclaims that spread across the pages of the local press in both cities.

The following account is based on material in the general and local periodical press; the hardware specialty journal, The Iron Age (beginning in 1872); and a variety of memoirs, business records, government documents, artifactual material, and secondary accounts. Except for the Burden Iron Works of Troy, New York, the Tremont Nail Works of West Wareham, Massachusetts, and several related manufacturers, the firms of the Middle Atlantic and New England states left few records. Many of the major manufacturers, such as the huge Boonton Nail Works in Boonton, New Jersey, disappeared completely during the late nineteenth century, and no records survived, either in research archives or in the records of succeeding corporations. Even the firms that existed in the Pittsburgh, Pennsylvania, area have left few traces. Some simply went out of business, and many switched to other products and were caught up in the Carnegie and United States Steel consolidations, again leaving few records behind. But in the Wheeling district, records of four firms have survived, and together with national and local journalistic accounts they reveal the forces that transformed small specialty manufacturers operated by mechanics into large, integrated firms operated by corporations--and then what happened when wire nailmaking presented its challenge.

The Rise and Decline of the American Cut Nail Industry

1
The Technology and the Market

> Cut nails...being an American invention substituted machinery for manual labor.
>
> J. Leander Bishop
> A History of American Manufacturers

The nail is an ancient implement developed by man whenever and wherever the technology to fashion artifacts from metal was possessed. Although a metal product, the nail properly belongs to periods and cultures in which populations relied heavily on wood, for the chief virtue of the nail was and still is efficiency in fastening wood to wood. In this capacity the nail was a central feature in architectural advances and in the development of many implements and even technologies, such as those based on wooden vehicles. Of course, the nail has also been used in other capacities, such as affixing the shoes to the hoofs of animals or in general and military construction work where wood was employed.

Historians have all but ignored the nail. Except for the references to the industry in standard works such as Clark's History of Manufacturers in the United States, Temin's Iron and Steel in 19th Century America, and Boorstin's The Americans, there are few secondary sources that deal with the subject. A few antiquaries have from time to time taken an interest in the nail as an object and have done some research into early manufacture and distribution. Henry C. Mercer, in his booklet, "Dating Old Houses," did some basic and pioneering research on the topic in the 1920s. During the last decade, an interest in historic preservation has prompted architectural historians to study nails and nailmaking. Lee H. Nelson, a historian for the National Park Service, published a pamphlet entitled "A Nail Chronology" in the early 1960s; Susan Buggey published a 1813 catalogue of nails in the Bulletin of the Association for Preservation Technology in 1976; and Peter Priess published an article on the wire nail in the same journal in 1973.[1]

Even in the nineteenth century, relatively few people wrote on the subject. The first American writer to give any attention to nail manufacturing was J. Leander Bishop. His History of American Manufacturers from 1608 to 1860, published in 1868, contains much information about the early history of nailmaking in the United States. A few other nineteenth-century writers, such as Horace Greeley, also made reference to the manufacture or use of nails. For the most part, however, information on the subject is confined to sources in which nailmaking was strictly incidental, such as census reports, or to the usual, and in this instance scarce, primary sources.[2]

The history of nailmaking in western Europe dates from the Roman invasions. Excavations of Roman sites in Kiserlentern, Germany, and Reading, England, have yielded nails as well as nail-making tools. An anvil from the Kiserlentern site and heading tools from the English site show that nailmaking was well developed as early as the third century A.D. --so well developed, in fact, that the same basic tools could be found thirteen hundred years later in colonial America.[3]

One of the few major advances in nailmaking prior to 1770 came during the fifteenth century when the English introduced the slitting mill, a device for cutting metal plates into thin strips which in turn were cut into nails. At about the same time, English ironmongers also developed the "penny" pricing system that was the first step toward standard size. Under this method of pricing, an eight pence, or eight penny, nail referred to the length of nail that sold for eight pence. By the late eighteenth century the length and weight became firmly related, and nails were sold by the pound instead of by length.[4]

Just when the first nails were brought to America is uncertain. Most likely the credit belongs to Norsemen who explored the East Coast. These seafarers, like those from other western European countries who came later, carried with them ready-made nails or materials from which nails could be made in order to fashion temporary repairs to their vessels.

When permanent settlement began in the early seventeenth century, the immigrants thought of nails as essential. Written and artifactual records from both the Jamestown and Plymouth settlements leave little doubt of the importance of nails for survival in the New World. The papers of the London Company, for example, show that nails were regarded as being as important as food, clothing, and weapons. An entry in the records of the London Company dated June 18, 1623, titled "a portion of the charges to furnish and transport six men to Virginia," listed nails as one of several essential items. Succeeding entries in the company records also show that from time to time varying quantities of "nayles" were shipped to the colony.[5]

Many sources testify not only to the importance but also to the scarcity of nails throughout the colonies until well into the eighteenth century. In 1645, for example, the House of Burgesses of Virginia enacted legislation that probibited the burning of houses for nails. In 1691 the Supervisors of Kent County, Delaware, ordered the old country courthouse burned in order to "get the nails." Similar instances of destroying buildings for nails are found in records from Pennsylvania and other colonies. There are many hints that on the American frontier structures were deliberately burned for nails. Military forts, structures that often contained large numbers of nails, were frequently abandoned as settlement advanced and had an uncanny record of destruction by fire.[6]

Just as it is impossible to assign a precise date to the first imported nails, so, too, is it difficult to determine with any precision when the first nails were made in America. The earliest settlers had the tools, and undoubtedly many were skilled enough to make nails. During the age of wrought nails the nail-making process was a two-phased operation. Wrought iron nail plates produced by tilt hammers (later by rolling mills) were cut into thin rods corresponding in thickness to the size of the nail shank. Once the nail rod had been made it could be cut and headed at a slitting mill or shipped to its destination and converted into nails by the purchaser. Since the cost of shipping nail rod was less than that of shipping nails, substantial amounts of imported nails used in the colonies probably came as rods that colonial blacksmiths converted into nails. In addition, nail rod was widely used for purposes other than nailmaking. Colonial craftsmen fashioned nail rods into such diverse objects as coopers' cressets, fire baskets, "mud spoons" (a stonemason's tool), trivets, various "S" hooks, gridirons, etc. The number of nail rod artifacts that have survived to the present day confirms that a significant portion of the nail rod was not used for nailmaking.[7]

Except for specialty nails, nailmaking did not require either high levels of skill or a large capital investment. Nail rod could be cut with a hammer and chisel on a common anvil using any fireplace as a source of heat. Although heading was a bit more complicated, a simple tool fashioned from wrought iron was all that was required for this task. There is ample evidence to suggest that during the late colonial period most of the nails for domestic use were made either by the user or by local cottage industries, while commercial naileries specialized in making nails for shipbuilding. Even large users, such as military engineers and large scale builders, often employed nailers to convert nail rod to nails on the site.[8]

Throughout most of the colonial period British mercantile policy discouraged manufacturing nail rod in the American colonies. Parliamentary acts of 1669, 1719, and 1750 specifically outlawed the manufacture of nail rod or the construction of the slitting mills that were necessary for nail rod production. The Parliamentary Act of 1750, for example, proclaimed that "from and after the 24th day of June, 1750, no mills or other engines for slitting or rolling iron ... shall be erected or hereafter such erection continue in His Majesty's colonies in the Americas."[9]

As was the case with other parliamentary acts regulating trade, the colonists, as well as the British officials, ignored laws prohibiting nail rod manufacture when entrepreneurs and legislators found it to their advantage to do so. An instance from the records of the General Court of Connecticut not only illustrates this open disregard for Parliament's rules but also provides insight into the importance attached to nailmaking. In May 1722, Ebenezer Fitch petitioned the General Court asking for a license to operate a slitting mill. The Court's affirmative response was accompanied by a clear statement of its view of the importance of nailmaking for the local economy:

> Whereas, Mr. Ebenezer Fitch represented to this court that divers gentlemen in company with himself are willing and desirous to set up a slitting mill upon the river called Stony Brook...to slit and draw out iron rods for nails and for other artificers of iron...and this court considering the great advantage such a mill will be to this government as well as to the neighbouring, have thought fit to encourage the same.[10]

The court officials granted Fitch a fifteen-year monopoly and included a provision that allowed him to erect a second mill if "any tax or duty shall be set upon the iron so slit." This final provision suggests that nails were also being produced in Massachusetts and anticipated the probability of some form of protection in that colony. Ten years later in a report to the House of Commons, the governor of Massachusetts did refer to a slitting mill and a nailery located in the colony. By 1750, when Parliament, in conjunction with the passage of an Act for the Encouragement of Importing of Pig and Bar Iron, ordered a survey of ironmaking establishments, the governor of Massachusetts reported that the rolling mills of Massachusetts were chiefly employed in making nail rod from which spikes and large nails were already made in great abundance and cheaper than they could be imported.[11]

Other sources contain information that confirms the existence of several iron works and nail mills in Massachusetts, Connecticut, and Pennsylvania during the two decades before the Americn Revolution. North Canaan, Connecticut, had three slitting mills; Sharon had several "nail shops"; and East Haddam, in Middlesex County, had a "nail factory." In Pennsylvania, nail makers could be found as early as 1703. By 1770, John Litle, in his "Account of Smiths and Nailers," noted dozens of nail manufacturers producing nails ranging in size from three to thirty penny.[12]

The geographic pattern that emerged before the Revolution continued well into the nineteenth century. Massachusetts, Connecticut, and Pennsylvania dominated the nail-making industry until the 1850s, when the western nailers, specifically those in the Upper Ohio Valley, became the largest manufacturers. Even as late as 1870 Massachusetts and Pennsylvania still accounted for a substantial portion of American nail output.[13]

Clearly, the colonies had developed a substantial nailmaking capacity by the outbreak of the American Revolution. How nearly self-sufficient the colonies were is debatable. Records from 1770 show that only 22,238 pounds of nails or nail rod were imported that year, a small fraction of the quantity necessary to meet the demands of the American market. This seems to indicate a sizeable domestic industry. Furthermore, the colonies were importing large quantities of Russian and Swedish iron, the most preferred for making nails during the late Colonial and Federal periods. This, too, suggests the existence of a sizeable industry. More direct evidence, such as records of a congressional debate in 1789, sheds some light on the status of nail production. Thomas Fitzsimmons, a congressman from Pennsylvania, claimed that the United States was self-sufficient in the production of spike and ship nails. Other congressmen, particularly the Southerners, objected that while the northern states were self-sufficient, the southern states still imported large quantities of nails and nail rod from abroad. Alexander Hamilton's report from 1791, which noted that the United States had imported 900 tons of nails or nail rod, gives support to the Southerners' argument that self-sufficiency was confined to the northeastern states. In short, while the precise degree of self-sufficiency is difficult to determine, it can be said that a sizeable American nail industry had evolved by the Revolutionary War period.[14]

Even with a sizeable industry, nails continued to be expensive and therefore relatively scarce. In 1800, for example, common sizes of nails sold for ten to fourteen cents a pound along the eastern coast and considerably more in the interior. The high cost was a result of the labor-intensive system of manufacturing that required semiskilled workers to spend hours doing tedious work.[15] The true nature of the work may be best comprehended by pointing out that nail manufacture was left, whenever possible, to slaves (in the South) and children. As noted previously, the process required two separate operations. Slitting, cutting the wrought iron nail plate lengthwise to produce a series of rods, occurred in a mill and was often divorced from the actual manufacture of nails. In 1795, Nathaniel Read, a Massachusetts nail maker, estimated that it required five men one full day to slit and bundle three tons of nail rod. He further noted that the customary price for slitting was $1 per 100 pounds. Consequently, the slitting phase added substantially to the cost of the finished product.[16]

The second portion of the process, during which the nail was shaped, required three steps--pointing, cutting, and heading. In the first step the nailer pointed one end of the nail rod. The most common form of point was produced by working the four surfaces of the nail rod to a point. Other nail points were made by flattening the end of the rod to produce a "bill," and still others received chiseled points which required that only two faces of the nail rod be brought to a point. Each type of point required the nailer to heat the nail rod and strike several blows with the hammer.[17]

Once pointed, a section of the rod corresponding to the length of the nail, with proper allowances for the head, was cut from the bar. Finally, the nailer forged a head on the blunt end of the nail. Although nailers used several techniques to form the head, the most common was to place the nail blank in a tube with a tapered hole large enough to accommodate the pointed end but narrow enough to prevent the nail from falling through. (See Figures 1 and 2.) The nailer then forged one of many types of heads. To fashion the rosehead, a fairly common type, the nailer flared the metal around the shank, producing a head with several facets. The common "T" shaped head was formed by splitting the upper portion of the shank, parting it, and then flattening the two appendages to form a "T" shape. The rose and "T" heads are only two of the most common styles. Many more (Figure 3) styles show up in nail samples and in literature such as the Royal Engineers Catalogue of 1812.[18]

Each type of head and point required slightly different amounts of material and time to make. John Litle, in his "Accounts of Smiths and Nailers," noted the number and weight of nails produced by several Philadelphia nailers in 1778. On January 5, one nailer producing 10d (ten-penny) nails averaged 58 to the pound while three days later the number was 63 to the pound. Similar variations also occurred in the rates of production as the point and head became more complicated. At most, a skilled nailer could produce a few thousand simple nails per day, and this factor alone kept prices high enough to discourage the liberal use of nails.[19]

The labor-intensive method of manufacturing essentially tied the volume of nail production to the number of workmen who could engage in the work without any possibility of per-unit increase in output or decrease in price. In an area such as the colonies, where the potential for widespread use of nails in wooden construction existed alongside a shortage of labor, such a system, theoretically at least, was not very suitable. Prior to trade interruptions of the Revolutionary War, imports could supplement domestic production and ameliorate the worst effects of limited supply, if not high prices. After the Revolution interrupted trade with Great Britain and disrupted the supply of imported nails, American inventors began to search for alternate ways of manufacturing nails. Jeremiah Wilkinson, of Cumberland, Rhode Island, traditionally has received credit for developing the nail-cutting technique. In 1775, Wilkinson produced textile card tacks by shearing thin slivers of metal from the ends of a metal plate instead of cutting them from a rod. As far as can be determined, Wilkinson never used this process to produce nails. However, Bishop, who commented on the subject in 1868, believed that the process was picked up by nail manufacturers in the area and applied to nailmaking.[20]

It is therefore difficult to say whether Wilkinson or someone else deserves the credit for transforming his cutting process. What is known is that inventors and manufacturers adopted the process and quickly began making refinements. In 1798, for example, two Pennsylvanians, Samuel Briggs and David Folsom, petitioned their state legislature to grant patents on nail-making machinery. Such devices were also submitted to the national patent office. In 1796, a large portion of the U. S. patents granted had been for new or improved nail-making machines. Between 1790 and 1820, patents for nail-making machines and improvements accounted for

Nail plate was cut into rods at a slitting mill.

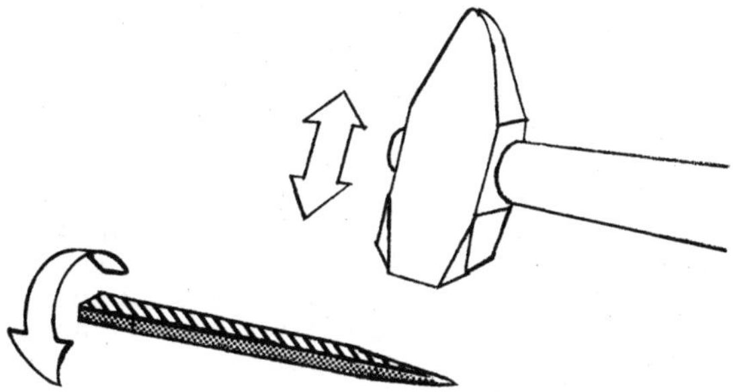

The nailer worked the heated nail rod to a point.
After each blow of the hammer, the nail rod was turned.

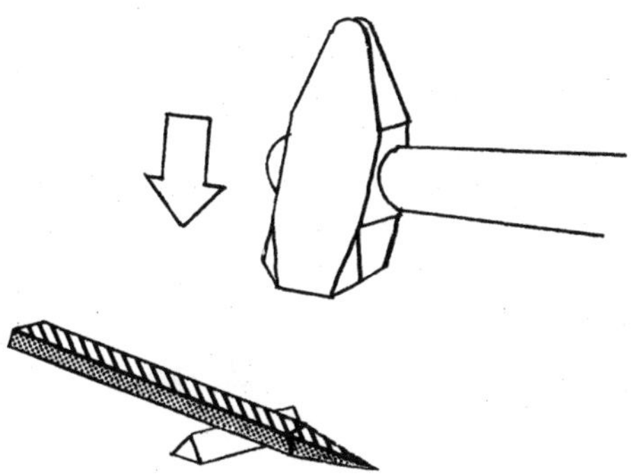

After the rod was pointed, the nailer, using a hammer and a "hardy," cut the pointed portion of the rod away.

Early Method of Nail Making

FIGURE 1

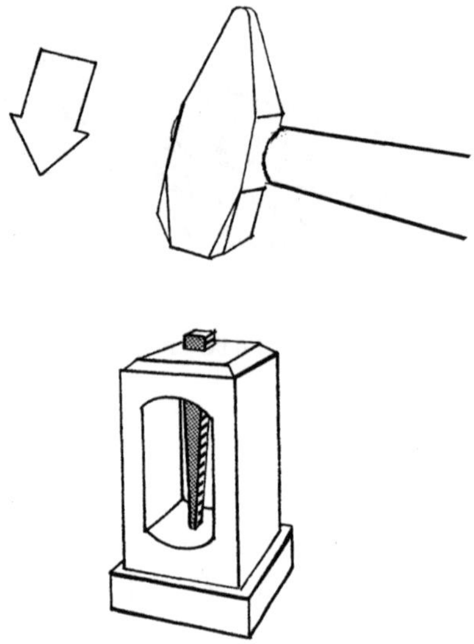

Using a device known as a header, the nailer flattened the upper portion of the nail rod. This illustration shows one of the common headers. The device had a tapered hole in the top that allowed the pointed portion of the nail to be inserted but held the unpointed portion above the surface.

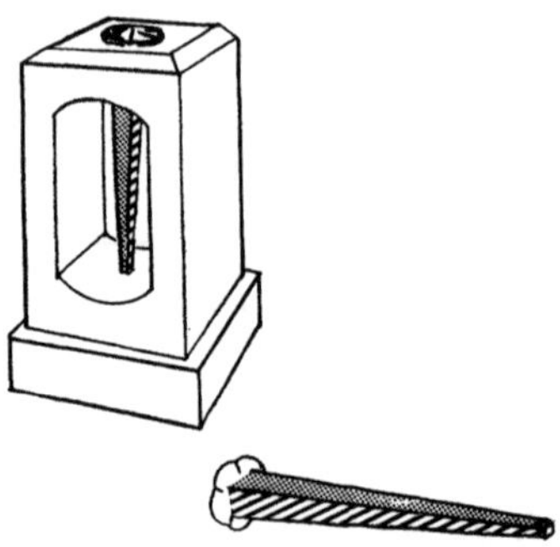

Once the nail was headed, a chisel or other device was inserted into the slot and forced up, releasing the nail.

The Header

FIGURE 2

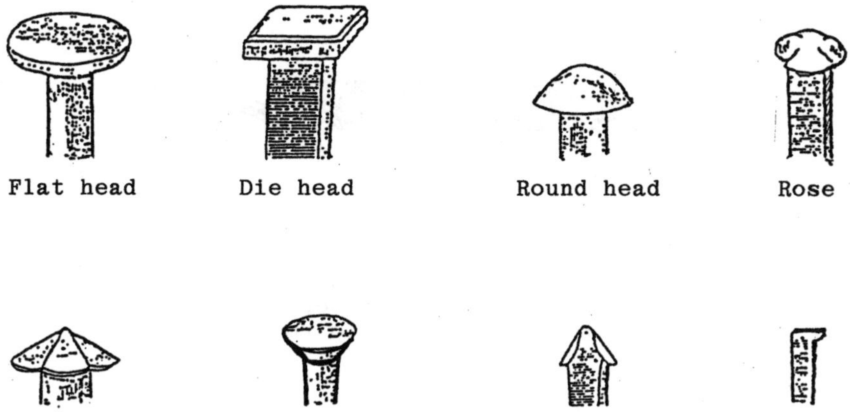

Common types of nail heads that appeared in an 1813 British Army supply catalog

FIGURE 3

slightly more than 2 percent of all of the patents granted by the U. S. Patent Office.[21] These figures suggest the extraordinarily important role of cut nail innovations in the history of American invention in the period of the early republic.

Inventors worked on two general types of machines during the late eighteenth century. Both types were designed to eliminate several of the manual steps in the nail-manufacturing process and thereby to speed up production. One group of inventors attempted to improve the wrought nail process by building machines that used dies to strike nails from the rod as it passed through the machine. One such machine patented in 1790 squeezed a bar of iron nails as the bar passed between heavy rollers with molds incised into their faces. Since only few samples of this type of nail have survived, it is apparent that large numbers were never produced.[22]

Most inventors chose a second path, one that built upon the concept introduced by Wilkinson's machine. Their machines were basically cutters that sheared nails from wrought iron plates, thus eliminating the need for slitting mills to cut nail rod. The plates were cut into widths corresponding to the lengths of the nails. Workmen then inserted the plate into a cutter, a machine that consisted of a fixed bed and a reciprocating blade. (See Figure 5.) As the blade struck, a small sliver of metal was cut from the nail plate. By constructing a cutter with a blade that struck at a slight angle to the path of the nail plate, it was possible to cut and

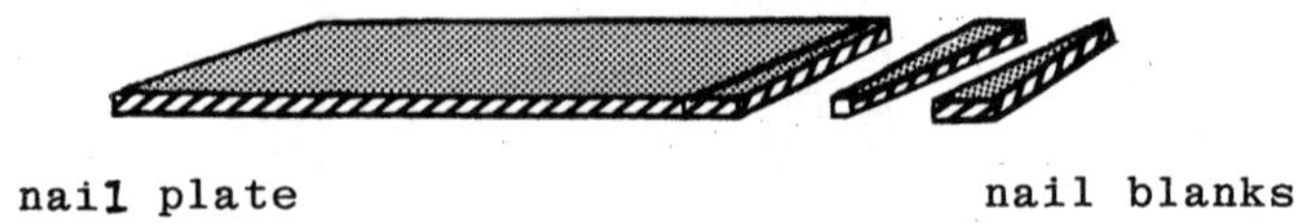

The Wilkinson process. Nails were cut from the end of the nail plate already pointed. This process eliminated the need for slitting the nail plate into rods.

FIGURE 4

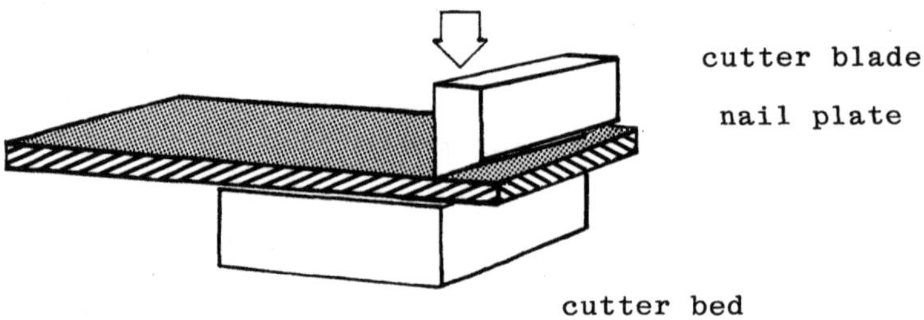

Schematic of nail-cutting machine.

FIGURE 5

point nails at the same time if the nail plate was flipped after each strike of the machine. The same end could be achieved with the blade perpendicular to the path of the nail plate if the plate were moved from side to side at an angle to the direction of the plate's movement.[23]

In 1797, Nathaniel Read (see Figure 7), a nail maker from Danvers, Massachusetts, described such a machine to Timothy Pickerington, secretary of state.

> My nail machine consists of a cutting lever of the common form...a stage upon which the nail plate is placed and forced into the jaws of the cutter by a pair of rippers and a small pully. Directly under the cutting tool is a small trough onto which the nail drops...the capacity of the machine is about 10,000 nails daily. With the same machine nails of any size from a 4d to a 20d can be made.[24]

The cutter had several advantages over the wrought nail machines that permitted the cut nail gradually to replace the wrought nail. Foremost, the cutter was less expensive to make. Simply put, the reciprocating blade cost less than a die. Read, in his letter to Pickerington, for example, said that it cost him only about $400 to make a prototype of his machine. The cut nail machine also had other attractive characteristics. As Read, quoted above, had noted, the size of the nail being produced could be varied by simple adjustments, whereas new dies had to be made and installed with each new size made on the wrought nail machine. Read emphasized this point again when he noted in another letter to Pickerington that with his machine only simple adjustments were necessary to make various sizes. Finally, the cutting machines significantly reduced the number of times nail plate had to be slit. This reduction not only lowered labor costs that went into the price of production of nail rods, but also allowed savings on material. Read commented, for example, that "the loss upon a quantity of iron slit into nail rods is about eight percent."[25]

Even with the advances in manufacturing technology, wrought nails, produced by hand, continued to be made for specific uses. The result was a dual market. Wrought nails, cut with the fiber of the nail plate running lengthwise in the shank of the nail, tended to bend very well, whereas cut nails, cut across the grain of the metal, tended to be brittle and broke very easily. This characteristic allowed the wrought nail to survive well into the nineteenth century for uses such as door battens.[26]

The last quarter of the eighteenth century was a critical time for the development of the new process. Not only was this the time when the innovation was born and when inventors began to make improvements that allowed application to manufacturing, but it was also a time when officials at both the state and national levels sought to encourage nail manufacturers through the adoption of several laws aimed broadly at stimulating all nailmaking but which, unwittingly it appears, disproportionately promoted cut nail manufacturing.

As was the case with many manufacturing and transportation enterprises, encouragement of nailmaking first occurred at the state level.[27] Three states attempted to stimulate the manufacture of nails during the Revolutionary War. In December 1774, the Provincial Assembly of Massachusetts recommended the manufacture of nails to the population of that state.[28] South Carolina, the second state to encourage the production of nails, acted in November 1775 with an offer of a 700-pound-sterling prize to the first citizen of that state would could slit 1,000 pounds of nail rods. No record of who,

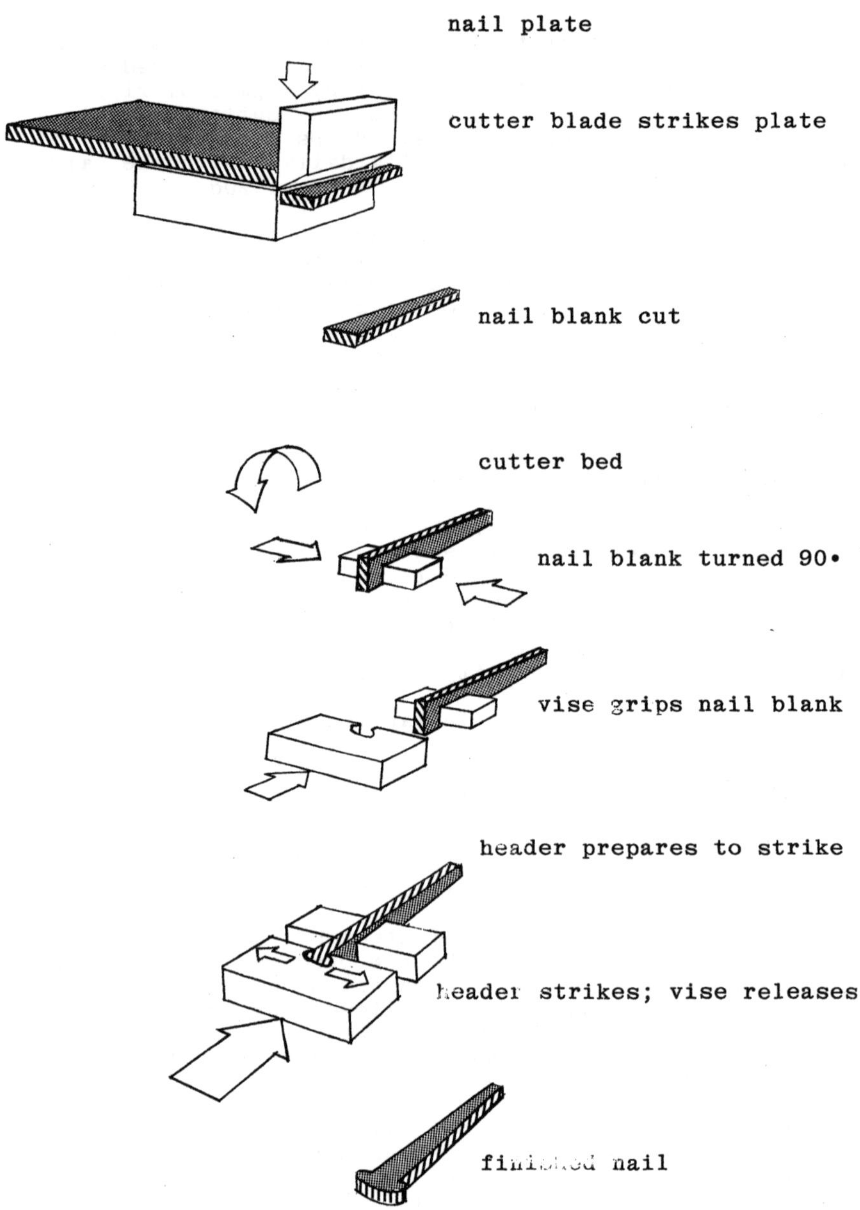

Cutting and heading steps

FIGURE 6

if anyone, collected the premium has survived. As late as 1810, census returns showed no slitting mills in that state.[29]

During the post-Revolutionary period, the legislature of Connecticut twice considered nail manufacturing. In 1786, the Legislative Council of Connecticut considered offering a premium for nail manufacturers, but the idea was rejected on the grounds that the industry in that state was well established and did not require stimulation. Nine years later, in 1795, the Council did act, passing a law to regulate the industry. In this first attempt to regulate nailmaking, the Connecticut legislators established fixed weights and lengths for wrought nails in the 2d-20d range that were being manufactured for sale or export. This law implicitly favored "cut nail" production. Because "cut nails" were of uniform size, they easily met the standards, while the all-wrought nails had to be manufactured much more carefully under the law.[30]

Official encouragement of nail manufacturers in the post-Revolutionary period was extended further in 1789 when Congress passed legislation placing a tariff upon imported nails. Even though several congressmen objected on the grounds that the country was nearly self-sufficient and that therefore the industry did not need protection, a tariff of one cent per pound was placed upon spikes and ship nails. This rate, set at 7 percent of the value as opposed to 5 percent for other finished iron products, established a pattern of high tariffs that held throughout the next century. Nails continued to be protected under the Tariff Acts of 1816, 1818, 1833, 1842, 1846, 1857, and 1862. The rate fluctuated from as low as 75 cents per hundred-weight to a high of 30 percent of imported value in 1846 and one cent a pound in 1862.[31]

The official position that held the nail to be an article of indispensable necessity influenced the growth of the industry during and immediately after the Revolution. State-level encouragement and the high tariffs passed by the national government stimulated interest in the industry. The congressmen who voted for the tariffs, and probably the state legislators who acted to encourage the industry, believed that they were encouraging a cottage industry. They failed to recognize that a major change was under way and that their acts were encouraging a new system of manufacture. Fisher Ames, a Massachusetts representative to the U. S. Congress, clearly described his view in 1789.

> It has become common for country people in Massachusetts to erect small forges in their chimney corners, and in the winters and on the evenings when little other work can be done, great quantities of nails are made even by children. These people take the nail rod iron of the merchant and return him the nails; and in consequence of this easy mode of barter, the manufacture is prodigiously great.[32]

Clearly Ames perceived that the action being debated would protect and foster the labor-intensive cottage industry. In fact, the new tariff gave added impetus for manufacturers to convert to cut nails, since it added a measure of protection to the additional capital investment cut-nail manufacturing demanded.[33]

With the new process developing and a fair measure of protection against foreign competition, the setting was right for the cut nail to begin to supplant the wrought nail. By 1800, not only was the cut nail finding a market, but the term cut nail had entered the American language. As early as 1790 Rufus Putnam specified cut nails for use in the construction of portions of Fort Campus Martius in Marietta, Ohio. Tench Coxe in his *Arts and Manufactures of the United States*, written in 1810, took note of the cut nail when he commented that

> the improvements of the system and tools...and particularly the introduction of the labor saving machines in their shops would be a very substantial benefit....The cut nail machinery has been very beneficially introduced into some of these shops....[34]

In the same report, Coxe went on to report that the nation had 410 naileries producing 15,727,914 pounds of nails; he did not, however, make any distinction between cut and wrought manufacturers.[35]

The cutting machine, while significant, did not represent either a notable mechanical advance or a true breakthrough in the rate of production. The early cutters were little more than modified blacksmith shears that shaped the shank and the point of the nail. Nailers were still required to forge the heads of most types of nails manually and this continued to pose a substantial production problem.

Nonetheless, the cutter was in another sense revolutionary. The idea of cutting nails from sheets of metal rather than bars jolted tradition enough to encourage a complete rethinking of the manufacturing process. Within twenty years after the cutter was first used, several mechanics and inventors could construct a totally automated production system--a remarkable change, particularly for an industry that had remained essentially unchanged for centuries.

Once it was established that nails could be cut from plates and once the basic principles of the cutter were understood, inventors began to make improvements that extended the capability of the machine. By the middle decades of the nineteenth century, nail-making machines had been sufficiently improved so that nails were truly mass-produced items, untouched by human hands during the manufacturing process.

As early as the 1780s, inventors conceived of a machine that automatically fed nail plate into the shears, cut the nails, and then headed them. Nathaniel Read was one of the first inventors to actually build such a machine. In 1792 he described his machine as being one that "feeds itself and cuts and heads the nails without any manual labor." He received a patent for such a machine and the model does exist to substantiate his claim. But there is evidence, in the form of an eyewitness account, that indicates that the heading device and the feeder did not work very well. Wilson Bentley, a minister from Salem, Massachusetts, visited the Read factory in 1810, a full decade after the invention was made, and recorded the following observations:

> The cutting machines are of different sizes with different motions. The large machine is fed by tongs led by a pulley. The smaller is fed by hand and can give 1,400 strokes in a minute. The machine for heading is not used since the first experiments, as it is found, heading is done better by hand than by any machine as yet invented, both as to the time and goodness of execution.[36]

Other accounts leave little doubt that the automatic headers were not used widely during the first decades of the nineteenth century. For example, John Wittaker, a Philadelphia nailer, used hand heading as late as 1820. The Digest of Accounts of Manufacturing Establishments in the United States in 1823 listed forty nail manufacturers. Under the equipment heading, many of the firms listed nail machines and heading tools separately, suggesting that the automatic header had not been perfected at this date.[37]

Precisely when the automatic header became practical is unknown. Henry Mercer and Lee Nelson, the only two researchers to study the subject, agree that machine-headed nails were not widely used until the 1830s. Both men based their conclusions on nails gathered from dated structures. Similar examinations undertaken as a part of this book confirmed their findings. About 4,000 nails dating from 1778 to examples taken directly from a currently operating cutting machine at the LaBelle Nail Works of the Wheeling-Pittsburgh Steel Corporation in Wheeling, West Virginia, were studied and seem to confirm Mercer's and Nelson's conclusions that not until the 1830s were many nails headed by machine.[38]

As Figure 8 shows, distinctive markings around the head make identification of machine-headed nails relatively easy. A few nails from early structures appear to represent attempts at automatic heading. Heads were irregular and the upper part of the nail shank shows evidence of compression which resulted from the heading vise gripping the nail along the narrow sides. Practical automatic headers became feasible only after mechanisms were designed to turn the nail blanks ninety degrees after it was cut, allowing the vise to grip the wider surface of the nail. This permitted a firmer grip and also prevented the upper portion from being crushed.

Pricing data also suggest that automatic headers were perfected only in the 1830s. No matter how efficient the cutters were, as long as heading was done by hand, nailmaking was labor intensive and the cost high. Between 1805 and 1825 nail prices remained constant at 9.5 to 9.9 cents per pound, except for the war years when prices were as high as 12.8 cents. In 1823, prices began a decline that continued until 1835 when prices reached an average of five cents per pound. A portion of the price decrease resulted from cheaper iron; but pig iron prices dropped by only 34.9 percent, while the price of nails dropped by almost 50 percent.[39] This decline in prices, taken in conjunction with the appearance of large numbers of automatically headed nails, suggests that the increased mechanization was beginning to reduce costs.

Next to the automatic header, the automatic feeder was the most important device introduced into the nail-making process during the nineteenth century. Like the header, the automatic feeder was experimented with from an early date. Read claimed in 1797 that his machine could automatically feed nail plate into the cutters; Bentley, in 1810, however, noted that Read's machines were manually fed. Patent records also show that several other inventors experimented with feeders, apparently with no more success than Read. Speaking in 1870, Shubal Wilder, a Newcastle, Pennsylvania, nailmaker, commented on the state of the nail-making machine, saying, "Machines have brought it [nailmaking] into a high state of perfection; the only thing now remaining to be done is the introduction of a reliable self-feeder." In the Upper Ohio Valley automatic feeders were not used until after 1875, and only then in emergency conditions created by strikes. The most frequent reason given for not using them was the waste of material they caused.[40]

A final innovation should be noted, although it was not directly associated with the nail machine. This machine, known as the rotary squeezer, was used in the manufacture of wrought iron nail plate and made it possible to produce cut nails with the grain of the metal running the length of the

Model of Read's nail-cutting machine (Bradlee, p. 96). Courtesy of the Essex Institute, Salem, Massachusetts.

FIGURE 7

Early Machine-Made Nails

The nail to the left is a machine-made nail. Markings on the nail provide much information about the manufacturing process and can serve to date the manufacture. Die marks that show clearly along the edges of the lower one-third of the nail indicate that the plate was moved from side to side (wiggled), a feeding method that was most prevalent in the late eighteenth century and the first two decades of the nineteenth century.

The head of the nail and the portion of the shank just below the head clearly indicate that this nail was headed by an early automatic header. The vise of the header gripped the nail shank, partially crushing it--a common problem with early automatic headers. (The nail to the right was hand headed. Hand-headed nails frequently have a bulge just below the head, which resulted from a worn heading tool.) Because header markings suggest that an early, imperfect heading machine was used, this places the probable date of manufacture for the nail on the left in the 1820s or early 1830s.

FIGURE 8

shank rather than crosswise. This allowed the manufacture of cut nails suitable for clinching and thereby increased the extent to which the cut nail impinged upon the wrought nail market.[41]

Henry H. Burden, owner of the Troy Iron and Nail Factory of Troy, New York, invented the rotary squeezer in 1836. Burden used the squeezer to produce wrought iron for spike and horseshoe nails. He also developed a spike machine in 1839 that manufactured railroad spike at the rate of 50 per minute. As a result of these two innovations, Burden's factory became a major supplier of spike for the expanding railroad system in the United States.[42]

By 1840, the technology for cut nail manufacture was complete except for the feeder. The cutter, the header, and the squeezer allowed the manufacture of nail plate and nail machines that could turn out large quantities of high-quality nails economically. A nail machine operating properly could strike 1,400 strokes per minute on smaller nails and 50 strokes per minute on spikes. It was this rapid production rate that allowed the cut nail to decline in price and led to the domination of the American nail market so completely that by 1870 wrought nails accounted for less than 5 percent of all the nails produced in the United States.[43]

The reign of the cut nail was relatively brief, however, and its demise was swift. By 1900, nails manufactured from cylindrical wires had all but replaced the cut nail. The "wire nail," as this new nail was called, came upon the scene almost as quickly as the cut nail had a century earlier. The U. S. Patent Office granted the first wire nail patent in 1877. Twenty-five years later, wire nail production had surpassed that of cut nails, and by 1920, only 8 percent of the U. S. nail production was cut nails.[44]

Because the cutter and related equipment so completely changed the nail-making process during the first half of the nineteenth century, the industry provides a particularly instructive example of the impact of mechanization. The major technological changes took place in the industry and had a direct impact not only on the price of the product but, as anticipated above, also on the organization of the industry. Two sets of statistics summarize the impact of the cut nail. By 1890, nails were available at less than 20 percent of their cost in 1800. Along with the declining price, there was a marked increase in the number of nails used. In 1810, Americans had used 2.18 pounds of nails per capita. Seventy years later, in 1880, the per capita use stood at 9.61 pounds, an increase of 340 percent. These statistics and others that will follow suggest the scope of changes that were taking place within the industry during the nineteenth century.[45]

The first national survey of nail manufacturing was conducted as a part of the 1810 census. Four hundred and ten manufacturers were listed, although there were certainly more, for the census did not take into account the chimney-side forges that Fisher Ames had spoken of in 1789. These 410 nail producers turned out slightly more than 15,700,000 pounds of nails. No mention of the number of employees in the industry or the capital invested was made during the 1810 census.

During the 1820 census, a partial list of nail makers was made that contained information on the number of employees and capital invested in the industry, but it omitted production statistics. For the period between 1820 and 1850, only scattered information is available, primarily in B. F. French's History of the Rise and Progress of the Iron Trade in the United States. After 1850, statistics abound in census reports and various industry publications.[46]

The most noticeable impact of the new equipment was the increase in the number of nails produced. In contrast to 1810 when American nail manufacturers had turned out about 15.7 million pounds of nails, forty years later production was at 206,500,000 pounds. This gross increase of about 1,300 percent in output and a per capita increase of about 340 percent clearly shows that what Douglass North refers to as "intensive growth" was occurring.[47]

If the technology had an impact on the growth of production, it also affected various other facets of the industry. The number of producers declined and the capital requirements increased. The 410 nail manufacturers listed in 1820 had dwindled to 87 by 1850. While the Digest of Accounts of Manufacturing Establishments in the United States in 1823 listed forty major nail firms that had a combined capital investment of about $300,990, the 1850 census listed the capital investment of the 87 firms manufacturing nails in that year at $4.4 million. This increase of 1,470 percent closely parallels the 1,300-percent increase in productivity suggesting that a close correlation existed between capital investments and productivity.[48]

As the output increased and the number of production units decreased, individual production units grew in size. The forty manufacturers surveyed in the 1823 report employed an average of 9.1 persons each. By 1850, the average size had grown to 60.1 employees per plant, an increase of about 660 percent in size. There are no reliable figures showing the total number of employees in the industry for the early period, so that overall fluctuations of employment cannot be charted with certainty. If the 9.1 average figure can be applied to the 410 naileries listed ten years earlier, it suggests that around 1810 about 3,000 persons were employed in the commercial nail manufacturing industry. In 1850, 5,237 individuals were so employed. If these figures are approximately correct, production per worker stood at between 4,200 and 5,000 pounds per year in the decade after 1810. By 1850, the average yearly production per employee had risen to 39,511 pounds.[49]

The increasing capital expenditure, the decline in prices, the trend toward centralization, and increasing worker productivity all suggest that mechanization was taking place. Since these changes were under way at a time when literary and artifactual sources show that new equipment was being introduced, it is safe to conclude that the industry was undergoing a technological revolution during the decades before 1850.

By the 1850s, the industry had attained a technological plateau, and there were no more dramatic innovations to be made until the wire nail was introduced later in the century. Between 1850 and 1870, production more than doubled--from 206,500,000 pounds to 443,000,440 pounds. Although a portion of this increase in productivity came from increasing individual productivity (from 39,500 pounds per employee in 1850 to 54,407 pounds per employee in 1870), a substantial part of it came from an expansion of the industry. During the period, the number of manufacturing units rose from 87 in 1850 to 142 in 1870. Capital investment also slowed, rising from $50,900 per plant in 1850 to $64,000 per plant in 1870.[50]

The statistical trends changed significantly again during the two decades after 1870. Between 1870 and 1886, cut nail production continued to increase, rising from 443,000,000 pounds to 816,000,000 pounds. Unlike earlier periods, when production increases were accompanied by a decreasing number of employees and concomitant gains in employee productivity, the 1870-1886 period witnessed a reversal of these trends. While production increased by 85 percent, the number of employees increased by 96 percent, and overall employee productivity actually declined by 6 percent.[51]

Several factors contributed to the changes that these statistics reflect. First, by the mid 1880s, the cut nail industry was badly overextended. In 1885, The Iron Age published reports that the capacity of the industry was 30 percent above demand. To cope with this condition, manufacturers during the late 1870s and the 1880s operated on "short time," closing plants for as much as six weeks per year. This affected the worker-productivity figures stated above. Second, throughout the 1870s and early 1880s, eastern manufacturers lagged behind the more modern western factories. In 1873, for example, Wheeling nail manufacturers averaged 159,800 pounds of nails per machine while Massachusetts manufacturers managed to produced only 66,300 pounds per machine. Finally, as already noted, there were no new technological developments introduced into the nail factories during the period. The cutter and header were universally in use by 1870 and, except for the automatic feeder that was being introduced during the late 1870s and early 1880s with heavy resistance from workmen, no changes were being made.[52]

The downward trend of prices continued throughout the 1870-1890 period. Prices stood at 4.4 cents per pound in 1870, declined to below 2.5 cents per pound during the late 1870s, rose to 3.4 cents per pound in 1883, and then began to drop gradually to 2 cents per pound by 1890. The decline in prices and relatively constant production levels are quite the opposite of earlier trends when prices were tied directly to productivity. After 1870, as will be developed in a later chapter, cost savings were related to efficiencies that resulted from industrial organization, refinements of the manufacturing process, and the prices of raw materials.[53]

In summary, then, it may be said that the cheaper prices and increase in production achieved during the first half of the nineteenth century resulted from the application of the cutter and header to the nail-making process. After the Civil War, the increased production resulted from adding more machines (to either existing or new plants), and the price declines came as a result of organization and manufacturing efficiencies. As has been noted and will appear below, the industry attained a certain technological maturity in the mid-nineteenth century, and the problems faced thereafter were those of organization and (after 1882) overproduction.

Sizeable increase in production and the accompanying decrease in the price of nails also suggest that basic changes were occurring in the industry. As the foregoing comments have pointed out, the application of new machines to ancient technology was a key factor. Technology alone, however, cannot account for all the growth even during the early years of the nineteenth century. Labor, capital, and market conditions all contributed to the growth and development of the nail industry, and each had a relationship to technology.

Few innovations were as perfectly suited to the environment in which they were developed as was the cut nail. Relatively scarce labor, abundant supplies of timber and the American reliance on wood for a wide range of uses, and linkages with other innovations in milling and architecture provided a set of conditions that encouraged the application of technology to nail manufacture.

Scholars such as H. J. Habakkuk have noted that labor was scarce and expensive during the eighteenth and much of the nineteenth centuries and have suggested that this created a favorable climate for the application of technology to manufacturing. The nail industry seems to confirm this theory. As we have seen, wrought nail manufacturing was a labor-intensive occupation with the gross output limited by the number of persons who could be enlisted to make nails. Contemporary observers were aware of the labor-intensive character of nail manufacturing and, in several instances, commented on the advantages of cut nail making in terms of the labor it saved. Read, for example, pointed out that his machine would permit labor savings. Coxe, in 1810, observed the overall advantage of cut nail machines as labor-saving devices. Finally, Bishop, in his three-volume History of American Manufacturers published in 1868, dwelt upon this theme at some length.[54]

The impact of labor supply on mechanization has been of particular interest to those who are interested in comparisons between the United States and other countries. It has been in such comparisons that the impact of the size of the labor market on technological developments has shown most clearly. When U.S. and English nail making are compared, labor supply and organizational differences appear to be most significant in decisions to introduce cut nail machines. Unlike England, where a large group of specialized nailers had a vested interest in the labor-intensive wrought nail, the United States received much of its domestic supply of nails from farmers and blacksmiths who viewed nailmaking as a secondary activity. The few full-time nailers who did work in New England and Pennsylvania nail factories had little to fear from the nail machine because the wrought nail remained much in demand for certain uses and, initially at least, was not affected by the cut nail.[55]

Furthermore, nail-making innovations were regarded with great patriotic pride. When cut nail machines were invented and brought into production, there was a feeling that they demonstrated American inventiveness. Bishop emphasized in several places that the nail machine was an American invention. George E. Sellers, a Philadelphia engineer, also commented upon the American origins of the cut nail. In a conversation with an Englishman, he recorded the following comments:

> I reminded him of the English prejudices that years before had led to the riots that destroyed nail cutting machines that Samuel R. Wood, of Philadelphia, was endeavoring to introduce in England. Wood...left England in disgust....I said it would be impossible to estimate or realize what the rejection of the cut nail had cost England. Mr. Donkin smiled as he said, "I have long been using in my pattern shop the American cut brads."[56]

Not only was there no opposition, but there were solid reasons for workmen to accept the machines. Since demand for nails was high, the more nails a workman could make the greater his income, and, as noted above, the nail machine permitted a dramatic increase in worker output. The cut nail machine and related improvements gave rise therefore to two entirely new occupations that were exceedingly profitable. The most profitable of these occupations was that of nailer, who was in fact a machine operator. The second occupation, feeder, was filled by a person who fed the plate into the machine.

Shubal Wilder, a nailer from Newcastle, Pennsylvania, recalled years later that "from 1825 to 1835, there was a great increase in the number of nail machines in factories in New England, New York, and all through New Jersey and Eastern Pennsylvania; consequently, there was a great demand for men to run the nail machines. Almost all the men kept coming to Massachusetts, on a hunt for nailers."[57] In fact, there appears to have been a shortage of trained nailers well into the 1870s. This constant demand for nailers and feeders insured that the jobs for both paid well. In 1874, Alexander Glass, a nailer who worked in Wheeling, earned between $15 and $20 per day, depending upon the size of nail he happened to be cutting. James Reeves, in an 1870 medical study of Wheeling, also noted that the nailer's job paid well. He observed that there were few nailers over 50 years of age working in the factories, not because of early death, "but the result of the wealth and independence which a few years in this business insures." The precise nature of the nailer and feeder jobs, the working conditions, and the pay scales will be discussed in some detail later in this book. Suffice it to say here that both were compensated well from the very beginning of the industry and that the cut nail machine meant wealth for all those who worked beside it.[58]

While labor supply and the acceptability of the machine by workmen had some role in the rapid acceptance of the process, other, and perhaps more important, factors must be considered. Foremost was the general availability of cutting machines. The cutter was simple and uncomplicated. Once the concept of cutting had been firmly established and its advantage seen, any mechanic could build a machine to do the work. A description of a machine used in Indiana County, Pennsylvania, in 1818, illustrates just how simple the cutters were.

> The machine used was propelled by one person using the right hand on one lever and the right foot on another lever. The left hand was occupied in manipulating the iron from which the nails were cut. Before cutting, the iron was brought to a red heat....After the nails were cut, they were taken to a place to be headed.[59]

In the eighteenth and early nineteenth centuries even crude equipment such as the cutter described above offered substantial savings over the hand-wrought process. But even the more sophisticated machines, such as the one developed by Read, could easily be copied. In 1797 Read complained that "a mechanic by the name of Bird...obtained in a clandestine manner access to the apartment where I had concealed the model of my machine, examined every part of it, and had its principles fully explained to him."[60]

The rapid introduction of cut nail technology was also aided by quick marketing of the machines by their inventors. Jacob Perkins, who invented a cutter in 1790, and Read, whose machine was patented in 1798, had their machines licensed very quickly. By 1809, Read's machine was being used in Massachusetts (22 at Malden), Pennsylvania, New Jersey, and Ohio. Wilder commented that the Read machine and the Perkins machine were the most widely used in 1825.[61]

Moreover, the cut nail machine was ideally suited for use in early nineteenth-century America because it could be used successfully in a variety of circumstances. For example, it could be powered by hand, as described by Wilder, by animal, by water, and later, by steam. One machine or many machines could be worked with reasonable expectation of profit, thus allowing nailmaking to be carried on in either small shops or large factories.[62]

The diversity of settings in which the nail machine could be used may be shown by citing a few examples. Massachusetts and Pennsylvania were the two leaders in nail production in 1810. In both of these states the machines were integrated into larger shops at a very early date. The Perkins Ironworks at Amesbury, Massachusetts, for instance, turned out 100 tons of cut nails in 1805. At the same time, Thomas Jefferson was using machines in his plantation shop, a very different sort of setting. A single machine such as one operated by horsepower in Zanesville, Ohio, or several machines such as those operated by the inmates at the New Jersey Prison, could turn a profit.[63]

Availability of iron was the only factor limiting use of the machine. From the 1750s until after 1800, nailers preferred Swedish and Russian iron for nailmaking. Shortly after 1800, the importation of Swedish and Russian iron declined, and nailers began to look to domestic sources such as the Pennsylvania ores for their supply. With this shift, nailers no longer had to rely upon coastal ports for iron supply, and the coastal locations lost much of their advantage and then their preeminence. As domestic iron supplies came into use, proximity to forges and rolling mills became more important. Coxe noted in 1810 that "the cut nail machinery has been very beneficially introduced into some...shops, near to the iron furnaces."[64]

Generally speaking, nail manufacturing developed along one of two lines as the cut nail machinery was introduced. On the one hand, existing metal-working establishments added nail-making capacity. Both Nathaniel Read and Jacob Perkins introduced their machines in conjunction with other items, such as chains and anchors. Coxe, in the 1810 report on manufacturers, noted that some shops had introduced nail-making machines, "insuring the profitable employment of all of the time not otherwise occupied." Ten years later, the census of manufacturers bore out this observation. Eight of the forty manufacturers listed in this census also manufactured other items such as domestic utensils, scythes, hoes, and hoops.[65]

For existing finished metal products manufacturers, the cut nail was an ideal product. The manufacturing process was simple, relatively inexpensive, and could be carried on with simple machinery. Furthermore, the nail market appears to have been relatively stable during the early part of the nineteenth century. Tariff laws not only protected manufacturers from imported wrought nails but foreign demand even opened an export market for American nails during the first decade of the century. Between 1807 and 1810, for example, Massachusetts nailers exported 280 tons of nails.[66]

While cut nails were second and third products in some manufacturing establishments, many factories and shops began to specialize in the production of cut nails by the second decade of the nineteenth century. Small and medium-size manufacturers grew up in Connecticut, Rhode Island, and Massachusetts, where producers had access to imported nail plate. Similarly, many manufacturers in the Pennsylvania iron region began production near the iron furnaces and rolling mills.[67]

By the second decade of the nineteenth century, the scale of some of the specialized manufacturers increased noticeably, signaling a movement toward the large-scale, integrated manufacture of nails. One of the first large manufacturers of nails was the Amesbury (Massachusetts) Nail Factory, incorporated in 1805.

This factory grew out of the Jacob Perkins nail innovation and contained both a rolling mill and a nail factory. A disastrous fire and difficulty in obtaining iron caused the mill to cease operation sometime around 1825. In 1809, Thomas Odiorne and several associates purchased the patent nail machine of Jesse Reed (not to be confused with Nathaniel Read) of Boston. Odiorne, in what was probably the first major attempt at large-scale nail manufacturing, established three plants--one at Malden, Massachusetts; one at Chester Creek, Pennsylvania; and one at Phoenixville, Pennsylvania. The two factories in Pennsylvania included rolling and slitting mills and between them had 52 machines. In 1838, the Phoenixville Ironworks added boiling furnaces, becoming the first specialized nail factory to produce its own wrought iron. Other large manufacturers included the Troy Iron and Nail Factory, founded in 1822 by Henry Burden. This factory, significant because its owner was the inventor of the rotary squeezer and the automatic spike machine, developed slowly from a small nail works to one that by mid-century had two forges, two rolling mills, and twenty-four puddling furnaces.[68]

As will be shown below, the first nail factories established in Wheeling were much like the Phoenixville and Troy works. They had boiling furnaces, rolling mills, and nail factories combined in a single operation. After the Civil War, the Wheeling nail makers went even further and purchased blast furnaces (later Bessemer converters), coal mines, iron mines, and transportation facilities.[69]

The existence of a sizeable market for large quantities of cheap nails was the final factor that promoted the use of cut nail equipment. From the earliest days of settlement, Americans relied on wood to meet a wide range of needs. It was in situations where wood had to be fastened to wood or wood to metal that the nail was most useful. The need was a significant one that was recognized during the nineteenth century. A writer for The Iron Age observed in 1882 that "the abundance of timber in America...urged the mechanics on in their efforts to make practical nail machines." The reliance upon wood and the need for nails in construction was intensified during the nineteenth century by the rapid growth of the nation. During the century, the population grew from 5.2 to 76.1 million and this alone placed a heavy demand on the housing industry.[70]

During the late eighteenth and early nineteenth centuries, three basic building styles were common in the United States. The log house, which has become so symbolic of the American frontier, was built by laying log upon log to form a wall that supported the roof. This type of construction required little skill, only a minimum number of tools, and few materials not found on or near the site of construction. The structure could literally be built without using a single nail, but many builders did manage to purchase or manufacture enough nails to make doors, window frames, and shutters.[71]

The log house was almost universally regarded as temporary shelter to be improved upon and replaced as soon as possible. The replacement house was often a frame structure. Large timbers were fitted together, usually with mortise joints to form a framework that supported the roof and provided a matrix for affixing the weatherboarding to make the walls. Such construction required a supply of nails for use in weatherboarding, roofing, windows, doors, interior woodwork, and floors. Even with this type of construction, however, nails could be replaced in many areas, such as the flooring, with wooden pegs.

In some areas, particularly the East, stone and brick construction was also common. Even this type of construction required nails for interior woodwork, roofing, windows, and door frames. For example, Thomas Worthington, the first

Senator from Ohio, constructed a large stone mansion near Chillicothe during the first decade of the nineteenth century. His records show that his workmen consumed over 600 pounds of nails in the construction of the roof and interior woodwork. The roofing alone required almost 33,000 shingle nails.[72]

Although the mortise frame and stone or brick structure was popular in the more settled areas, it was not well suited for the needs of the growing country. Both types of building relied heavily upon the ready availability of construction materials at or near the site of construction. In addition, both required skilled artisans such as masons and carpenters and consumed considerable amounts of time in construction.

As the country grew and settlement pushed on to the western prairie, supplies of wood and other construction materials were less available than they had been in the East. The traditional log house that had served eastern settlers well could not be constructed with ease on the prairies. Furthermore, the boom-town character of many of the western mining and railroad construction settlements required rapid construction of temporary structures where artisans, such as carpenters, were often in short supply. These conditions gave rise to a new type of structure that depended on precut lumber and smaller and lighter framing members.

The new type of building became known as the "balloon frame" or "basket frame." Like the log cabin that was so symbolic of the advancing frontier east of the great prairies, the balloon frame was the first dwelling for the western settlers. It shared with the log cabin two important characteristics. Both could be constructed quickly, and neither required the services of a skilled carpenter.

Although it is impossible to determine precisely when or where the "balloon frame" construction was first used, there is considerable evidence that it appeared in Chicago about 1833 when George W. Snow, a New Hampshire lumber dealer, constructed St. Mary's Church. The style of building used by Snow was so intimately associated with Chicago that for some years during the 1840s it was referred to as the "Chicago frame" technique of construction. Harry E. Pratt, a resident of Chicago in 1833, later described the new structures and the conditions that led to their development as follows:

> Nearly all the buildings put up that year were, what was aptly described as balloon frames. That is, 2" x 6" joists for sills, studs 2" x 4" toed onto the sills by nails, a strip of inch board for plate and, if one story strips of inch boards for the joists....It required but little mechanical skill to build one. It was not uncommon to see one rise in a single day and constitute the next day a snug home for a young and enterprising couple.[73]

Pratt also described the conditions that existed in Chicago at the time. The town was a bustling boom town sorely in need of buildings but woefully short of materials and skilled labor.

> The town was full of strangers and more flocking in daily. All was activity and enterprise, and preparations for building everywhere. No mills had yet been started in the pine forests of Lake Michigan and the timber brought in from across the lake was mostly white wood. Some was brought up from the Wabash by teams....However, the country was then so wet much of the time the roads were so bad that it was difficult and expensive to move lumber from them [sawmills on the Wabash] to Chicago.[74]

From Chicago, the new style of buildings spread very rapidly. In 1835, Solon Robinson described a model home in The American Agriculturist by saying that "it [the house] is particularly intended for the new settler, and is to be built on a balloon plan, which has not a single tenon or mortise in the frame...all the uprights are held together by nails...and just as good and far cheaper than ordinary frames." Others, including G. E. Woodward in his book, Woodward's Country Homes, and Horace Greeley, one of the authors of Great Industries of America, noted the "balloon frame" and attributed to it some significance. Greeley commented:

> The method of construction with wood known as balloon framing is also the most important contribution to our domestic architecture....The heavy beams, the laborious framing, and the use of mortise and tenons have all been replaced...so that a single man, and a boy can put up a house, such as formerly, for its raising, required the combined force of a village. There is hardly better evidence of the American spirit...than the introduction of this new style of building, and it has really been the most efficient cause of the rapidity with which, in modern times, our villages and towns spring into existence.[75]

The essential ingredients in the balloon frame were the nail and the precut timber. As already noted, the development of the cut nail machine assured the capability of supplying large numbers of nails at reasonable cost by the 1830s. In 1833, when Snow built his Chicago "balloon frame," for example, nails already sold at an average of 5 cents per pound and the price was rapidly declining. The cutnail machine, along with new milling equipment that made predimension lumber readily available, coincided with the need of the western environment to provide a new type of building. The new building, in turn, stimulated demand for nails and prompted additional growth in the nail industry.[76]

Greeley's view that the balloon frame was evidence of the American spirit was indeed accurate, for it rested squarely upon the nail industry, and the numerous innovations that produced it were largely products of the American environment. Greeley and other writers pointed consistently to the labor-saving characteristic of the balloon frame which came primarily as a result of the replacement of the mortise and tenon with the nail. As significant as the savings in time was, the replacement of the skilled mechanic with the unskilled workman in the construction industry was even more important.

Estimates vary on the amount of savings. In 1869, one writer said that the balloon frame could be constructed for "forty percent less money that the mortise and tenon frame."[77]

The two American innovations, the balloon frame and the cut nail, not only relied upon each other but also may be seen as a direct outgrowth of the physical environment and the economy where labor was at a premium. Both stand as monuments of sorts to the American ideal of efficiency and mass production. The cutter and the automatic header speeded up the rate of production of nails, reduced the amount of labor required by the industry, and introduced efficiencies in materials use through savings on slitting and through the standardization of the product. Likewise, the balloon-framed house could be constructed faster than previously used housing types, at less cost, and with less labor.

At the same time that Snow was constructing St. Mary's Church in Chicago, David Agnew, a Pittsburgh iron master, was looking at Wheeling, West Virginia, as a possible site for the manufacture of nails. Attracted by a sizeable supply of coal that could be used to fuel furnaces and steam engines, Agnew constructed a puddling, rolling, and nail factory that within a few decades was to be the foundation for the largest single group of nail manufacturers in the country. Between 1833 and 1900 Wheeling mills produced approximately 50 million kegs of nails, most of which were used in the American West. By 1890, it could be fairly said that there were few communities between the Ohio and the Rockies that did not have nails made in Wheeling, West Virginia, holding at least some of the dwellings together.[78]

Because the birth of the nail industry in Wheeling not only coincides closely with the development of the balloon frame house but also with the perfection of the automatic nail header, this segment of the nail industry developed at a point when the major innovations in the industry were complete and when the market was beginning to expand. Alfred D. Chandler, author of The Visible Hand, observed that "modern business enterprise rose as the volume of business activities reached a level that made coordination by management more efficient and more profitable than market coordination" and that "such an increase in volume of activity came with new technology and expanding markets." The Wheeling nail industry had the benefits of new technology and an expanding market.[79]

Notes

1. Victor S. Clark, History of Manufacturers in the United States 1607-1860 (3 vols., New York: Peter Smith, 1949); Peter Temin, Iron and Steel in 19th Century America (Cambridge, Mass.: The MIT Press, 1964); Daniel J. Boorstin, The Americans: The National Experience (New York: Random House, 1965), pp. 155-158; Henry C. Mercer, "Dating Old Houses," Old Time New England, April 1924; Henry C. Mercer, Ancient Carpenters' Tools (Doylestown, Pa.: The Bucks County Historical Society, 1929); Lee H. Nelson, "A Nail Chronology," The American Association for State and Local History, Technical Leaflet #48; Susan Buggey, "Supplying Building Materials to the British Army in the Colonies: An Illustrated Document," The Association for Preservation Technology Bulletin VIII (1976), pp. 87-92; Peter Priess, "Wire Nails in North America," The Association for Preservation Technology Bulletin V (1973), pp. 87-92.

2. J. Leander Bishop, A History of American Manufacturers from 1608 to 1860 (3 vols., Philadelphia: Edward Young & Company, 1868); Henry Dickerson Scott, Iron and Steel in Wheeling (Toledo: Caslon Co., 1929); Horace Greeley et al., The Great Industries of the United States (Hartford, Conn.: J. B. Burr, Hyde & Co., 1872).

3. Mercer, Ancient Carpenters' Tools, pp. 238-244; Kenneth M. Wilson, "Nailers' Anvils at Old Sturbridge Village," The Chronicle of the Early American Industries Association, June 1960, p. 1; "Nail Headers," The Chronicle of the Early American Industries Association, November 1961, p. 36; Dionysius Lardner, The Cabinet Cyclopaedia (London: Longman, Rees, Orme, Brown & Green, 1831), pp. 193-196.

4. James M. Swank, History of the Manufacture of Iron in All Ages and Particularly in the United States from Colonial Times to 1891 (Philadelphia: American Iron and Steel Association, 1892), pp. 48-49.

5. Susan M. Kingsburg (ed.), The Records of the Virginia Company of London (4 vols., Washington: Government Printing Office, 1936), IV, p. 227; C. A. Weslager, The Log Cabin in America (New Brunswick, N.J.: Rutgers University Press, 1969), p. 119.

6. Nelson, "A Nail Chronology," p. 3; Arthur C. Bining, Pennsylvania Iron Manufacture in the Eighteenth Century (New York: Augustus M. Kelley, 1970), pp. 62-63.

7. Lawrence S. Cooke, "Nail Rod and Some of Its By-Products," The Chronicle of the Early American Industries Association, March 1961, pp. 6-7. The prevalence of artifacts made from nail rod can be seen by examining almost any museum collection that contains examples of early American metal.

8. Abridgments of the Debates of Congress from 1789 to 1856 (New York: D. Appleton & Co., 1857), I, p. 38.

9. Bishop, Manufactures, I, pp. 491, 623-624.

10. Charles J. Hoadly, The Public Records of the Colony of Connecticut from May 1717 to October 1725 (Hartford, Conn.: Lockwood & Brainard, 1872), p. 312.

11. Ibid., p. 313; Bishop, Manufactures, I, pp. 483, 503, 519; Bining, Pennsylvania Iron, pp. 150-153, 179-183.

12. Robert A. East, Business Enterprise in the American Revolutionary Era (New York: Columbia University Press, 1938), p. 19; Florence S. Marcy Crofut, Guide to the History and Historic Sites of Connecticut (2 vols., New Haven: Yale University Press, 1937), I, pp. 188, 189, 279, 420, 443; John Litle, "Accounts of Smiths' and Nailers' Work Received from January 19, 1778-October 1, 1779," MS, Library, The American Philosophical Society, Philadelphia.

13. Clark, History of Manufacturers, I, p. 222; Tench Coxe, A Statement of the Arts and Manufacturers of the United States of America for the Year 1810 (Philadelphia: A. Cornman, 1814), [p. 11]; Francis A. Walker, The Statistics of the Wealth and Industry of the United States Compiled from the Original Returns of the Ninth Census (Washington: Government Printing Office, 1872), p. 617; Bishop, Manufactures, III, pp. 446, 617.

14. Committee on Historical Statistics of the Social Science Research Council, The Statistical History of the United States from Colonial Times to the Present (Stamford, Conn.: Fairfield Publishers, Inc., 1965), p. 765; Bishop, Manufactures, I, pp. 499, 500, 523, 629; Abridgments of the Debates of Congress from 1789 to 1865, I, p. 38; Bishop, Manufactures, II, p. 35; B. F. French, History of the Rise and Progress of the Iron Trade of the United States from 1621 to 1857 (New York: Wiley & Halsted, 1858), pp. 12, 13.

15. Committee, Historical Statistics, p. 124; Thomas Senior Berry, Western Prices before 1861 (Harvard: Cambridge University Press, 1943), p. 248; Gen. John Johnston, "Account Book of Gen. John Johnston, Indian Agent, Ft. Wayne, Indiana, 1802-1811," p. 9, MS, Library of the Ohio Historical Society, Columbus; John Litle, "Accounts of Smiths' and Nailers' Work Received," entries for January 5 and January 8, 1778.

16. Bishop, Manufactures, II, p. 34; Swank, History, pp. 49, 188; Coxe, Arts and Manufactures, p. xxxi; Francis B. C. Bradlee, "The Salem Iron Factory," Historical Collections of the Essex Institute, April 1918, pp. 103-104; Albert S. Bolles, Industrial History of the United States (Norwich, Conn.: The Henry Bill Publishing Co., 1881), p. 218.

17. Susan Buggey, "Supplying Building Materials to the British Army in the Colonies: An Illustrated Document," The Association for Preservation Technology Bulletin VIII (1976), pp. 94-118; Nelson, "Chronology," pp. 6-7.

18. Buggey, "Supplying Building Materials," pp. 94-118. This article is largely a reprint of the Royal Engineers Catalogue and contains one of the best graphic descriptions of wrought nails found during this study; Mercer, "Dating Old Houses," Old Time New England, April 1924, p. 171.

19. There are no reliable data on production rates for wrought nails. John Litle's "Account Book" does give numbers of nails produced for several nailers. John Willson, February 14, 1778--6,725/10d; John Willson, June 6, 1778--1,200/10d; Edward Reamer, January 22, 1778--2,565/10d; John Blackburn, February 14, 1778--8,761/10d. From these and other accounts in Bishop, it is clear that any production over 6,000 (10d) per day was excellent. On February 14, 1778, when John Willson produced 6,725 nails, he had at the end of the day

produced 134 pounds, or about one and one-third kegs of nails.

20. Bishop, Manufactures, I, p. 388; H. J. Habakkuk, American and British Technology in Nineteenth Century (Cambridge, England: The University Press, 1962), pp. 17-28, 172.

21. Bishop, Manufactures, I, pp. 498, 571. The number of patents for nail machines was arrived at by counting the listings of patents granted between 1790 and 1836. See Commissioner of Patents, A List of Patents Granted by the United States from April 10, 1790 to December 31, 1836 (Washington: Government Printing Office, 1872), pp. 7-690.

22. Lardner, The Cabinet, pp. 197-199; Horace Greeley, et al., Great Industries of the United States, p. 1072. At least a few innovators attempted to produce cast nails (Nelson, "Chronology," p. 6). They were too brittle and would not stand up to the carpenter's hammer. Occasionally, a sample of a cast nail will show up in an old structure or in the collections of museums. During the course of this study, approximately 4,000 nail samples were studied plus numerous photographs of nails. The sample ranged from nails taken from a fortification (Ft. Laurens) constructed in 1778 to modern cut nails taken directly from a currently operating cutting machine at the LaBelle Nail Works. No samples of machine wrought nails were found.

23. Mercer, "Dating Old Houses," pp. 172-175; Nelson, "Chronology," pp. 3-10. This description is also based upon examination of nail machines at the LaBelle Nail Works of the Wheeling-Pittsburgh Steel Corporation. The machines, which are still in operation, date to the late nineteenth century. In addition, the company has wooden foundry patterns for machines that date from the 1850s.

24. Bradlee, "The Salem Iron Factory," pp. 110-111.

25. Ibid., pp. 103-104, 110.

26. Nelson, "Chronology," pp. 4-9.

27. For a general discussion of state encouragement of manufacturing and transportation, see Alfred D. Chandler et al., The Changing Economic Order (New York: Harcourt, Brace & World, Inc., 1968), pp. 148-165.

28. Bishop, Manufactures, I, pp. 498-499.

29. Ibid., p. 619.

30. Ibid., p. 519.

31. Abridgments of the Debates of Congress, I, p. 38; Bishop, Manufactures, II, p. 485; F. W. Taussig, The Tariff History of the United States (New York: G. P. Putnam & Sons, 1930), p. 51; French, History of the Rise and Progress of the Iron Trade, pp. 15-18; Walter Lowrie and Matthew St. Clair Clarke (eds.), Documents, Legislative and Executive, of the Congress of the United States from the First Congress to the Third Session of the Thirteenth Congress, Inclusive (9 vols., Washington: Gates & Seaton), VIII, pp. 854-855; Hunt's Merchant Magazine XLIV (1861), p. 496.

32. Bishop, Manufactures, I, pp. 498-499; Abridgments of the Debates of Congress, p. 38.

33. Bishop, Manufactures, I, pp. 498-499.

34. Coxe, Arts and Manufactures, p. xxxi.

35. Ibid., [p. 11.]

36. Bradlee, "The Salem Iron Factory," pp. 99, 109-114; Commissioner of Patents, A List of Patents, pp. 11-13, 22.

37. Mercer, "Dating Old Houses," p. 174; Digest of Accounts of Manufacturing Establishments in the United States in 1823 (Washington: Gates & Seaton, 1823), pp. 2-31.

38. Mercer, "Dating Old Houses," pp. 173-175; Nelson, "Chronology," pp. 3-11.

39. Committee, Historical Statistics, p. 124.

40. Bradlee, "The Salem Iron Factory," pp. 110, 111, 113; Swank, History, pp. 448-449; Commissioner of Patents, A List of Patents, pp. 270, 377, 646; Commissioner of Patents, Report for 1856 (Washington: Cornelius Wendell, 1857), I, pp. 222.

41. Bishop, Manufactures, II, p. 634. "Clinched" is a term used to describe a nail that was driven through a board and then bent at a 90• angle.

42. Ibid. For a discussion of Burden, see Paul J. Uselding, "Henry Burden and the Question of Anglo-American Technological Transfer in the Nineteenth Century," The Journal of Economic History, XXX, pp. 312-337.

43. Bradlee, "The Salem Iron Factory," p. 111.

44. F. H. Kindl, The Rolling Mill Industry (Cleveland: Penton Publishing Co., 1913), p. 41; Peter Priess, "Wire Nails in North America," pp. 89-90.

45. Committee, Historical Statistics, pp. 7, 123-124.

46. Coxe, Arts and Manufactures, [p. 11]; French, History of the Rise and Progress of the Iron Trade, pp. 15, 18, 20, 23, 25, 71; Digest, 1823, pp. 2-31.

47. Coxe, Arts and Manufactures, [p. 11]; Walker, The Statistics of the Wealth and Industry of the United States, III, p. 617; Bishop, Manufactures, III, p. 486; Douglass C. North, Growth and Welfare in the American Past (Englewood Cliffs, N.J.: Prentice-Hall, Inc., 1966), p. 31. Figures on productivity are based on prices for the year.

48. Coxe, Arts and Manufactures, [p. 11]; Walker, The Statistics of the Wealth and Industry of the United States, III, p. 406.

49. Digest, 1823, pp. 2-31; Bishop, Manufactures, III, p. 486; Coxe, Arts and Manufactures, [p. 11].

50. Walker, The Statistics of the Wealth and Industry of the United States, III, p. 617.

51. Ibid., p. 396; Statistics of the American and Foreign Iron Trades for 1899 (Philadelphia: The American Iron and Steel Association, 1900), pp. 56-57; Twelfth Census of the United States Taken in the Year 1900 VII, pt. 1 (Washington: Government Printing Office, 1902), p. 9.

52. The Iron Age, April 2, 1885; The Wheeling Intelligencer, March 7, 1874, April 26, 1875, and May 10, 1875.

53. Committee, Historical Statistics, pp. 123-124. Figures cited are computed based on data contained in The Iron Age, April 6, 1876; Walker, The Statistics of the Wealth and Industry of the United States, p. 617; Scott, Iron & Steel in Wheeling, p. 40.

54. Habakkuk, American and British Technology, p. 17; Bradlee, "The Salem Iron Factory," pp. 111-112; Coxe, Arts

and Manufactures, p. xiv; Bishop, Manufactures, I, p. 500; Bishop, Manufactures, II, p. 634.

55. Eugene S. Ferguson (ed.), "Early Engineering Reminiscences (1815-1840) of George Escol Sellers," U.S. National Museum Bulletin CCXXXVIII (1965), pp. 125-126; Scientific American Supplement I (1876), pp. 89-90. Also see Hunt's Merchant Magazine, November 1851, p. 578; Bishop, Manufactures II, pp. 153-154.

56. Ferguson, "Early Engineering Reminiscences," pp. 125-126.

57. Swank, History, pp. 448-449. The scarcity of skilled nailers to operate the growing number of machines tends to support Paul Uselding's argument that labor scarcity was at least partially a result of technological change. See Lewis D. Cain and Paul J. Uselding (eds.), Enterprise and Economic Change (Kent, Ohio: The Kent State University Press, 1973), p. 77. I have no interest in addressing the differences between Habakkuk and Uselding except to note that the nail industry may in fact prove that both theories are correct. It seems that initially labor scarcity as reflected through high labor costs did prompt the development of the cut nail machine and related innovations. In turn, however, these machines created a need for specialization and, in fact, there resulted a shortage of nailers and feeders.

58. Robert L. Plummer, Sixty-Five Years of Iron and Steel in Wheeling: Reminiscences of Alexander Glass, n.p., n.d., p. 13. This printed volume is in the library of the West Virginia Historical Society at Charleston, West Virginia; James E. Reeves, M.D., The Physical and Medical Topography of the City of Wheeling (Wheeling: Wheeling Daily Register, 1870), p. 23.

59. Swank, History, p. 449.

60. Bradlee, "The Salem Iron Factory," p. 110.

61. Charles I. Pettingell, "Powow River Industries," The Essex Institute Historical Collections LXXXII (1946), p. 322; Bishop, Manufactures, II, pp. 124-125; Swank, History, pp. 448-449.

62. Swank, History, pp. 448-449; J. F. Everhart, History of Muskingum County, Ohio (Columbus, Ohio: A. A. Graham, 1882), p. 88.

63. Coxe, Arts and Manufactures, [p. 11]; Pettingell, "Powow River Industries," p. 321; John F. Kasson, Civilizing the Machine, Technology and Republican Values in America 1776-1900 (New York: Grossman Publishers, 1976), p. 24; Everhart, History of Muskingum County, Ohio, p. 88; Kathleen Bruce, Virginia Iron Manufacture in the Slave Era (New York: The Century Co., 1931), p. 129.

64. Bishop, Manufactures, I, p. 629; Coxe, Arts and Manufactures, p. xxxi.

65. Ibid.; Digest, 1823, pp. 7, 10, 14, 15, 28.

66. Bishop, Manufactures, II, pp. 153-154.

67. Ibid., I, p. 629; Crofut, Guide to the History, I, pp. 188, 189, 279, 420, 433; Bishop, Manufactures, II, pp. 125, 126, 131; Ronald L. Michael, "Cut Nail Manufacture: Southwestern Pennsylvania," p. 99.

68. Bishop, Manufactures, II, pp. 111, 125, 126, 634; Pettingell, "Powow River Industries," p. 321; Bishop, Manufactures, III, p. 478.

69. Committee, Historical Statistics, pp. 123-124; "The Minutes of the Meetings of the Board of Directors and Stockholders of the LaBelle Iron Works (Bailey, Woodward & Company) from January 28, 1868 to September 20, 1873," MS, records of the Wheeling-Pittsburgh Steel Corporation, Wheeling, West Virginia, p. 23; "A Letter from John Griffen, Iron Master 1878; A Description of Improvements in the Manufacture of Iron, Pennsylvania, 1843-1878," Journal of Economic and Business History III (1930-1931), pp. 687-695.

70. The Iron Age, September 22, 1881; Committee, Historical Statistics, p. 7.

71. Weslager, Log Cabin in America, p. 225.

72. "Bills for Repairs on House," Worthington Papers, MS in the collections of the Ohio Historical Society, Columbus.

73. Harry E. Pratt, "Chicago in 1833 and 1834," Journal of the Illinois State Historical Society XXVIII (1935), pp. 11-12; Mable McIlvaine (ed.), Reminiscences of Chicago during the Forties and Fifties (Chicago: The Lakeside Press, 1913), pp. 6-7; Sigfried Giedion, Space, Time and Architecture, The Growth of a New Tradition (Cambridge, Mass.: Harvard University Press, 1949), pp. 281-289.

74. Pratt, "Chicago in 1833 and 1834," pp. 10-11.

75. Herbert Anthony Kellar (ed.), Solon Robinson: Pioneer and Agriculturist, Selected Writings (3 vols., Indianapolis: Indiana Historical Bureau, 1936), I, pp. 553-558; Greeley, Great Industries of the United States, p. 41.

76. "Manufactures of the United States," DeBow's Review XVII (1854), pp. 632-635; Committee, Historical Statistics, pp. 122-123.

77. Walker Field, "A Reexamination into the Invention of the Balloon Frame," Journal of the American Society of Architectural Historians II (1942), pp. 7-8.

78. Scott, Iron and Steel, pp. 7-8.

79. Alfred D. Chandler, Jr., The Visible Hand: The Managerial Revolution in American Business (Cambridge, Mass.: The Belknap Press, 1977), p. 8.

2
Founding the Nail Industry 1834-1860

> You have been pleased to refer...to my connection with the iron interest of Wheeling. It would be vanity in me to appropriate to myself the honor, although I may have been the moving cause...in bringing about the grand results that have been achieved in the iron manufacturies of the city.
>
> E. W. Stephens
> The Wheeling Intelligencer
> April 9, 1856

When American settlement breached the Allegheny Mountains during the last quarter of the eighteenth century, the Upper Ohio Valley was the first stop for the westward-bound travelers. Protection provided by several military forts encouraged many of the earliest travelers to take advantage of the federal land policy and remain in the area between Pittsburgh and Fort Henry. Once established, the settlers were in a position to profit from the continued western migration, first as provisioners for the parties traveling west and then, because of the relatively easy water transportation, as suppliers to the growing population in the lower Ohio and Mississippi valleys. The profit to be reaped from commerce, the expense and difficulty of importing eastern manufactured goods, and the availability of key natural resources provided the impetus for traders to become manufacturers as soon as capital, skill, and natural resources were available.

The residents of Wheeling, Virginia, like their contemporaries in several other towns along the upper reaches of the Ohio River, were quick to take advantage of the opportunity offered by their unique location. By 1820, Wheeling had become a minor commercial town located at the junction between a land route to the West and the Ohio River. As early as the third decade of the nineteenth century, the commercial interests in Wheeling were beginning to shift their attention from commerce to manufacturing. Within this context, the manufacture of nails began and flourished, slowly at first, but more rapidly as the century progressed.

The Upper Ohio Valley felt the influence of two larger urban centers, Pittsburgh and Cincinnati, which played an important role in the economic and cultural life of the entire region. Because of its close proximity to Pittsburgh, Wheeling was always influenced by the economic life of the "Iron City." Cincinnati, a down-river town, exerted less direct influence, and yet because the market for nails made in Wheeling lay to the south and west, and because Cincinnati was a major distribution center, that city, too, was of substantial importance. Much of the information on western nail prices, for example, has been drawn from the quotations on the Cincinnati market.[1]

Although the success of the Wheeling nail industry was rooted in broad economic factors, such as favorable markets, location, natural resources, and excellent transportation facilities, purely local conditions and specific individuals played a significant part in its establishment and growth. As has been found in the histories of other nineteenth-century cities, personalities and local pride, expressed in urban boosterism, so typical of the Midwest during the early decades of the century, were of substantial importance. Local, and a few industrial, historians who have given attention to the nail industry have in fact tended to place much emphasis on the role of a handful of individuals who established the first mills. Some writers have portrayed the founders as visionaries, while others, including some of the participants, have viewed these men as simple mechanics looking for a place and circumstances in which to practice their trade. The inescapable conclusion is that as a group, the founders were neither visionaries nor simple craftsmen. They were speculators whose motives were not unlike the land speculators or town promoters of the era.

The period between 1830 and 1865 was a time of transition. Isaac Lippincott, in his classic (1914) <u>Economic History of the Ohio Valley</u>, took the 1830s as a transition date that divided the "pioneer period," during which commerce was the major nonagricultural activity, from the "mill period" in which manufacturing evolved. This interpretation seems to be essentially correct if somewhat overstated. Richard Wade, author of <u>The Urban Frontier</u>, the best of the scholarly works on the early history of the Ohio Valley, was perhaps more accurate, if less precise, in his assessment of the period. Western towns, he said, were "cradled in commerce but while very young showed remarkable manufacturing promise." It was in these three decades that the infant towns of the Upper Ohio began to leave the cradle, although, to follow Wade's figure of speech, they never ventured far from its nurture.[2]

Manufacturing first grew up in and around Pittsburgh. The early factory products (iron, glass, and ceramics) answered the needs created by the local provisioning trade. Settlers moving west in the 1790s and the first decades of the nineteenth century typically abandoned their land vehicles south and east of Pittsburgh and took first to the Allegheny and then to the Ohio River for the final leg of their journey. Pittsburgh and the neighboring settlements were handy places to stock up on needed supplies and to replace tools what were too bulky for the land journey or that were destroyed during the trip over the mountains. As early as 1789, Pittsburgh newspapers advertised the products of such diverse manufacturing trades as cabinet making, upholstering, locksmithing, and sickle and scythe making. In addition to the supply trade stimulated as settlers moved west, the military campaigns launched against the Indians from Pittsburgh and Cincinnati in the 1790s also stimulated the provisioning trade. A decade and a half later, the military expeditions of the War of 1812 had a similar impact.[3]

As the new settlers became customers for the products of the towns and cities of the Upper Ohio Valley, the growing market and the availability of natural resources (coal, iron, sand, and clay) stimulated manufacturers to undertake a wide variety of enterprises at an early date, just as in Pittsburgh. Iron manufacturing began in the Upper Ohio Valley as early as 1798 and spread throughout western Pennsylvania and eastern Ohio during the early decades of the nineteenth century. In addition, the manufacture of glass, textiles, and ceramics, to name only the most prominent, grew up not only in the Pittsburgh area but in other towns along the Ohio River such as Steubenville, East Liverpool, and Wheeling. In 1818 and 1819, two English travelers, Thomas Hume and Timothy Flint, took note of the manufacturing in the Upper Ohio Valley when they journeyed separately through the region. Hume commented on a "glass works" at Wellsburg, then known as Charlestown, and a woolen manufactory, a cotton mill, a paper mill, an iron foundry, and "tanyards" at Steubenville. Flint, in addition to commenting on the works mentioned by Hume, described an iron furnace, a fulling mill, and a carding mill near the mouth of Beaver Creek, and two earthenware manufacturers in Steubenville. Flint also took note of "a considerable number of artisans" and the fact that the machines in the several establishments of the region were "wrought [powered] by steam."[4]

Another natural characteristic of the region that influenced the growth of manufacturing was the poor quality of the land. After the first settlers had taken up the valley lands, the availability of prime agricultural land was limited. Particularly after better agricultural regions farther to the west opened up in the 1840s and 1850s, labor could be more profitably employed in commercial and manufacturing activities. For example, in rural counties such as Monroe County, Ohio, population actually began to decline after 1850. By contrast, there was a noticeable influx of rural workers into the potteries at East Liverpool toward the end of this period.[5]

The single most important restraint on the development of manufacturing was the lack of capital and a related shortage of currency. Throughout the early decades of the century, eastern investment was noticeably limited even in the more developed cities such as Pittsburgh, Cincinnati, and Lexington. All through the Ohio Valley, businessmen were left to their own devices to raise the money needed for equipping factories, constructing buildings, and procuring other facilities needed for production.[6]

The capital that did accumulate locally was almost always generated locally, and from one of two sources. The profits from commerce, specifically the provisioning trade, have already been noted. Writers, such as Wade and Lippincott, have given great weight to the importance of this source of capital, concluding that trade was of importance as a stimulus for manufacturing. Its importance as a source of capital, however, which is a different matter, has been much overstated. While there can be little question that men such as Colonel James O'Hara and John McClung, two Pittsburgh manufacturers, used profits from commercial ventures to begin manufacturing enterprises, the source for much of the early manufacturing capital was land speculation.[7]

Steubenville, Ohio, provides an example of a direct link between land and manufacturing enterprises. The early history of this place has received little notice even though travelers visiting the region during the early years of the nineteenth century consistently noted the industrial character of the town. During the second decade of the nineteenth century, Steubenville and the towns in the immediate vicinity were second only to Pittsburgh in manufacturing. Steubenville was the location of the U.S. Land Office between 1800 and 1821. As a consequence, currency was present in a greater proportion than in other cities, since land was one of the few things that could not be purchased through barter. And, in fact, one individual, Bezaleel Wells, a land speculator who had amassed large holdings in the old Seven Range land survey area, was responsible for the founding of the textile industry that flourished in and around Steubenville after 1810.[8]

A similar, but less obvious, situation existed at Wheeling. Archibald Woods, an ex-military man who had settled in Wheeling in the late eighteenth century, accumulated a sizeable fortune from Ohio land sales. Woods, in concert with his brother and Johnathan Paull, purchased much of the land that now comprises Monroe and southern Belmont counties and in 1813 founded the town of Woodsfield, selling off the surrounding lands. The money Woods realized from this venture eventually went into the organization of the Bank of Northwest Virginia at Wheeling. During the 1830s and 1840s this institution, one of only two banks in Wheeling, provided resources for the expanded nail industry and a share of Wheeling's subscription to the Baltimore and Ohio Railroad.[9]

As a region, then, the Upper Ohio Valley had advantages of location in relation to markets, the availability of good transportation, a good supply of natural resources, and if not liberal, at least an adequate, source of capital. Early efforts to develop manufacturing that were successful, largely in the Pittsburgh area, soon spread, and by the 1830s manufacturing was beginning to become an important part of life in the Ohio Valley. Moreover, manufacturing continued to develop over the course of the nineteenth century, and as the region evolved it became one of the country's largest iron and steel, chemical, and coal-producing areas.

Wheeling, described in 1821 as a "miserable Virginia country town, which can never be more that 200 yards wide" by one of its detractors, was located approximately seventy miles south of Pittsburgh on the east side of the Ohio River. The town had grown up in the general vicinity of Fort Henry, a military outpost established prior to the American Revolution by the colony of Virginia to counter the claims that Pennsylvania had made to the panhandle region and to control the Indian population of the area. After the Revolution, Fort Henry, like Fort Pitt, was a stop for people--settlers, speculators, and others--traveling south along the Ohio River. Perhaps the most notable residents of the area during the pioneer era were the Zane family. Although Betty Zane, the frolicsome young heroine of later novels, has received most of the notice, it was her father, Ebenezer Zane, who left the largest imprint on Wheeling. In 1796, he cut a trail west and south across Ohio to Maysville, Kentucky. This trail, and later the National Road and the Baltimore and Ohio Railroad, made Wheeling an important crossroads town. An English traveler by the name of Cummings, who visited Wheeling in 1808, commented that Wheeling was important "on account of its situation where the great post roads from Philadelphia, Baltimore, and the northern parts of Virginia unite and cross the river, on the route through the states of Ohio and Kentucky to Tennessee and New Orleans." Ten years later Flint, a traveler already mentioned, made essentially the same observations. And the editor of the Western Herald noted in 1816 in verse:

> Wheeling has secured her roads,
> Come wagoneers, come hither and bring your loads.
> Immigrants, come hither and build a town,
> And make Wheeling a place of renown.[10]

In addition to the favorable location along land routes, Wheeling also had a fortunate location on the Ohio River. Located farther south than Pittsburgh dry weather less frequently halted river navigation at Wheeling, and the port was therefore more accessible. This was an important consideration as early as the first decade of the nineteenth century when Wheeling was chosen as the western terminus of the National Road. With the rise of steam navigation on the western rivers after 1820, Wheeling's location was even more critical. With the availability of cheap, regular upriver navigation, a new dimension was added to the economic activity of the Upper Ohio Valley. For the first time, raw materials from the Lower Ohio Valley and elsewhere along the Mississippi River system could be imported, freeing merchants and manufacturers from exclusive reliance upon upriver sources. Since a major iron-manufacturing center, the Hanging Rock region of Ohio and Kentucky, lay to the south of the city, the availability of upstream transportation and the dry season port were of some importance to the establishment of iron-working estabishments in Wheeling.[11]

All of these factors encouraged Wheeling to develop a vigorous, mixed economy during the early decades of the nineteenth century. Because of its roads and river location, the city did a substantial business in trans-shipping. Goods arriving by the National Road from the east were transferred to river craft for shipment downriver. In addition, Wheeling was a stopping point for easterly bound goods arriving by land along the National Road or by boat from downriver. Wheeling businessmen also engaged in some raw material processing. At an early date, coal was mined along the river banks for use in steamboat boilers, and at least one large sawmill, operated by the Hubbard family, supplied lumber for export and for local boatyards. In the days before steam power, flatboats, keelboats, and even a few ocean-going schooners were constructed in Wheeling boatyards. After steamboats came into use, Wheeling boat builders constructed steamboats along with other craft. As early as 1819 Hume observed construction of a stern wheeler in Wheeling "to go, they say, 1,800 miles up the Missouri River." Steamboat construction stimulated other manufacturing. By the late 1820s at least one boiler works and a foundry were located in the city. In addition to supplying the boat builders, these establishments probably provided castings and equipment for the early agricultural implement manufacturers who had located west of Wheeling in Ohio.[12]

Wheeling merits more attention than historians have given it heretofore. To date, for example, a comprehensive history of the city has not been written. While this study is not intended as a history of Wheeling, mention of some of the more important local events must be made. One of the enticing characteristics of Wheeling was the liveliness of the community. The constant competition with Pittsburgh colored almost every enterprise undertaken by the Wheeling business community. During the first two decades of the nineteenth century, when Wheeling's population never exceeded 1,200 persons, a serious rivalry between the two towns seemed almost ridiculous. After Pittsburgh's fortunes were tarnished by the economic collapse brought on by the panic of 1818, Wheeling's prospects brightened. When Wheeling was selected over Pittsburgh and Steubenville as the western terminus for the National Road, local optimism rose and continued throughout the first half of the century. While the competitive spirit was embodied in many events ranging from boat racing to dog fights, the most significant manifestations were the Wheeling bridge case and the Baltimore and Ohio Railroad.[13]

In 1848, several businessmen in Wheeling, in concert with the city government, decided to construct a bridge across the main channel of the Ohio River to Wheeling Island where connections could be made with an existing bridge over the back channel of the river and thereby to the Ohio shore. Pittsburgh raised objections because the height of the bridge obstructed the passage of steamboats with high stacks. A lengthy court fight ended with a Supreme Court order that the bridge be removed, but Wheeling interests took their case to Congress and successfully thwarted the court by having the bridge declared a mail route.[14]

At the same time that the bridge controversy was under way, two railroads intimately connected with the cities of Pittsburgh and Wheeling were racing each other to become the first rail connection with the Ohio River. The Pennsylvania Railroad managed to nose out the Baltimore and Ohio in 1852.

During the race westward the city of Wheeling became so interested in beating the Pennsylvania Railroad that its businessmen subscribed to Baltimore and Ohio stock, even going so far as to pick up part of the obligation originally subscribed by the state of Virginia.[15]

Just as local boosterism became entwined with the bridge and the railroad, so too the nail industry became inextricably involved with Wheeling's community pride. In the 1850s, Wheeling slowly crept up on Pittsburgh, the major western nail producer, and by the beginning of the postwar era was within striking distance. In 1874, The Wheeling Intelligencer finally declared victory. "Wheeling now justly claims to be the greatest nail manufacturing city in the United States," wrote the editor of the Intelligencer. Pittsburgh conceded defeat a year later when The Iron Age, published in Pittsburgh, compared the two towns. "It has been supposed that Pittsburgh could compete with any other point in the country," the editor wrote, "but it transpires that Wheeling is now doing the leading nail business." Several writers, such as Daniel J. Boorstin and Richard Wade, have taken note of the importance of boosterism and "urban imperialism," pointing out that they were frequently bound up in the ambitions of businessmen and newspaper editors like those associated with the Wheeling and Pittsburgh nail industries. The most that can be concluded here is that a sharp rivalry between Wheeling and Pittsburgh prevailed throughout the nineteenth century and frequently surfaced when the nail men met to discuss the affairs of their business.[16]

It was in this economic and social context that commercial nail manufacturing began and grew in the Ohio Valley during the first half of the nineteenth century. The first factories were in Brownsville, Mercer, and Washington, Pennsylvania. But in the first years of the nineteenth century, Pittsburgh became the nail-making center of the West. In 1807, Pittsburgh had four nail mills producing about forty tons of cut and wrought nails annually. Two decades later, in 1831, the city's mills were turning out 2,096 tons or about 42,000 kegs of nails per year. When Wheeling entered the nail business in 1834, Pittsburgh was the unquestioned leader in the West. Even so, as late as the mid-1830s, eastern nails, principally from Boston, were marketed throughout the Ohio Valley at a price generally 1-2 cents higher per pound than the two major Pittsburgh brands--Juniata and Pittsburgh Common.[17]

Pittsburgh was not the only western town to produce nails during the early decades of the nineteenth century, of course. Zanesville, Cincinnati, and even Wheeling had small nail manufacturers from a very early date. These small shops were geared primarily to produce for a local market and only infrequently engaged in the export of nails. Until Wheeling's later entry into the national market, the Pittsburgh mills were the only ones to seize upon the possibilities for broad marketing that the Ohio River Valley transportation system offered. By mid-century, eight Pittsburgh manufacturing establishments were each producing in the range of 20,000 or more kegs of nails per year and two factories, the Juniata

Works and the Lyng-Painter & Company Works, were each turning out more than 50,000 kegs per year.[18]

The first Wheeling nail mill was a direct product of the Pittsburgh manufacturing community. In 1832 (or 1834, depending upon which source is used), two Pittsburgh iron manufacturers--Peter Schoenberger and David Agnew--visited Wheeling seeking a location for a puddling works. Both Schoenberger and Agnew were experienced iron manufacturers and both would play an important role in the American iron manufacturing community in the decades to come. Peter Schoenberger was most noted as an entrepreneur in the Pittsburgh iron community and at his Juniata Works, near Pittsburgh, was the first western iron master to use the rotary squeezer. David Agnew, who had been the manager of Schoenberger's Juniata Works, had the distinction of being, in conjunction with his brother, the first eastern iron manufacturer to use Lake Superior ore, at the Sharon Iron Works in Sharon, Pennsylvania, in 1853.[19]

At least a part of Schoenberger's interest in Wheeling resulted from his friendship with Thomas Sweeney, a local foundry owner. Sweeney, as an old man, commented upon the founding of Schoenberger's works. "In about 1834," Sweeney told a newspaper reporter, "I was instrumental in getting Dr. Schoenberger, of Pittsburgh, a warm friend of mine, to buy property and build a rolling mill on the site of the present Top Mill." While Sweeney's friendship may have been important, Schoenberger almost certainly knew of advantages offered by the Wheeling area. The availability of the large and cheap supply of coal suited for use as a fuel in puddling and in the operation of steam equipment had been known for many years. Comments by travelers in the first and second decades of the century and later articles in both Hunt's Merchant Magazine and DeBow's Review made reference to Wheeling's coal supply. A writer in the latter source noted during the 1840s that coal was cheaper in Wheeling than in any other western city. Locating mills in close proximity to fuel supply was not an uncommon practice. Puddling operations were in fact frequently located nearer to fuel sources than to iron supplies because fuel was more expensive to ship than was pig iron.[20]

Sweeney in his comments about the Schoenberger mill confirmed that access to deep-river transportation during the dry season played an important part in Schoenberger's decision to locate his mill in the Wheeling area. Scott and other writers have maintained that Schoenberger intended to ship pig iron from western Pennsylvania to Wheeling. The lack of transportation during dry seasons would have prevented such shipments, and since this was widely known it is unlikely that Schoenberger ever attempted to use Pennsylvania pig iron. Actually, Schoenberger and the others who located mills in Wheeling during the prewar era were looking downstream to the Hanging Rock region of Ohio for their supply of pig iron. Published reports of steamboat cargoes and their origin show that a considerable portion of the iron used in the Wheeling puddling mills in fact came from the Hanging Rock region and later in the century from the Iron Mountain and Pilot Knob region of Missouri.[21]

In addition to the value of deep-water navigation for pig iron shipment, Wheeling's position offered advantages for the marketing of the finished product. The river provided access to growing western and southern markets. Furthermore, the National Road provided a good land transportation route for shipping products such as nails to the interior of Ohio and Indiana after the western section of the road was completed in 1833. Although there is no solid evidence to support the claim, the opening of the Ohio canal system may have been another factor that led Schoenberger to consider Wheeling. With canal ports south on the Ohio at Marietta and Portsmouth open by 1834, and at the mouth of the Little Beaver to the north, Wheeling manufacturers had direct water transportation to Cleveland and to the Great Lakes.[22]

The importance of Wheeling's position along transportation routes was intensified in the late 1840s when the Baltimore and Ohio Railroad did finally choose the city as its western terminus. The arrival of the railroad in 1852 coincided with the organization of several new nail firms and with the construction of new mills in close proximity to the railroad lines. While there is scant evidence from the prewar era of heavy reliance upon rail transportation for the transportation of raw materials or finished products, the business community in general and the nail mills specifically saw the railroad as a positive factor. The nail makers, initially at least, were more interested in the market for spikes which the railroad offered than in its possibilities for transportation. This view of rail transportation changed in the late 1850s when the Baltimore and Ohio pushed westward to Cincinnati and when the nail mills added blast furnaces. By 1865 the railroads were becoming important as transporters of both raw materials and finished goods.[23]

Along with fuel and transportation, the presence of capital to finance the mill operations made Wheeling, as has been noted, an attractive spot. While there can be little question that Schoenberger, with some help from Agnew, financed the first mill, capital generated locally financed the bulk of the expansion that took place in the area after 1845. Between 1845 and 1870 there was a perceptible flow of money from commerce and real estate to manufacturing enterprises in and around Wheeling. Old land speculators such as Noah Zane, Archibald Wood, and Thomas Wood, early merchants like Daniel List and Thomas Paul, and prominent attorneys such as Gibson Lamb formed the Bank of Northwest Virginia, an establishment that, as previously noted, played an important role in the development of nail factories and Wheeling in general.[24]

A second bank that had a direct association with the nail industry was the Merchants and Mechanics Bank of Wheeling, founded in 1834. Like the Bank of Northwest Virginia, the Merchants and Mechanics Bank was formed by old mercantile families, such as the family of the Quaker merchant, Israel Updergraff. The close relationship that existed between this bank and the nail industry continued from the founding of the bank. For example, David Agnew, manager of Top Mill, was a founder, director, and major stockholder in the Merchants and Mechanics Bank. After the Civil War, J. N. Vance, president of the Riverside Mill, also served as president of the bank, and two other prominent "nail men," Samuel Laughlin of the Benwood Company and L. S. Delplain of the Wheeling Iron and Nail Company, served as vice presidents.[25]

In addition to the money made available through the two banks mentioned above, money flowed directly from commercial or land enterprises to the nail industry. In 1852, for example, James C. Acheson sold his interest in a stage line and invested the proceeds in the Benwood Mill. A. Wilson Kelley liquidated his considerable land holdings in the 1850s and invested his money in the Belmont Mill. And merchants such as Crispin Oglebay, L. S. Delaplain, and Samuel Laughlin had begun to invest money accumulated through their merchandising establishments in the nail industry in the late 1840s and early 1850s.[26]

Although it would be inappropriate to regard them as reasons for the establishment of the nail industry at Wheeling, two factors--tariff policy and general economic expansion--must be taken note of. Both Henry Scott, author of Iron and Steel in Wheeling, and Earl May, author of Principio to Wheeling, a history of the Crescent Iron Works, claimed that during the three decades before the Civil War the fluctuations in tariff rates had an impact on nailmaking in the Ohio Valley. Both authors relied heavily upon The Wheeling Intelligencer for information, and particularly on a series of articles that appeared in this newspaper in 1874. Scott and May, like the writer in the Intelligencer, concluded that industrial fortunes rose and fell with the tariff. Such a conclusion, while having some basis in fact, deserves much scrutiny, for the evidence does not permit so simple and direct a conclusion.[27]

It is of central importance to note that the American cut nail manufacturers had little foreign competition. The cut nail was developed as and continued to be an American implement throughout the century. Except for speciality nails, few nails were imported. During the sixteen years between 1828 and 1844, for example, the average yearly import of nails was only twenty-four tons, or less than 500 kegs, and the single largest yearly import (in 1830-1831) was only 101 tons. Imports remained relatively high in the two following years, fifty-six and ninety-five tons respectively, but thereafter declined dramatically. This pattern would suggest that tariffs were of marginal importance, since the heaviest imports came while the "Tariff of Abomination" was in force. Especially for western nail manufacturers, therefore, the tariff was of little consequence. The first mill in Wheeling was established during the era of compromise tariffs, and the Pittsburgh manufacturers prospered, if production is used as a measure, after the "Compromise Tariff" of 1833.[28]

If tariff policy did have an impact, it appears to have been that it widened the price range between eastern and western nails. High tariffs on imported iron and nail plate disproportionately affected eastern manufacturers, who relied heavily upon imported Swedish and Russian iron. Although determining the precise impact of the tariff is difficult, it is possible to note that in the 1820s and 1830s, eastern nails were consistently more expensive than western nails. In the 1820s, nail prices were generally quoted by both manufacturer and size; however, in the early 1830s, the former designation was dropped and prices were listed only by size. This is perhaps unfortunate since the continued distinction by manufacturer as well as size would have permitted comparisons of prices between those manufacturers who relied on imported iron and those who used domestic iron. The most that can be said is that it seems reasonable to assume that the high tariffs on imported iron in 1828 and the corresponding high levels of tariff during the 1830s certainly did not improve eastern prices in relationship to those of western manufacturers.[29]

During the period between 1839 and 1855, eastern manufacturers' production declined in general and the number of nails shipped west greatly diminished. Figures contained in Hunt's Merchant Magazine, for example, showed that the value of products of Massachusetts nailers declined by almost three-quarters between 1839 and 1855. A part of this decline can be attributed directly to the lower prices per unit of output. But even when a 33-percent decrease in price is taken into account, the net decline in production was something more than 40 percent. Hunt's magazine also provides evidence that shipment from eastern nailers to the West declined during the 1840s. Between 1846 and 1849, for example, the number of kegs shipped west from Philadelphia declined from about 184,000 kegs to just slightly more than 70,000 kegs, a reduction of 50 percent in the space of four years. This period of declining eastern nail production and shipping coincides closely with an expansion in the production of both the Pittsburgh and the Wheeling nail manufacturers noted previously.[30]

While the price differential (some of which resulted from tariffs on iron) between eastern and western nail manufacturers was a significant factor in the disapppearance of the eastern nail from the West, the general growth that was taking place in the Midwest and in those southern states bordering the Mississippi appears to have been largely responsible for the rapid growth of western manufacturing. During the twenty years after 1830, Ohio, Indiana, Illinois, Michigan, and Wisconsin had a combined population increase of more than 3 million persons and was by far the most rapidly growing area of the country. In addition, Kentucky, Tennessee, Alabama, and Mississippi had a population increase of 1.5 million persons and were, as a group, the second fastest developing region in the nation. Based on average household size of 5.55 persons in 1850, a minimum of 827,000 residential structures would have had to have been constructed in these regions to accommodate the increased population. In addition to the residential construction needs, an indeterminate number of business structures, churches, schools, other buildings, and an expanding railroad and canal system created a demand for nails. The supposition that population growth and the resulting economic activity stimulated commercial activity in the Upper Ohio Valley is supported by transportation statistics. Between 1831 and 1835, for example, the number of craft passing through the canal at Louisville increased from 826 per year to 1,611 and tonnage increased from 76,323 tons to 200,143 tons. Furthermore, estimates made by Timothy Pitkin placed the surplus of exports over imports of the Ohio Valley in 1834 at $18-$20 million and the exports of Wheeling at a surplus of just over $1 million.[31]

Transportation, fuel supply, markets, and the other elements noted in the preceding pages therefore all contributed to a generally favorable environment for the launching of the nail-manufacturing industry in Wheeling. While it is doubtful that Schoenberger or Agnew carefully weighed the importance of many or all of these conditions, information from later sources suggests that the more obvious ones--fuel and transportation--were considered important by both men. But even with these advantages, Wheeling did not enjoy immediate success as a site for nail manufacturing. For more than a decade, Agnew and Schoenberger's mill continued to be the sole manufacturer of nails in the Wheeling area.[32]

By latter-day standards, Schoenberger's mill was a small enterprise. Insofar as can be determined, no contemporary descriptions of the mills have survived. An article in The Wheeling Intelligencer in 1874 suggested it was "designed for the general manufacture of bar, sheet iron and nails in accordance with the usual customs of the day." Fragmentary information from other sources suggest that the mill has six puddling furnaces, a steam-powered tilt hammer, a rolling mill, and either twelve or fourteen nail machines. Maximum capacity of a mill of this size would have been about 20,000 kegs per year.[33]

Between 1834 and 1840 the mill was owned by Schoenberger and Agnew, with Agnew as the operating partner. All accounts suggest that the mill was a prosperous one. Agnew quickly settled into the community. He helped found and became the president of the Merchants and Mechanics Bank. He participated in local politics. During the 1830s he was also part owner of at least one blast furnace in the Hanging Rock region of Ohio. While the firm of Schoenberger and Agnew weathered the panic of 1837, Agnew's other business enterprises, probably the furnace mentioned above, drove him into bankruptcy sometime around 1840. Schoenberger purchased Agnew's interest and leased the mill to Greisener and Tallant, two workmen who had been associated with the mill during Agnew's tenure as manager.[34]

Even less is known about the operations of the Schoenberger mill after Greisener and Tallant took over than during the Agnew and Schoenberger days. The newspapers reported that the partnership, "with but limited resources at command barely sustained themselves, but made no money." While the poor showing of the works between 1840 and 1845 was frequently blamed on tariff reductions; it was more likely the general decline in nail prices after 1840 and the lack of business skill of the two partners that caused the problems.[35]

The struggling partners of the Schoenberger mill, commonly referred to as Top Mill after 1840, finally succumbed to bankruptcy in the spring of 1845, and a firm formed by E. W. Stephens, who like Agenew was an experienced iron master from western Pennsylvania, took over the mill. Stephens' experience and his capital, reported to have been about $75,000, revived the faltering mill. Immediately after assuming control of the works, he set about expanding and improving the rolling and the nail mills. One of his decisions was to employ Edward and George Norton, two nailers from Pittsburgh, to take charge of the nail works. With the arrival of Stephens and the two Nortons, the triumvirate that was to establish Wheeling as a nail-making center had been assembled. Over the course of the following decade and a half, these three men, along with two other Norton brothers, organized more than a dozen firms and built five mills.[36]

Even in their lifetimes they were regarded as the founders of the industry. They not only built, reorganized, and sold mills but recruited and trained nailers and tapped local sources of capital as expertly as any trained broker. Moreover, they expanded their business activities over the entire Upper Ohio Valley, speculating in various phases of the iron business in Ohio, Kentucky, and Missouri. They also embarked upon a publicity campaign to convince the western market that Wheeling nails were the best nails manufactured in the West. A writer using the pseudonym of "An Old Mill Employee" commented in 1874 that the success of Top Mill and others with which Stephens was associated could be attributed to "the unprecedented popularity of what was known as the Stevens nail."[37]

Stephens and the Norton brothers operated Top Mill for just over two years. In 1847, Stephens was embarrassed financially by the loss of $100,000 in an iron-mining venture in New Jersey and was forced to bring Edward P. Schoenberger, the son of Peter Schoenberger, and two other anonymous partners into the firm that operated Top Mill. Shortly after this change, Edward Norton left Top Mill and, along with Stevens, who retained his interest in Top Mill, and three other nailers, John Hunter, William Fleming, and Robert Morrison, organized Hunter, Morrison & Company. The newly organized firm undertook the construction of Virginia Mill, Wheeling's second nail factory, and the first to limit production solely to nails. A report in <u>Debow's Review</u> in April 1848 contained reference to Top Mill and noted that another "establishment of the same kind is progressing." By August, a writer in <u>Hunt's Merchant Magazine</u> briefly mentioned Virginia Mill, noting that "only in part filled with machinery [it] is turning off about 1,000 kegs of very superior nails per week."[38]

Designed by Edward Norton and Thomas E. Lewis, an English millwright who had settled in Pittsburgh, Virginia Mill was considerably larger than Top Mill. About two years after it opened, forty machines were operating, making the factory comparable to any of the Pittsburgh mills in operation at the time. Like Top Mill, the particulars of its construction are not available, and since the mill was demolished in 1852 to make way for the Baltimore and Ohio Railroad terminal, there is little written or graphic evidence to depict the physical appearance of the mill.[39]

Edward Norton's stay with Hunter, Morrison & Company was a short one. By 1849 Norton had withdrawn to form a new firm. The old company reorganized under the name of Hunter, Fleming & Company, and Edward Norton organized Norton, Bailey & Company. The new firm included, besides Edward Norton, who invested about $8,000, his brother F. D. Norton and eight other nailers who had been employed at either Top Mill or Virginia Mill. The partners raised $40,000 among themselves for the construction of a new mill which they named Belmont Mill. While Belmont Mill was smaller than Virginia Mill (having only eighteen machines), the new mill did introduce to the Wheeling nail manufacturers two important innovations--the Burden rotary squeezer and the bullhead roller. The squeezers completely replaced the old tilt hammers that were used at Top and Virginia mills and greatly improved the quality of the nail plate. The bullhead rollers permitted the production of a narrower nail plate and eliminated the need for cutting the nail plate from larger sheets. Furthermore, the squeezer and roller had the combined effect of producing nail plate that could be cut so that the direction of the grain of the metal ran the length of the nail. Thus the Belmont nails were the first made in Wheeling suitable for use as door battens and other uses that previously required hand-wrought nails.

Like Hunter, Fleming & Company, the firm that built Virginia Mill, Norton, Bailey & Company was a short-lived one. In November 1851, William Bailey and six of the partners withdrew from Belmont Mill, selling their interest to Edward Norton, Henry Moore, James C. Acheson, and F. D. Norton. Moore, a wealthy farmer, had taken a small share in the old firm sometime after its founding in 1849. When Bailey and the others withdrew, Moore purchased about one-half of the interest ($36,000). Acheson, who had been a part owner of a stage firm operating along the old National Road, took about $10,000 worth of the interest sold by Bailey and the withdrawing partners. The two Norton brothers purchased the remainder ($21,000) of the withdrawing partners' interest.[40]

Bailey and the nailers who left Belmont Mill formed a new partnership known as Bailey, Woodward & Company, which was to become one of the most stable firms in the Wheeling nail industry. The new firm purchased four acres of land south of Wheeling and by the fall of 1852 had planned and constructed a new mill. Christened LaBelle Mill, the new facility had eight boiling furnaces, two heating furnaces, a muck mill, a skelp mill, and twenty-five nail machines. While LaBelle Mill incorporated both the squeezer and the bullhead rollers that had been introduced at Belmont Mill, there is no evidence that LaBelle Mill contained any other important innovations.[41]

Bailey, Woodward & Company was different in one significant aspect from its predecessors. When the new partnership was formed, those men who signed it agreed that if any member of the firm wished to sell his interest, it had to be offered to the remaining partner who had the least interest in the firm. If that partner refused or could not purchase the departing interest, it was then offered to the next partner, and so on. Only after each partner had declined could the interest be sold to someone outside the firm. A restriction of this sort hints that the members of the new firm were concerned with stability and that Bailey and his partners were aware of some of the more unfortunate effects of partners leaving mills to establish new ones.[42]

After Norton and Biley left Top Mill, the firm that Stevens helped put together to operate, the mill struggled and then failed. A completely new firm, Johnson, Sweeney & Company, organized and took over operations of Top Mill in 1849, changing its name to the Missouri Iron Works, but they managed to run the mill with only "varying success," as a reporter in The Wheeling Intelligencer phrased it. Operations at Virginia Mill followed much the same pattern. When Norton, Bailey, and the others withdrew, the firm operated "but with tolerable success" until 1852, when the Baltimore and Ohio Railroad purchased the mill site. At that point the company reorganized, and John Gill, a local banker, became the major owner. In 1853, Gill moved the equipment from the old Virginia Mill south of Wheeling and began work on a new mill located on McMechen Farm. This new mill, known locally as the Benwood Iron Works, began operation in late 1853. However, according to accounts in The Wheeling Intelligencer, "misunderstandings and constant dissatisfaction prevailed resulting in the frequent changes of administration, under none of which much success was achieved."[43]

Norton and his colleagues appear to have engaged in a bit of a game. They organized a firm, constructed a factory, showed a profit, and then sold their interest to local businessmen, who found it difficult to continue operations because those who knew the business withdrew to form a competing company. Edward Norton, who was widely hailed as a practical nailer of the first order, also had a talent for business affairs that seemed to escape the attention of his contemporaries. In addition to participating in the design of three nail mills, he served as the "business partner" in several firms in which he had the responsibility for making contracts, purchasing the raw materials, selling the products of the establishments, and generally "attending to the finances." Furthermore, Edward's brother George went into the shipping business as captain of an Ohio River steamboat. Since a well-defined marketing system had not yet appeared, George probably played a crucial role as a salesman for his brother's product. Edward appears to have also made certain that his most recent mill was superior in one way or another to the one that he had just abandoned. Virginia Mill was larger than Top Mill; and at Belmont Mill the rotary squeezer and bullhead rollers were introduced.

Norton's success shows clearly in the figures of the various sales and resales. When he came to Wheeling in 1845 he was not, insofar as can be determined, an investor at Top Mill. When Norton, Bailey & Company organized in 1849, Edward Norton invested $8,000; two years later, when the firm reorganized, he purchased an additional $17,000 worth of the withdrawing partners' stock, bringing his total holdings to $25,000. By 1868, when Norton left Wheeling, his holdings were in excess of $100,000 at the Wheeling mills plus an undetermined amount at the two mills in Ironton, Ohio.[44]

A new element was introduced into the nail industry with the organization of Bailey, Woodward & Company. The firm purchased enough excess land around the new LaBelle Mill site to build houses for the partners and hired workmen, thus bringing into existence the region's first company town. For this firm, and the Benwood Company that followed suit the next year, the company town was a result of a decision to locate the mill outside of the city of Wheeling. The decision to move out of Wheeling was apparently prompted by two concerns. First, space was at a premium in Wheeling, a town that was sandwiched between the Ohio River and a mountain. Second, moving south of the city placed the firms closer to the Baltimore and Ohio Railroad, which ran south for several miles along the Ohio River to the Bellaire Bridge where it crossed the Ohio River. Initially the company towns were simply accommodations for workmen, including the partners. By the late 1860s, these settlements began to assume some of the characteristic features that have historically been associated with mill towns. Script came to replace part of the workmen's wages, rules to regulate saloons and even promoting of certain religious denominations appeared in the 1870s and 1880s. And in the late 1870s and 1880s, rents were used as a tool for breaking strikes.[45]

One interesting, and it might be said possibly unique, feature of the company towns in Wheeling was the role they played in attracting merchants to the industry. Crispin Oglebay, a substantial grocery and drygood merchant, who became one of the more prominent "iron men," first entered the nail business through his contracts to operate the Benwood company store. Another merchant, L. S. Delaplain, also appears to have first gained an interest in the industry through the operation of a company store.[46]

The new settlements, one of which became the city of Benwood, West Virginia, seemed to have given additional permanence to the mills. LaBelle Mill remained the property of Bailey, Woodward & Company until it was incorporated as the LaBelle Iron Company in 1875. The new corporation, made up largely of the old partners and their descendants, continued to operate the mill and maintain an interest in the company town until 1921, when it became a part of the Wheeling Steel Corporation. After several upheavals in the 1850s, the Benwood Iron Works settled into a similar pattern and like LaBelle eventually became a part of the Wheeling Steel Corporation.

During the time (1847-1853) when Norton and his associates at Wheeling were building new mills, the economics of nail marketing changed rapidly. The partners found that the price of nails was declining. Between 1847 and 1852, for example, nail prices dropped steadily from $4.50 per keg to $3.13 per keg. At the same time, demand, at least in the West, was growing. At Cincinnati, nail imports increased from 56,130 kegs per year in 1846 to 83,761 kegs per year in 1851, for example. Pittsburgh factories, like those at Wheeling, were expanding to meet the increased demand, increasing production betwen 1846 and 1850 from about 86,000 kegs per year to more than 269,000 kegs per year.[47]

That the price of nails fell during a time when demand was high raises several questions. If traditional market forces were at work, the opposite trend would have been expected. Although it is impossible to assert with certainty, three conditions may account for the falling prices in the face of increasing demand. First, transportation costs were falling. Both North and Taylor have noted the decline in freight costs over the first half of the century and specifically during the 1850s for river craft. Transporation costs were also being reduced by canals. Two canals, the Ohio and Erie and the Hocking, crossed the Hanging Rock region, and since much of the pig metal that arrived at Wheeling originated in this area, these two canals contributed to the declining costs of transportation. With the cost of water transporation declining, the price of nails shipped to areas along the Ohio River would have reflected at least a portion of the savings. In addition, the cheaper transportation costs provided by canals reduced the price of nails in inland regions. Furthermore, the impact of railroads was being felt. The completion of the Baltimore and Ohio Railroad to Wheeling in 1852 has already been noted. Four years later, the road was completed to Cincinnati, a major market area for Wheeling nails. In addition to the Baltimore and Ohio, other railroads, particularly the southern lines out of Cincinnati, may have been important as shippers of nails to the southern states. Exports of manufactured iron products from Cincinnati increased dramatically (1400 percent) between 1846 and 1853. Since Cincinnati did not have a nail industry, a portion of the increased imports noted above were being transshipped to the southern states by rail.[48]

The decline in the cost of pig iron during the 1846-1852 period also accounts for a portion of the price decline. T. S. Berry, in his study of Cincinnati prices, noted that between 1846 and 1852 prices for pig iron receded from $31.50 per ton to $24.50 per ton, or about 22 percent. French observed the same trend in the East in his history of the iron trade. This decrease alone would have accounted for a substantial portion of the decline in nail prices.[49]

A final consideration in nail prices must be the technology that was being applied to the craft and the organization of the production units. While a more detailed analysis of this increase will be made below, it should be noted that prices were beginning to reflect decreases in production costs during the early 1850s.

Beginning in 1853, nail prices increased both nationally and in the West. The increase of about $1.75 per keg in 1853 was related to a corresponding increase in the cost of pig iron. On February 26, 1853, *The Wheeling Intelligencer* carried a notice that the Wheeling nail manufaturers were raising the price of nails 25 cents a keg as a "consequence of heavy increases in pig metal." Manufacturers throughout the West also came under pressure to increase wages in late 1853. Wheeling manufacturers acceded to employee demands for wage increases for boiling and puddling in late December. The increase in the price of pig metal continued in 1854 and 1855; nail prices, however, began to slide downward as production capacity and demand became more closely matched and as the impact of the panic of 1857 was felt by the industry. This trend continued until 1861 when wartime demand sent the prices shooting upward once more.[50]

During the 1850s, increased costs from materials and labor largely offset gains in efficiency and in transportation costs. Prices fluctuated form $3.13 per keg in 1852 to $4.76 per keg in 1854, but at the end of the decade prices were 15 cents per keg higher than in 1850. The experience of the 1850s showed clearly that costs, and prices, were in good part at the mercy of the iron market. If this central fact of life for the nail industry was lost on men who directed the firm in the 1850s, the high costs and difficulty in procuring iron during the Civil War emphatically pointed it out during the 1860s. Beginning in the mid-1850s and for the two decades thereafter, one of the major objectives of the Wheeling nail firms was to counter these fluctuations in price and supply in the pig iron market.

The early 1850s, when declines in cost were outnumbering declines in price, was a time of considerable activity in the Wheeling mills. It was during this period that the LaBelle, Belmont, Virginia, and Benwood mills were planned or built, and when Top Mill was expanded. After 1853, when prices rose accompanied by even higher costs, the impetus to organize new mills slackened. During the remainder of the 1850s, however, two new factories, indirectly related to nail manufacture at first, were established, and the older ones began to expand and move cautiously toward operating on a larger scale. In both the new mills and all but one of the older mills, the constant shifting of owners that had characterized the preceding years continued on an even more grandiose scale.

The railroad fever that seized the Ohio Valley in the 1850s was responsible for one of the largest ventures undertaken by the Wheeling iron manufacturing community. Taken by the potential for financial success that a rail mill, located at the western terminus of the Baltimore and Ohio Railroad, could have, E. W. Stephens, who had been the organizer of the nail factory at Top Mill in 1840 and a sizeable investor in Virginia Mill, set about organizing a rail factory. In company with John Gill and George Hardman, local bankers, and with the backing of Edward Norton, Stephens began the task of raising money for the new mill in 1852. The plans called for purchasing 9,000 acres of coal lands, obtaining a blast furnace, and constructing a mill that was to have fifteen double puddling furnaces, three trains of muck rolls, two squeezers, and a variety of other equipment.[51]

Stephens, Gill, and Hardman raised enough capital locally to construct the mill during the winter of 1853 and spring of 1854. Shortly after completion of the mill (named Crescent Mill because it paralleled the curvature of Wheeling Creek), Stephens, Gill, and Hardman were joined by Chester Hubbard, an attorney, state representative, and heir to a sizeable sawmill fortune, and Henry Moore, and the firm was incorporated with an authorized stock of $1 million. The three original partners subscribed about $300,000, mostly in the form of the mill that they had recently completed, and the new incorporators, Hubbard and Moore, put up $200,000, largely in lands and other securities. To raise the remainder of the money needed to purchase the blast furnace and about 9,000 acres of additonal land in Marshall County, West Virginia, the firm turned to John B. Gardner of Boston and Joseph Whitaker of Philadelphia. Whitaker eventually purchased a sizeable block of stock, but no other outside investors were enticed by the rosy predictions of prosperity the organizers promised. A brochure published by the Crescent Manufacturing Company informed potential investors that the hills surrounding Crescent Mill were layered with deposits of fire clay, sandstone, soapstone, coal, cement lime, and limestone. The minerals were to be mined until the hills were flattened and the lots were to be sold as real estate at $2,000 each.[52]

The company failed during the panic of 1857, only a few months after Stevens had sold his stock and left Wheeling for Kentucky, where a few years later he would once again team up with Edward Norton and go into the nail business at Ashland, Kentucky, and Ironton, Ohio. After the collapse of the Crescent Manufacturing Company, Chester Hubbard and the other partners reorganized it and operated Crescent Mill until 1865, when the property was sold. The Whitaker family, already a noted iron family from Principio, Maryland, then purchased the majority of the holdings and operated the mill until it merged with the Laughlin Nail Company later in the century to form the Whitaker Glessner Corporation. Crescent Mill was the only one of the Wheeling mills that did not manufacture nails. Throughout its history the mill manufactured rails, sheet iron, and, in the 1880s, structural and architectural iron. The mill, and a closely associated enterprise, the Wheeling Corrugating Company, also produced large quantities of corrugated roofing, metal tubs, and similar materials in the 1880s and 1890s.[53]

The Crescent Manufacturing Company is important here because it introduced Wheeling to the national financial community. The campaign to raise capital stock for the corporation drew attention, and during the 1850s and 1860s two easterners invested heavily in Wheeling firms. In addition to Whitaker, W. L. Hearn, a New Yorker, invested in a small wire mill and converted it into the fifth Wheeling nail factory.[54]

The organizers of the Crescent Manufacturing Company were also the first in Wheeling to attempt to build a vertically integrated organization. Although the venture was criticized by the iron men of the 1870s as a speculative scheme, Stevens and his fellows attempted to collect under single ownership a mill, a blast furnace, and coal lands and other mineral holdings needed to operate an iron mill.[55]

Finally, the Crescent Manufacturing Company was the first of the Wheeling mills to incorporate. From the very beginning of the industry, the firms that operated the mills were partnerships or were owned by single individuals. Capital was raised from partners--usually skilled workmen--or local businessmen. As already noted, these partnerships were volatile, subject to disintegration when the partners decided to separate. When a partner, such as Stevens, suffered financial embarrassment, as he did in 1847, the entire partnership was affected. The partnerships were distinctly limited in the amount of capital they could raise. After the Civil War, the entire nail manufacturing community would learn that the partnership arrangement could not raise the capital needed for expansion and would emulate the corporate organizational pattern of the Crescent.[56]

The last mill to be organized during the prewar period was Eagle Wire Mill, founded by Eliphalet C. Dewey, a Cadiz, Ohio, native. Precisely when the mill was formed is unknown. Scott claimed that the mill dated from 1852, but in 1849 a visitor to Wheeling reported in Hunt's Merchant Magazine that a new mill in Wheeling was manufacturing cables for the suspension bridge that was under construction. If this reference was to Eagle Mill, it dates from earlier than has been generally thought. The wire mill operated until sometime in 1855, when Dewey went into bankruptcy. The mill stood idle for three years, until Chauncey Dewey, the father of the organizer, reopened it. After a fire, Orville Dewey, a brother of the founder, reorganized the firm and began manufacturing railroad spikes and wagon axles. The firm of Dewey, Vance and Company struggled through the Civil War, continuing to be the smallest of the group of Wheeling manufacturers. In 1867 William L. Hearn, "a retired capitalist from New York City," joined the firm, putting up enough money to construct a new mill. From that time until the firm joined the National Tube Corporation in 1898, it, along with the LaBelle and Benwood mills, enjoyed a reputation for being one of the more solid and prestigious firms in the city. While LaBelle was known for its solid management and conservative technology, Riverside Mill, operated by Dewey, Vance and Company, gained a reputation for engineering advances and technological sophistication. It was the first firm to build a Wheeling blast furnace, the first to employ an engineer, and the only firm regularly to seek patents on innovations that it developed.[57]

Between 1856, when Orville Dewey reorganized Eagle Wire Mill, and 1869 no new factories were built in the Wheeling area. Change in ownership continued as before, with firms rising and disappearing as the fortunes of individual partners rose and fell. A review of the history of Virginia Mill, organized by Norton and Stevens in 1847 and abandoned by them in 1849, illustrates the path that ownership typically took. Immediately after Norton left the firm it was reorganized under the title of Fleming, Hunter and Company. After the Baltimore and Ohio Railroad Company purchased the Virginia Mill site in 1852, the firm that operated it was reorganized under the title of Gill, Fleming and Company and rebuilt at Benwood, south of Wheeling. With the financial setbacks suffered by Gill in the Crescent Manufacturing Company, the partnership was expanded to include A. Wilson Kelley, a farmer turned manufacturer. Eventually J. J. Holloway, a banker from Bellaire, Ohio, was admitted to the partnership. In 1857, Kelley purchased the interest of Holloway and Gill and operated the mill until 1864, when the courts ordered it sold to satisfy debts. At this point Edward Norton once again became associated with the mill, financing it in concert with several local businessmen and organizing a firm under the name of Norton, Mendenhall and Company.[58]

The instability of the firms and the top management of the mills was one of the features of the business environment during the early years frequently noted by later observers. The second generation "nail men," those who replaced Norton, Stephens, Gill, and Moore, were particularly critical of their predecessors. The periodic "swarming" of an earlier day appeared unthinkable to the corporate men who exercised control over the mills in the 1870s and 1880s. Actually, the frequent change of ownership, when viewed in perspective, had a salutary effect on the industry. The familiar pattern of "organize and sell" attracted capital to industrial ventures not only in Wheeling but in other towns in the Ohio Valley, and not only in the metal trades but also in glass and ceramics. Furthermore, the organize-and-sell pattern provided a method for bringing capital and skill together. Because of the technical nature of the nail industry, laymen could not easily plan, organize, and put into operation a production unit. Once organized and staffed, however, a layman did have a reasonable chance of succeeding.[59]

In the case of the nail industry, the pattern of organization that produced a succession of mills was the foundation for the leadership that the Wheeling firms exercised after the Civil War. The expertise of Norton and, to a lesser degree, Stevens and Bailey assured the technical soundness of the industry. As observed above, each of the Wheeling mills was equipped comparably with those of its competitors at Pittsburgh and by 1860 was on the average larger.[60]

As unstable as ownerships appeared, there was a moderately successful attempt to structure related businesses--besides iron production--that would assure the success of nail manufacturing. Most notably, there were several attempts to organize packet lines in Wheeling during the 1850s. Previous reference has been made to E. W. Norton's brother George as a steamboat captain and to the relationship he bore to several nail enterprises. Other lines, such as the Sunfish Line and the Union Line, also appeared, and among the organizers and owners were J. C. Acheson and Thomas Sweeney, men who had interest in two of the city's mills. While it cannot be demonstrated beyond question that a firm causal relationship existed between shipping and nail manufacturing, there can be little doubt that nail makers profited from the home-owned transportation.[61]

Several local businesses had begun to service the machinery demands of the nail mills by the eve of the Civil War. The Sweeney Foundry, L. Spence Foundry, and the Center Foundry turned out nail machines, boilers, and other equipment needed by the factories, for example, Foundry patterns currently in the possession of the Wheeling-Pittsburgh Steel Company's LaBelle Works date from the prewar period with a few having stamped dates as early as 1860.[62]

The overpowering presence of Edward Norton, the organizer and salesman, and the men he enticed and led into enterprise after enterprise tended to obscure another group of individuals who were less entrepreneurially oriented. These men, skilled mechanics and craftsmen, attracted to Wheeling by Norton personally and by the rapid growth of the mills after 1850, served as stabilizing elements for the mills and the industry in the ever-changing ownership and management milieu. Two such men were John Altmeyer and his son, Jacob, who emigrated to Wheeling from Pittsburgh in 1850. These two men worked as nailers at Top Mill and Belmont Mill during the 1850s and by the 1860s and 1870s served as mill managers. Others such as Henry Babcock and David Spaulding had been nailers in Massachusetts before they went to Wheeling in 1854. Like the Altmeyers, these two men, skilled mechanics when they arrived, quickly moved into what would be later called middle management.[63]

These four men, and several dozen like them, were a stabilizing force that kept mills operating while Norton and his colleagues speculated. Long after Norton and Stevens had left Wheeling, the names of the nailers and puddlers who arrived in the 1850s remained associated with the industry. They provided the technical skills to keep the mills operating, taught the crafts to the new workmen, and exercised a general leadership role at the mill level. One of the more famous of this group was Nicodemus Reister, a German who learned the nailers trade as one of the original apprentices at Top Mill at the age of fourteen. By the early 1860s he had become manager of Belmont Nail Mill. In this position he was so popular with the workmen and so respected by the ownership of Belmont that the new blast furnace engine in 1872 was formally christened "Old Nick" in his honor.[64]

Although most of these men owned stock in the companies for which they worked, only a few, most notably David Spaulding, ever rose above the level of mill manager. In fact, most placed more allegiance to their craft than to the particular company at which they were employed. Jacob Altmeyer and a younger brother, as well as Reister, for example, lost their positions in 1886 when they refused to teach their crafts to the new nailers.[65]

Men like Jacob Altmeyer and Reister were young men when they arrived at Wheeling in the 1850s. Throughout the 1860s and 1870s, and into the 1880s, they bridged the gap between the owners and top-level managers on the one hand and, on the other hand, the men on the nail line and at the furnace hearth. Their stature at the mills was further reinforced by their standing in the community. Reister, for example, served on the city council, was a director of the People's National Bank, and was a stockholder in the Wheeling Electric Railroad Company in the 1880s. All enjoyed, in addition to the respect of workmen and owner alike, a standard of wealth that made them the envy of other classes of workmen. Henry Scott, who was just entering the factories as Reister and Altmeyer were in their prime, referred to them as the plutocrats of the laboring force.[66]

In several ways the growth of the industry at Wheeling paralleled the development of the nail industry in Pittsburgh. Technologically, Wheeling was even with Pittsburgh by the mid-1850s and maintained parity until the great strike of

1886. Likewise the organizational forms, partnerships, and close relationships with banks were also similar to those that developed in Pittsburgh.[67]

Wheeling diverged from the Pittsburgh firms, however, in two important areas. First, in the 1850s Wheeling manufacturers individually and collectively became more specialized, concentrating their full attention, except for Crescent Mill, on nail production, while Pittsburgh manufacturers tended to diversify, producing nails as only one of many products. This specialization in Wheeling intensified throughout the 1860s and into the 1870s and led the producers there to view themselves as nail manufacturers rather than iron masters. Indeed, it was not until the late 1870s that the Wheeling newspapers began to refer to the Wheeling manufacturers as iron makers instead of "nail men" or nailers.

Nailmaking in Wheeling also developed much more rapidly than in Pittsburgh. If the arrival of Stevens and the Norton brothers in 1845 is taken as the beginning of the industry, all of the mills were constructed within a ten-year period and, except for Eagle Wire Mill, which later became the Riverside Nail Works, they grew out of the efforts of Norton and Stevens, or men like Bailey who were associated with Norton. After a decade during which new production units were added, the nail manufacturers abruptly changed direction and began an internal expansion of existing facilities. Belmont Mill, which had eighteen machines when it went into operation in 1849, had more than quadrupled its size (eighty machines) by 1860; Benwood grew from forty-five to sixty-five machines; and LaBelle increased in size from twenty-five to eighty-three machines. But the expansion went beyond just adding machines. Two firms, LaBelle and Belmont, added blast furnaces in 1855 and 1857, respectively. In both instances, the Wheeling mills were in advance of competitors in Pittsburgh, who did not add furnaces until 1859. In both cities the prewar furnaces were regarded as experimental. It would take the Civil War market to prove their worth and the profits of that war to provide the capital for this movement to continue.[68]

In April 1853 the editor of The Wheeling Intelligencer walked through the town and recorded his impressions of what he saw for his readers. Referring to the "lower part of center Wheeling," the editor reported "a cluster of manufacturies and busy mechanics, enough by themselves to fill a small town," and he concluded, "This part of her town is bound to shine." The miserable "country town that could never be more than 200 yards wide" had begun to shed its commercial heritage and was moving firmly toward manufacturing. Combining favorable location, liberal fuel supplies and a healthy portion of local capital with imported skills and a growing market, the town was to become the nail-manufacturing center of the West in the late 1860s and remain so until 1886.[69]

Notes

1. Richard C. Wade, The Urban Frontier: Pioneer Life in Early Pittsburgh, Cincinnati, Lexington, Louisville, and St. Louis (Chicago: University of Chicago Press, 1964), pp. 323-327; Thomas S. Berry, Western Prices before 1861 (Cambridge, Mass.: Harvard University Press, 1943), pp. 272-274. Wheeling is referred to as being located in Virginia prior to the Civil War. After 1863, when West Virginia was organized, it is referred to as Wheeling, West Virginia.

2. Isaac Lippincott, A History of Manufacturers in the Ohio Valley to the Year 1860 (New York: The Knickerbocker Press, 1914), pp. 129-197; Wade, Urban Frontier, p. 43.

3. Ibid., pp. 46-48; Louis C. Hunter, "Influence of the Market upon Technique in the Iron Industry of Western Pennsylvania up to 1860," Journal of Economic and Business History I (1928-1929), p. 245; Lippincott, History of Manufacturers, p. 52; Victor S.Clark, History of Manufactures in the United States (3 vols., New York: Peter Smith, 1949), I, pp. 339-340; Beverley W. Bond, Jr., The Foundations of Ohio (Columbus: The Ohio State Archaeological and Historical Society, 1941), pp. 319, 343.

4. Wade, Urban Frontier, p. 44; Reuben Gold Thwaites (ed.), Early Western Travels, 1748-1846 (31 vols., Cleveland, Ohio: A. H. Clark Co., 1907), IX, p. 34; X, p. 79.

5. Annual Report of the Secretary of State to the Governor of the State of Ohio for the Year 1872 (Columbus, Ohio: Nevins & Myers, State Printers, 1873), p. 361; Tucker Sutherland, Ohio Almanac (Lorain, Ohio: The Lorain Journal Co., 1967), pp. 124, 128.

6. Wade, Urban Frontier, pp. 44-48; Douglass C. North, Growth and Welfare in the American Past (Englewood Cliffs, N.J.: Prentice-Hall, Inc., 1966), p. 83.

7. Louis C. Hunter, "Financial Problems of the Early Pittsburgh Iron Manufacturers," Journal of Economic and Business History II (1930), pp. 521-523; Wade, Urban Frontier, pp. 43-45, 48.

8. W. H. Hunter, "The Pathfinders of Jefferson County," The Ohio Archaeological and Historical Publication VI (1898), pp. 210, 238-245, 249; William T. Utter, The Frontier State (Columbus, Ohio: Ohio State Archaeological and Historical Society, 1942), pp. 129-130.

9. Charles A. Wingerter, Greater Wheeling and Vicinity (Chicago: The Lewis Publishing Co., 1912), pp. 300-302.

10. Wade, Urban Frontier, pp. 324-325; Bond, The Foundations of Ohio, pp. 187, 388-390; Thwaites, Early Western Travels, IV, pp. 112-113, IX, p. 105.

11. Wade, Urban Frontier, p. 325; The Wheeling Intelligencer, February 29, 1884.

12. Henry Dickerson Scott, Iron & Steel in Wheeling (Toledo, Ohio: Caslon Co., 1929), p. 7. Henry D. Scott wrote this volume in the late 1920s while president of Wheeling Steel. At the time, he had been associated with the Wheeling nail and, later, steel firms for almost fifty years. While he clearly had some biases, the volume contains many useful observations and information that are not available elsewhere.

Scott's comments and his observations are treated as a primary source in the period after 1870. Prior to that date his comments must be taken as secondary. He did have access to certain business records of the prewar factories that seem to have disappeared, and internal evidence suggests that he relied heavily upon The Wheeling Intelligencer. Thwaites, Early Western Travels, X, p. 78; H. Morgan to Dana Hubbard, letter, September 18, 1835, Hubbard Family Papers, West Virginia University Archives.

13. Wade, Urban Frontier, pp. 322-326.

14. Scott, Iron & Steel, p. 17; George R. Taylor, The Transporation Revolution 1815-1860 (New York: Harper Torchbooks, 1968), p. 93.

15. Scott, Iron & Steel, p. 16; Earl C. May, Principio to Wheeling 1715-1945 (New York: Harper & Brothers, 1945), pp. 109-116.

16. The Wheeling Intelligencer, March 7, 1874; The Iron Age, April 15, 1875, p. 11; Daniel J. Boorstin, The Americans: The National Experience (New York: Random House, 1966), pp. 115-133, 161-168.

17. James M. Swank, History of the Manufacture of Iron in All Ages and Particularly in the United States from Colonial Times to 1891 (Philadelphia: American Iron and Steel Association, 1892), p. 216; Clark, History of Manufactures, I, pp. 340, 546; Berry, Western Prices, p. 262.

18. Ronald L. Michael, "Cut Nail Manufacture: Southwestern Pennsylvania," Bulletin of the Association for Preservation Technology VI (1974), no. 1, pp. 102-104.

19. Scott, Iron & Steel, p. 7.

20. The Wheeling Intelligencer, February 29, 1884; "Coal and Iron Trades of the Ohio Valley," The Merchant's Magazine (May 1847), p. 454; J.D.B. DeBow (ed.), DeBow's Commercial Review of the South and West, (August 1855), p. 207; Peter Temin, Iron and Steel in Nineteenth Century America: An Economic Inquiry (Cambridge, Mass.: MIT Press, 1964), p. 92.

21. The Wheeling Intelligencer, February 29, 1884; April 23, 1853; Scott, Iron & Steel, p. 7.

22. The Merchant's Magazine (February 1841), p. 199. This publication suggests that in 1839 and 1840 the Ohio Canal was transporting large quantities of nails. Wheeling was located about midway between two canal ports that provided access to the Great Lakes shipping routes.

23. The Wheeling Intelligencer, April 23, 1853, provides some indication of the general attitude toward and view of the railroad and manufacturing in general. The nail manufacturers appeared to look to water transportation in the 1850s primarily because the raw material came from the West and the market for the nails lay to the west and south. Not until after the Civil War was the rail network sufficiently well developed to begin to supplement water transportation.

24. Scott, Iron & Steel, pp. 19, 38; History of the Upper Ohio Valley (2 vols., Madison, Wisc.: Brant & Fuller, 1890), I, p. 347.

25. The Wheeling Intelligencer, January 6, 1872.

26. Scott, Iron & Steel, p. 39; The Wheeling Intelligencer, February 7, 1874; History of the Upper Ohio Valley, I, pp. 325, 330-332, 471.

27. Scott, Iron & Steel, p. 13; May, Principio to Wheeling, p. 104; The Wheeling Intelligencer, February 2, 1874.

28. B. F. French, History of the Rise and Progress of the Iron Trade of the United States from 1621 to 1857 (New York: Wiley and Halsted, 1858), pp. 27-30; Michael, "Cut Nail Manufacture," pp. 102-104.

29. Berry, Western Prices, pp. 272-274.

30. "Iron Trade of Philadelphia with the Interior," The Merchants' Magazine and Commercial Review XVIII (1848), p. 311; "Iron Trade of Pennsylvania in 1848 and 1849," Ibid., XXII (1850), p. 582; "Produce and Manufacture of Massachusetts," Ibid., I (1839), p. 274; Ibid, XXXV (1856), pp. 496-497.

31. Social Science Research Council, The Statistical History of the United States from Colonial Times to the Present (Stamford, Conn.: Fairfield Publishers, 1965), p. 13; Lippincott, History of Manufacturers, pp. 142-143.

32. The Wheeling Intelligencer, February 29, 1884.

33. Scott, Iron & Steel, p.8; The Wheeling Intelligencer, February 2, 1874.

34. The Wheeling Intelligencer, February 2, 1874.

35. Ibid.; Scott, Iron & Steel, p. 14.

36. The Wheeling Intelligencer, April 9, 1856; Scott, Iron & Steel, p. 14.

37. The Wheeling Intelligencer, February 2 and 5, 1874.

38. Scott, Iron & Steel, pp. 14-15; J.D.B. DeBow (ed.), "Commerce and Prosperity of Western Cities," DeBow's Commercial Review of the South and West V (April 1848), p. 376; "Iron Works at Wheeling, Virginia," The Merchants' Magazine and Commercial Review XIX (1848), p. 230.

39. The Wheeling Intelligencer, February 5, 1874; Scott, Iron & Steel, p. 15.

40. The Wheeling Intelligencer, February 7, 1874; Scott, Iron & Steel, pp. 15-17.

41. The Wheeling Intelligencer, February 18, 1874; Scott, Iron & Steel, p. 19.

42. The Wheeling Intelligencer, February 18, 1874; Scott, Iron & Steel, p. 18; The Steubenville Daily Herald, July 27, 1885.

43. The Wheeling Intelligencer, February 2, 5, and 20, 1874.

44. Scott, Iron & Steel, p. 16; Oliver I. Taylor, Directory of Wheeling and Ohio County, (Wheeling: The Daily Gazette, 1851), p. 69.

45. The Wheeling Intelligencer, February 5 and 18, 1874; The Benwood Iron Works, "Minutes of Stockholders' and Directors' Meetings from June 29, 1864-January 21, 1880," pp. 132, 361, MS in possession of the Wheeling-Pittsburgh Steel Corporation, Wheeling, West Virginia.

46. The Benwood Iron Works, "Records," p. 13.

47. Council, Statistical History, p. 124; French, History of the Rise and Progress of the Iron Trade, p. 173;

"The Iron Trade of Europe and the United States," The Merchants' Magazine and Commercial Review XVI (1847), p. 589; Michael, "Cut Nail Manufacture," pp. 102-104.

48. Taylor, The Transportation Revolution, pp. 135-138; Frances P. Weisenburger, The Passing of the Frontier: 1825-1850 (Columbus: Ohio State Archaeological and Historical Society, 1941), pp. 97-99, 104-105, 112-113; Berry, Western Prices, p. 257; French, History of the Rise and Progress of the Iron Trade, p. 173.

49. Thomas S. Berry, "Wholesale Commodity Prices in the Ohio Valley, 1816-1860," The Review of Economic Statistics XVII (1935), p. 32; French, History of the Rise and Progress of the Iron Trade, pp. 146-148.

50. Council, Statistical History, p. 124; Berry, "Wholesale Commodity Prices," p. 32; The Wheeling Intelligencer, February 26 and December 29, 1853.

51. Scott, Iron & Steel, pp. 20-23.

52. Ibid.; The Wheeling Intelligencer, October 11, 1855; "Trustees Sale of Valuable Ironworks, Mineral Lands, and Etc.," broadside in collections of the West Virginia Historical Society, Charleston, West Virginia; Scott, Iron & Steel, p. 23.

53. Ibid., pp. 20-23, 127, 170; Directory of the Iron and Steel Works of the United States (Philadelphia: The American Iron and Steel Association, 1901), p. 239; Directory of the Iron and Steel Works of the United States (Philadelphia: American Iron and Steel Association, 1882), p. 131; The Wheeling Intelligencer, April 9, 1856; May, Principio to Wheeling, pp. 120-125.

54. The Wheeling Intelligencer, February 25, 1874.

55. Ibid., February 2, 1874.

56. Scott, Iron & Steel, pp. 14, 16.

57. Ibid., p. 24; The Wheeling Intelligencer, February 25, 1874.

58. The Wheeling Intelligencer, February 7, 1874.

59. This topic is discussed more fully in Chapter 3.

60. Size of the Wheeling mills in 1860 is taken from The Wheeling Intelligencer, February 5, 7, 10, 18, 20, 25, 1874. Size of the Pittsburgh mills is taken from Michael, "Cut Nail Manufacture," pp. 104-105; George H. Thurston, Directory of the City of Wheeling and Vicinity for 1859-1860 (Wheeling: The Daily Intelligencer, 1859), p. 140.

Wheeling		Pittsburgh	
Benwood	40 machines	Juniata Works	84 machines
Belmont	80 machines	Graff, Bennett & Co.	30 machines
LaBelle	65 machines	Catherine Lorens	28 machines
Top Mill	40 machines	Hailman Ralinst Co.	40 machines
Eagle	48 machines	Lyng, Painter & Co.	82 machines
		Lloyd & Black	13 machines

61. The Wheeling Intelligencer, February 11 and March 12, 1874.

62. Ibid., April 23, 1853, and January 5, 1854.

63. *History of the Upper Ohio Valley* I, pp. 214, 216, 229, 230.

64. Ibid., pp. 414-415; *The Wheeling Intelligencer*, January 16, 1874. The *Intelligencer* reported, "The engine, we understand, is to be called 'Nick Reister,' in compliments, we suppose, to the efficient management of the Belmont."

65. Benwood Iron Works, "Minute Books January 27, 1880-August 4, 1892," pp. 186, 190; Belmont Nail Company, "Minutes of the Stockholders' and Directors' Meetings July 11, 1879-January 28, 1890," pp. 208, 214. Both manuscripts are in the possession of the Wheeling-Pittsburgh Steel Corporation, Wheeling, West Virginia.

66. *History of the Upper Ohio Valley*, I, p. 214; Scott, *Iron & Steel*, p. 13.

67. Hunter, "Financial Problems of the Early Pittsburgh Iron Manufacturers," pp. 527-530.

68. Data on the size of the mills was taken from a series of articles that appeared in *The Wheeling Intelligencer* on the following dates in 1874: January 10, February 2, February 5, February 18, February 20, February 25, and February 26.

69. *The Wheeling Intelligencer*, April 23, 1853.

3
Wheeling: The Nail City 1860-1880

> Wheeling now justly claims to be the greatest nail manufacturing city in the United States and we propose to give enough figures to substantiate these claims.
>
> The Wheeling Intelligencer
> March 7, 1874

The two decades after the Civil War were a time of change for the American nail industry. Beset with declining prices for nails, rising iron costs, a generally unfavorable economic climate resulting from the panic of 1873, and a decline in increasing productivity that characterized the prewar period, the entire industry underwent major changes. Although the eastern manufacturers were most affected, all of the nail manufacturers except those in the Wheeling area found business tenuous at best and impossible at worst. The nail manufacturers that had grown up in and around Wheeling before the Civil War were not only the exception but, throughout much of the period, were conspicuous for their ability to prosper and expand. While most of the industry fought to maintain price levels, the Wheeling firms, as a matter of policy, opted for reductions in prices. When competitors reduced wages, the Wheeling firms maintained and even raised the rates of many workmen to attract manpower from the troubled eastern mills. And, as the eastern mills reduced production capacity, the Wheeling mills added machines and even built new plants.

To contemporary observers, Wheeling's success was incomprehensible, and all the more so because of the relative insignificance of the prewar mills in Wheeling. The puzzlement of the industry was stated most succinctly by the editor of The Iron Age in 1875 when he asked, "How is it that Wheeling is now doing the leading nail business?" With a change in tense this question becomes the theme for consideration here. How was it that Wheeling came to do the leading nail business?[1]

The availability of rather complete corporate records, as well as an excellent body of production and pricing data and the observations of people both within and outside the industry, provides a combination of sources that allow examination of several Wheeling (and other) firms during the late 1860s and 1870s. The sources permit comparison and contrast of the business strategies and allow some conclusions to be drawn about how successful various approaches to internal organization and marketing were.

While there is no suggestion that the nail industry as a whole or the Wheeling segment in particular was typical, it does provide an opportunity to view at close range some of the forces that shaped the postwar business environment. These include economic pressures that led to vertical integration, and the impact that integration had on management structure and operational philosophy. Since not all of the nail manufacturers in the country responded in the same manner, an examination of the industry also permits some understanding of how effective alternative actions were and, ultimately, the impact that these diverging manufacturing approaches had on intra-industrial relations. Finally, the development of the Wheeling nail industry after 1865 is significant because it was among the first manufacturing groups to use cost accounting as a substantial management tool.

Eighteen sixty was selected as the beginning point of this chapter because the Civil War was an important catalyst, at least for the development of the Wheeling firms. The suggestion that the war was important in stimulating industrial development runs counter to what many scholars who have studied business in the mid-nineteenth century have concluded. Thomas Cochran, Douglas North, Glenn Porter, and others have shown that the war, at least in other industries, was either a retarding influence or of little significance. In certain quarters of the nail industry this widely accepted theory holds true; however, at Wheeling and in the western mills in general, the wartime economy was significant and, in fact, determinative for later development.[2]

The following analysis owes much to Oliver Williamson and his book, Markets and Hierarchies. His observation about the relationship between markets and management hierarchies and his view of transactions provide a most intelligible framework for examination of the Wheeling firms. While more traditional approaches to business development could be applied, none offered so good an explanation, particularly of the differences between individual firms, as Williamson's.[3]

Alfred D. Chandler's work in the rise of professional management was also most useful. As the following discussion will show, the urge to control markets and internal conditions, which Chandler associates with the professionalization of management, was a considerable force in the Wheeling mills. The corporate records referred to above clearly show a change as the craftsman-owner was displaced by people with new skills and very different philosophies. It appears, however, that some of the important elements of the attitude that Chandler associates with the professional manager preceded the arrival of the professional manager and may, in fact, have been the cause rather than the effect of professionalization.[4]

By the eve of the Civil War the six nail factories in Wheeling already formed the city's largest manufacturing community. Even so, the size of operations were small compared with what they would be in the postwar era. In 1860, the mills had a combined total of 250 machines and employed about 500 workmen at peak periods. While precise figures on capital investment in the prewar factories are not available, none except the Crescent Works appears to have cost more than $70,000. During and immediately after the war the scale changed dramatically. At the end of 1873, the Wheeling firms employed 3,500 workmen, operated 625 nail machines, and had a capital investment in machines, factories, blast furnaces, and related equipment of more than $5 million. According to The Iron Age, Wheeling firms by 1875 formed the largest single group of nail manufacturers in the country and accounted for 37 percent of the nation's nail-making capacity.[5]

On February 23, 1872, The Wheeling Intelligencer published an article titled "A New Era in the Manufacture of Iron in Wheeling." In this article and six others published in 1874 A. W. Campbell, editor of the Intelligencer, and another writer, probably Ben Fisher, one of the original nailers at Top Mill, evaluated the history of the nail industry and of each mill. Each article addressed and puzzled over a single question--what accounted for the success of the industry in Wheeling? "Tremendous energy," "cheap fuel," "supplies of raw materials," and the quality of the "Wheeling nail" appeared over and over as the reasons for the success of Wheeling's nail industry in each of these articles.[6]

Shortly after the Intelligencer articles of 1874 ended, The Iron Age raised the same question. "It has been supposed," the editor noted, "that Pittsburgh could compete with any other point in the country...but it transpires that Wheeling is doing the leading nail business." The editor concluded that Wheeling's success resulted entirely from a "particular devotion to nails" and a freedom from "trade union influences."[7]

To a degree, each of the conclusions arrived at by the writers of the articles that appeared in the Intelligencer and The Iron Age was correct. As noted in the preceding chapter, cheap fuel obtained from huge coal supplies in and around Wheeling, abundant raw materials from the Hanging Rock region, and a devotion to nailmaking were present, as were transportation facilities and accessible markets. Yet none of these factors could account entirely for the vigorous growth of the industry in the late 1860s and early 1870s.[8]

In fact, the initial reason for the growth came largely from the wartime economy. During the Civil War, both the demand for nails and the price of nails showed a noticeable increase. Prices, for example, increased from $3.13 per keg in 1860 to $7.08 per keg in 1865, and the net profit for Wheeling firms ranged as high as $1.55 per keg. In addition to the brisk nail trade, the Wheeling mills also did a profitable business in the manufacture of armor plate. Just after the beginning of the Civil War, Edward Norton and James Acheson leased Top Mill, idle since 1858, and for two years they made naval armor plate for the Union river fleet.[9]

By the end of the war every mill in the area had recorded high profits. LaBelle Mill showed a profit of $164,780 in 1866, and while specific data is not available on the earnings of other mills, their dividend records show that they were "literally coining money," as a local newspaper story suggested.[10]

Although demand was good and profits were high, there was but a minor expansion of production facilities during the war. Only two mills added large numbers of new machines--the Belmont, forty, and the Benwood, thirty-eight--during the war years. Two reasons account for the lack of expansion until after the war. First, the pig metal supply was erratic and, when available, expensive. Only the firms such as Belmont, which had access to the Mendenhall furnace, the LaBelle, which owned its own furnaces, had a regular supply of pig metal at a reasonable cost. Second, not everyone associated with the industry was interested in reinvesting the profits. Several individuals were content to take excess profits as dividends. Other individuals, such as Edward Norton, continued the build-and-sell cycle that had prevailed before the war or took profits as capital gains. Norton, for example, bought into and sold out of a least two firms in the Wheeling area between 1861 and 1867, using the profits accumulated from the transactions to finance new factories in Ironton, Ohio.[11]

Two firms, the LaBelle Works and the Riverside Works, retained much of the wartime earnings as undivided profits. As late as 1874, the company records of LaBelle showed $350,491 in undivided profits accumulated largely during the 1860-1866 period. By contrast, in the other firms--Belmont, Benwood, and the Wheeling Iron and Nail Company--the partners took most of the profit from the business. The net result was that many of the profits that could have been reinvested were siphoned away and, although several individuals became wealthy as a result of their association with nail works, those businesses emerged from the war with but limited resources.[12]

The actions of the partners in these latter firms were not unusual. As was observed in the preceding chapter, the industry from its very birth involved a speculative urge. That two firms did choose to establish a pattern of holding profits for reinvestment was in fact a significant departure from the past and was one that put them in an advantageous position after the wartime economy had cooled.

Toward the end of the 1860s profits declined. Earnings began to slump as the price of nails dropped by more than $2.60 a keg between 1865 and 1870. To compound the problem, pig iron prices held relatively high until after the panic of 1873. Caught between declining prices for the finished product and the high cost of materials, the Wheeling firms looked for ways to survive. Very quickly, the manufacturers concluded that the market price for pig iron was excessive and that the solution to the dilemma they faced lay in circumventing the market as the determinant of price. In order to accomplish this they decided, during the decade after the Civil War, to construct blast furnaces and thereby internalize the production of pig metal. This decision was a critical one. Oliver Williamson has observed that a change in the assignment of a major "transaction," such as the one under consideration here, has ramifications that are far-reaching and pervasive, particularly for the internal-management hierarchy. To a considerable degree, much of the change that occurred in the 1870s was either the immediate or long-range effect of this decision on the management, structure, and operations of the Wheeling firms.[13]

By 1865, two firms--LaBelle and Belmont--had operating blast furnaces. LaBelle had constructed two furnaces at Steubenville between 1862 and 1864. The firm that operated Benwood had leased the furnace built by Cyrus Mendenhall at Martins Ferry, Ohio, in 1858. Mendenhall had operated his furnace independently until 1862, when LaBelle had leased it. With the completion of its furnace at Steubenville the LaBelle lease lapsed, and Belmont first and then, near the end of the Civil War, Benwood took a lease on the Mendenhall furnace. Both LaBelle and Benwood had, as already noted, gained a stable supply of metal from their venture into the furnace business. The advantages were not ignored by other firms and by those individuals interested in the well-being of the industry. The Wheeling Intelligencer, for example, frequently published articles about blast furnaces in the late 1860s and editorially commented in 1872 that "a large amount of money will be saved in freight and profit if pig metal can be manufactured in Wheeling."[14]

By 1870 most of the mills were committed to proceed with furnace construction. Riverside, in 1871, was the first to begin construction. During the next four years, each of the mills built furnaces--The Wheeling Iron and Nail Works, 1872-1874; the Belmont Company, 1872-1875; the Bellaire Nail Company 1872-1873; and the Benwood Company, a second one, in 1874. All of the new furnaces represented the state of the art for the time. Stacks ranged from 60 to 75 feet in height and bosh sizes varied from 15 to 18 feet. All were hot blast, utilizing either Player or Tate ovens; all had capacities of 50 to 70 tons per day; and all were fueled by coke.[15]

Three men designed and were associated closely with all of the Wheeling furnaces built after the Civil War. William Pollack, of Youngstown, Ohio, who designed and constructed the Riverside furnace, had a long association with Wheeling firms. During the 1870s and into the 1880s, he was employed by several firms as a troubleshooter, called upon to assist when problems arose with furnace operations. William Tate, a native of England and a resident of Pittsburgh who had gained fame as an inventor of the Tate hot blast oven, and William Bird of Pittsburgh designed and built the other Wheeling furnaces. These included the furnaces at the Wheeling Iron and Nail Works, the furnace at the Bellaire Nail Works, the furnace at the Belmont Company, and the second furnace at the Benwood Company. The furnaces at each of these firms therefore bore striking resemblances to each other, and the Wheeling Iron and Nail Company furnace and the Bellaire Nail Company furnace were exact duplicates of each other.[16]

Compared with other parts of the mills, the blast furnaces were expensive, costing nearly $200,000 in the 1868-

1872 period. Owners of the mills where the partners had drained off much of the wartime income were forced to reorganize operations, incorporate, and issue capital stocks and bonds to obtain the money. When this occurred, an entirely new group of men gained controlling interest in three of the nail firms. A number of the men who purchased large blocks of stock were already well-seasoned entrepreneurs when they purchased large blocks of stock. John Ingham, referring to these men, noted in his study, The Iron Barons, that the Wheeling mills attracted more men from business backgrounds that did the iron industry of other cities. Although the new men had experience in business, many were not strangers to the nail industry. In fact, a number of them had been nonworking partners or had invested in the industry during the 1850s. Crispin Oglebay, a grocery merchant, and L. S. Delaplain, a drygoods merchant, took control of Benwood in 1868, replacing Edward and George Norton and C. M. Mendenhall. Chester D. Hubbard, a politician and lumber merchant, Henry Hornbrook and G. K. Wheat, boatyard owners, and Alexander Laughlin, owner of a wholesale drug firm, took control of the Wheeling Iron and Nail Company, replacing the old Acheson, Bell and Company in 1869.[17]

The events that led Hubbard, Hornbrook, Wheat, and Laughlin to take control of Top Mill illustrate the conditions that forced the old working partners from control. At the beginning of the Civil War, the firm headed by Edward Norton and James Acheson operated Top Mill. With lucrative contracts for the manufacture of armor plate in hand, the mill should have been well situated. During the war the mill was sold or reorganized three times, and on each occasion, one or more of the partners sold to remaining partners or to outsiders who, in turn, took substantial profits from the mill to pay for their interest. After the war, the company simply did not have sufficient capital resources to purchase the needed blast furnace. A statement from the directors' meeting of May 4, 1869, shows the problem the firm faced. Moses B. Cox, a director, noted: "It was well known that all the profits in the iron business just now was [sic] in the blast furnace and it gave the mills who had furnaces such an advantage that they could go on making money while other mills...would be compelled to wind up before a great while." In June 1869 the company dissolved, and Hubbard, Wheat, and Hornbrook purchased its assets for $200,000, formed the Wheeling Iron and Nail Company, and began raising money for a blast furnace.[18]

The new owners shared several characteristics. As noted, all had experience in businesses outside of the nail industry. Several were wholesale merchants who had experience in managing businesses in which success depended upon long-term performances, buying low and selling high, and on the management of cash flow. It was just these skills that the nail industry required. The mills had to be put on a firm footing and the speculative nature of the business replaced with long-term planning if the Wheeling manufacturers were to succeed. Furthermore, the industry needed an eye for financial detail. Because of the large quantities of nails produced, a fraction of a cent loss per keg or a few cents difference in the price paid for iron could mean the difference between a profit and a loss. With the technology of the industry well established, business acumen came to play a more important role in shaping its history.[19]

A number of newcomers were also associated with banks. J. N. Vance, president of the Riverside Mill, William Bailey of the LaBelle Company, L. S. Delaplain of Benwood, and A. W. Kelley of Belmont were on the board of directors of the Merchants Bank, for example. In addition, Henry Hornbrook and A. W. Campbell of the Benwood were directors of the First National Bank of Wheeling. Furthermore, several of the new men were directors of railroad companies, insurance firms, or glass companies. In short, they were in a position that permitted them to secure loans and to market stocks and bonds. This position, along with their personal wealth, helped in raising capital for the mills.[20]

By 1871, the new men were firmly in control of the industry. As a group they showed a strong interest in building their businesses. In addition to the blast furnaces, they added to the boiling departments, rolling mills, nail factories, and even such new units as keg and gas works. Between 1865 and 1874 Benwood, for example, added eight boiling furnaces and thirty-six nail machines. During this period, the total number of machines in the Wheeling area increased from about 240 to 625.[21]

As the new men came to control the firms, bringing with them new skills and new attitudes, the holdovers from the old working partners group were pushed aside. Edward Norton and his brothers liquidated their interest in Belmont in 1868 after a disagreement (the nature of which is unknown) and moved to Ironton, Ohio, to devote full time to two nail works in that area. By the early 1870s, The Wheeling Intelligencer actually criticized some of the departed nail men. Of Stephens, a writer for the Intelligencer said, "He listened to the wonderful tales of oily tongued Eastern speculators...and in a short time was relieved of a clean $100,000." As for Agnew, the writer commented that "a multitude of ill-advised enterprises engaged his attention and absorbed his capital." And John Gill's interest in "various schemes had wasted a major part of a handsome fortune," according to the Intelligencer.[22]

For the new owners, acquiring the blast furnaces was the first order of business. The problems attendant to the construction of the blast furnaces were sizeable, particularly for men who had no experience as iron masters. At first, they had to familiarize themselves with the state of technology. The construction process usually began with the directors or a committee of the directors visiting furnaces, observing operations, and discussing their plans with the builders of furnaces that they had visited. The first stop was western Pennsylvania, followed by visits to the Mahoning Valley and Cleveland. The visits were followed by the selection of a builder and then negotiations for a price. William Tate, who constructed three of the furnaces, designed and supervised the construction in return for 25 cents per ton on each ton of metal produced during the first year of operation. Pollack, who designed the Riverside furnace, was paid a fixed sum.

Even though individuals were hired to design and supervise the construction of the furnaces, procuring supplies for construction materials and finding subcontractors remained the job of the directors.[23]

From reports published in the Intelligencer it was apparent that the firms gave careful thought to a full range of considerations and carefully studied not only the furnace design but also that of auxiliary equipment. "Messrs. Dewey, Vance and Company of the Riverside Works," the Intelligencer reported, "have, after careful examination and investigation of the cost of facilities for getting materials used in the manufacture of pig iron, compared with other localities, determined upon building a blast furnace." Three years after the Riverside furnace was complete, a reporter from the Intelligencer examined the operation of several mills and noted that the design of auxiliary equipment at the furnace was one of the key elements in the financial success of the Riverside's operation. A system of overhead railroads and conveyors that allowed iron ore to be moved directly from freight cars to the furnace mouth, the reporter claimed, saved the company $8 per day in labor costs. It was in the context of decisions such as this that evidence of a new philosophy of operations, one that emphasized efficiency and long-term growth, began to emerge.[24]

In addition to the problems associated with the decision to build blast furnaces, the boards were faced with the task of controlling, directing, and evaluating major construction projects while at the same time attending to the operations of manufacturing units. Before the blast furnace building era, managing partners made most of the decisions about operations. During the furnace construction era, the old management structure that was composed of working partners of more or less equal standing who managed various units of the plants was abandoned at all but LaBelle. The boards of directors began to exert control over operations through alternative mechanisms. First, the boards began to organize into committees, which were charged with responsibility for studying specific issues and making operating decisions related to those issues. Second, the boards began to leave the supervision of daily operations of the plants and daily supervision of production to the president and secretary, who exercised authority through a series of subordinate employees and collected information needed by the committees for decision making.[25]

In short, the management of the firms became more structured, in large part due to the needs that rose directly out of blast furnace construction. Additional needs, resulting from operational problems, discussed later in this chapter, built upon the system of committees, and by the 1880s the managerial structure was beginning to take on the distinctly modern look frequently associated with the rise of professional managers.

The blast furnace construction era introduced the Wheeling nail manufacturers to other segments of the iron industry. The inspection trips that Wheeling directors made to Pittsburgh and Youngstown first brought these men into contact with

The Belmont Nail Works 1877. This view of the Belmont Nail Works shows the various "departments" and their spacial relationship to each other. The buildings to the far left were the blast furnace and casting shed. The large building in the center of the drawing housed the puddling department and the large building to the right was the nail factory. Raw materials that arrived by rail and riverboat were off loaded near the blast furnace. Nails were loaded aboard trains or riverboats at the opposite end of the factory complex. (Scott, pp. 10-11)

FIGURE 9

A typical nail cutting machine of the type used at Wheeling, ca. 1875. The Iron Age, February 6, 1879, p. 43.

FIGURE 10

their counterparts in these two cities. A subtle change in viewpoint began, and the nail men of Wheeling increasingly began to think of themselves as iron manufacturers who specialized in nailmaking. The change was first noticeable when the firms adopted new names. The Belmont Nail Works, for example, became the Belmont Iron and Nail Works. A. W. Campbell, who not only was a major stockholder in the Benwood Company but also was editor of the Intelligencer, noted the change in the early 1870s when he commented that the manufacture of pig iron was "a legitimate outgrowth of our great nail business." By the end of the decade, Campbell commented, "Wheeling is most widely known as an iron manufacturing point," and he described the Riverside Works as a manufacturer of "pig iron, bar iron, and all kinds of nails."[26]

This change in self-image, almost unnoticed at the time, proved to be important to the development of the industry. When, in the mid-1880s, the wire nails supplanted the cut nails, the firms easily shifted to other products such as tin plate that utilized existing facilities.

In the process of building blast furnaces, the nail industry had a major impact on the business community of Wheeling. Except for the Riverside Mill, which relied heavily upon suppliers from the Youngstown area, a considerable amount of the equipment and most of the construction materials continued to come from the Wheeling area. Moorehead and Sons of Wheeling manufactured boilers; Cecil and Company Foundry of Wheeling and the Center Foundry cast pipe, furnace plate, and other parts. In addition, the Spence Foundry of Martins Ferry manufactured engines for both the furnaces and the nail mills. Each of these companies had been associated with the riverboat construction industry prior to the blast furnace boom. Each became progressively more involved in the nail and iron industry during the 1870s and 1880s. These firms and several others in the area provided equipment for the industry during the rest of the century.[27]

In addition to the firms directly associated with the production of machinery and furnace parts, the furnace-building era also provided a tremendous stimulus to the construction trades. Dozens of contractors provided lumber, bricks, and other construction materials needed for furnaces and auxiliary buildings and an undertermined but certainly large number of men were employed in building the structures. Between 1871 and 1875, the blast furnace construction projects pumped something over $2 million into the Wheeling economy. That activity alone softened the effects of the panic of 1873. "The financial panic, which threatened to swamp the entire country like a tidal wave," the editor of The Wheeling Intelligencer observed, "did not reach us even with the foam of its dashing." Prosperity resulting from the furnace and nail factory construction, along with the prestige that came from having the state capital moved to Wheeling in 1875, guaranteed the city and surrounding area a booming economy during the hard times that came in the middle part of the decade.[28]

By 1875, all of the furnaces were complete and in operation, and the effect on the community was noticeable. A visitor wrote, "There is a particular sordidness about these ironmaking towns...the air is constantly filled with 'blackies'... [that] descent upon one in greasy, filthy masses as if the contents of some plutonic featherbed had been shaken loose overhead....The all-pervasive spirit of soot must," the visitor speculated, "smirch even the immortal souls of the citizens." If anyone voiced concern about the pollution, it escaped notice of those in a position to record the complaint. Instead of complaining, many of the residents looked with amazement at what they saw and upon the prosperity that the transformation was bringing. "Every day," a writer for the Intelligencer reported, "hundreds of people to whom the manufacture of pig iron has heretofore been an unsolved mystery, gather at the works to witness the casting, and they look with awe upon the fiery stream....[which] is to most of them something not only new but beyond comprehension."[29]

As the preceding comments have suggested, the blast furnaces consumed much of the attention of the boards of directors and attracted considerable interest from contemporary observers. To suggest that installation of the furnaces was the only innovation, however, would be to completely misinterpret the events of this era. Other, less dramatic changes (expansion of mills, substituting boiling for puddling, new keg factories, etc.) were taking place. By the middle of the 1870s, the Wheeling firms had built manufacturing complexes that were well in advance of the rest of the industry. In 1876, the Wheeling mills averaged 96 machines per plant while the national average was 55.7. Furthermore, the Wheeling mills, as contemporary observers noted, were more efficient. Between 1870 and 1873, Wheeling manufacturers averaged 1,598 kegs of nails per machine each year. During the same time, Pennsylvania manufacturers averaged 1,329 kegs per machine and Massachusetts manufacturers averaged only 663 kegs per machine.[30]

The price of nails in the mid-1870s suggests that the changes that had taken place at Wheeling were having an impact. In 1875, when the national average price for 10d common nails was $3.42 per keg, the Wheeling firms were selling at $2.85 per keg. A few firms in western Pennsylvania and the large Boonton, New Jersey, nail works matched and, on occasion, bettered the Wheeling price, but the eastern mills, particularly those in Massachusetts and New York, could not compete. In 1875, the Parker Mill at Bridgewater, Massachusetts, for example, was selling nails at $3.61 per keg, fully 76 cents more per keg than the Wheeling firms. Even the few firms that were matching the Wheeling price were doing so by jeopardizing profits. Although selling within 3 cents of the Wheeling price, the Boonton Iron Works, for example, was making only 4 cents per keg, while the Wheeling manufacturers were realizing a clear profit of 34.8 cents.[31]

With comfortable profit margins, the Wheeling firms were able to force competitors to either sell at a loss or retreat from markets where Wheeling nails were being sold. Eastern manufacturers were completely excluded from the western market and were all but driven from the southern markets by the early 1870s. The Boonton, New Jersey, works referred to above attempted to meet the Wheeling price competition in the

South. By late 1875, the firm had ceased operating its nail factory and turned to other products. The western competitors fared somewhat better because they had a much larger market and exerted pressure to maintain prices through the Western Nail Association. Even so, the Wheeling mills kept the Pittsburgh nail manufacturers near the brink of bankruptcy throughout much of the 1870s. By the end of the decade, several had ceased nail manufacturing completely, and those that continued diversified so that profits were no longer completely dependent upon nails. Wheeling's competitive pressure was so effective that by 1880 there was not a single large firm in western Pennsylvania that produced only nails.[32]

Any one of several factors--more efficient technology, the vertically integrated structure, the economics of scale, or superior marketing opportunities--might have individually or in combination accounted for the success of the Wheeling mills. It is the contention here that none of these were determinative and, indeed, mills that were far less successful yet more integrated, larger, and equally equipped can be found during the 1870s.

As noted above, the Wheeling mills were "state of the art" manufacturing establishments. They used the same type of machines, very similar puddling furnaces, and generally the same type of subsidiary equipment as competitors in the East and West. Certain mills, such as Riverside, made advances in unloading equipment and, as a group, the Wheeling mills had more horsepower available than competitors, particularly in the East. These differences were minor and could not account for the advantage that Wheeling enjoyed in the marketplace.[33]

Nor can the advantage be attributed solely to the integrated structure of the Wheeling mills. The Boonton works in New Jersey and at least three of the Pennsylvania mills (Graff, Bennet and Company; Kimberly, Carnes and Company; and a firm owned by William H. Brown at New Castle, Pennsylvania) had integrated backward into pig iron production during or immediately after the Civil War. The Boonton Works failed in late 1875. The three others survived until after 1880, but none approached the success of the Wheeling mills.[34]

Like technology and structure, scale alone does not appear to have been the critical factor. The Boonton works was almost 20 percent larger than any of the Wheeling mills; two Pittsburgh firms (the Anchor Nail and Tack Works and the Juniata Nail Works) and the Fall River Iron Works at Fall River, Massachusetts, were larger than the smallest of the Wheeling firms. Yet none of these factories were consistently as efficient or profitable as those in Wheeling.[35]

The primary distinguishing characteristic of the Wheeling mills was their management system. Simply put, the Wheeling firms were better managed individually and as a group than were their competitors. The impact of the management may be seen by contrasting the Wheeling mills with the Boonton works. As noted above, the Boonton works was large (135 machines in 1870) and vertically integrated. Like the Wheeling mills, the firm owned blast furnaces, a puddling mill, a rolling mill, a nail factory, and a keg works. Moreover, like the Wheeling firms, the Boonton works expanded, adding a new blast furnace and thirty-five nail machines between 1868 and 1875. From a distance, there appears to have been an almost complete parallel between the Wheeling mills and the Boonton mill.[36]

On closer examination, however, there were important operating differences that led one to prosper and the other to falter. During the early 1870s, for example, the Boonton works averaged 8 percent fewer nails per machine than the least efficient and 17 percent fewer than the most efficient of the Wheeling mills. In addition, the Boonton works had a much higher waste metal ratio than the Wheeling mills. In 1870, 8.5 percent of the nail plate manufactured by the New Jersey works was not converted into finished nails. This compared with 4 percent at the LaBelle works in Wheeling. More importantly, both productivity per machine and waste metal ratios worsened at the Boonton works between 1860 and 1876, while they improved at Wheeling.[37]

With roughly equal size, comparable equipment, and similar structure, the different rates of efficiency suggest that management was a key factor. This supposition is further reinforced by the patterns exhibited at the Boonton works. Declining efficiency in the face of increasing size and complexity implicate the ability of management to serve as a coordinator and controller of operations. Likewise, increasing operating efficiency at Wheeling during a period of expansion suggests that management was performing well and making necessary adjustments to meet the needs of the new conditions.

In evaluating the success of the Wheeling firm, then, a closer examination of the management system may be in order. As already observed, a complete change in the top-level management of three firms occurred between 1868 and 1871. Actually, the change began with the founding of the LaBelle works, continued with the reorganization of the Riverside mill, and concluded with the new owners at Belmont, Benwood, and the Wheeling Iron and Nail Works. Although there were notable differences among individual firms, the change was characterized by the abandonment of the speculative "build and sell" approach to profits, and the emergence of a more long-term view that saw profits as a function of productivity.

Until the late 1860s, management and technical skills were inseparable elements. Norton and Stevens, who were master nailers, represented the prototype of successful managers. Indeed, it was widely assumed that only the craftsmen could become managers. In his farewell speech (1856) Stevens, speaking to the craftsmen of Wheeling, commented:

> I fully appreciate the feeling . . . coming as it does from those . . . who are best qualified to express an opinion of the management. Look around you and you will see who are the owners and managers of the most successful establishments in this city. The answer will be the workingman--mechanics. With true heartfelt pride I say it, myself being a mechanic.[38]

As long as the mills remained small and the individual units few, the craftsman manager functioned effectively. One man could subjectively evaluate the performance of all the workmen in a department and, since the firms were essentially a three-stage--puddling, rolling, and nailmaking--operation, the internal transactions were relatively simple and easy to coordinate. As the mills grew, it became more difficult for the working manager to subjectively evaluate performance of all the workmen and effectively coordinate the various departments. The blast furnace further complicated coordination and required much of the top manager's attention. No one at Wheeling had experience in operating blast furnaces, which by their very nature were more difficult to manage successfully and keep technologically current than were other units. Moreover, the operation of the blast furnace was most critical. If the furnaces did not produce metal more cheaply than the market, the firms that had integrated would be at a competitive disadvantage in relation to those who had not. In short, conditions that prevailed after integration mitigated against the working partners' management system and exerted pressure toward change.

This pressure was intensified by the arrival of the new managers, who took control after the decision was made to integrate. Not having the technical background to exercise subjective evaluation of the productivity of workmen and facility, faced with the demands of the new furnaces and integrated structure, and having a primary interest in the profits, the new managers had to devise new mechanisms for collecting and assessing information about operations, relaying decisions to lower level supervisors, and, most importantly, coordinating the flow of materials.

The committee system discussed earlier in this chapter represents one attempt at structuring a management system. It bore some resemblance to the old working partners meetings insofar as it attempted to concentrate both policy and implementation decisions in the same group of men. Although reasonably effective in dividing tasks among board members and investigating external questions, such as those attendant to blast furnace constructions, the committee system did not aid the evaluation or coordination of the daily operations of the plants. The lack of technical knowledge and the inability to quickly evaluate factory performance forced the development of a hierarchy of paid employees who translated policy into action and collected and evaluated performance data. By the early 1870s, two parallel management structures were emerging --one based on technical skills that implemented decisions and the other based on business skills that collected and evaluated information.

The second structure was more important and more responsible for the increasing efficiency of the Wheeling mills. It was associated with a sophisticated cost accounting system that became the most innovative and determinative element of Wheeling management.

While historians have taken note of the development of sophisticated accounting systems in the pre-Civil War railroads, there has been an assumption that industrial cost accounting, except for isolated instances, did not develop until very late in the nineteenth century. Michael Chatfield, who has studied and written extensively on the subject, concluded in his book, A History of Accounting Thought, that "until the twentieth century accounting data was not widely used as a direct aid to industrial decision making." Marc Jay Epstein, author of The Effect of Scientific Management on the Development of Standard Cost Systems, arrived at a similar conclusion. "The status of cost accounting in 1875," he wrote, "was that of an unsophisticated art." A. C. Littleton, in his classic pioneering work, Accounting Evolution to 1900, dated the introduction of cost accounting in the last decade of the nineteenth century.[39]

In the examination of the history of cost accounting, many researchers, particularly those whose interests lie in accounting or the history of accounting, have relied heavily upon published accounting literature. Although literature published in Europe and the United States during the early and mid-nineteenth century contains elements of industrial cost accounting, it was not until 1875, when two Englishmen, Emil Garcke and J. M. Fells, published their book, Factory Accounts, a work suggesting the integration of cost and financial accounts in a double entry system, that the first modern book appeared on the subject. Four years later G. P. Norton, another Englishman, published an article titled "A Manufacturer's Trading Account", in the Accountant that addressed the subject of profitability in multi-unit enterprises. These two works, along with The Cost of Manufacturers and the Administration of Workshops Public and Private (1885) by Henry M. Metcalf, an American, are generally thought to have marked the beginning of cost accounting.[40]

A few studies have gone beyond the accounting literature and focused directly on the records and management decisions of individual firms. H. Thomas Johnson in his studies of the DuPont powder mills and the Lyman Mills Corporation of Boston, Massachusetts, has addressed the subject. The latter study, which focused on the period between 1850 and 1865, indicates that the firm was using a cost accounting system by the mid-1850s; the author concluded that cost accounting systems "may have been widely used, long before historians had supposed." The development of cost accounting in the Wheeling firms tends to support this supposition.[41]

Although Johnson's study makes no effort to address the broad question of when cost accounting was generally introduced, it should be observed that the research on the subject suggests two points that may be salient in considering the question. First, cost accounting techniques were frequently regarded as industrial secrets and were therefore not widely published. Second, cost accounting does not appear to have originated with accountants. Epstein notes, for example, that a significant portion of the nineteenth-century material on cost accounting appears to have come from engineers such as H. M. Lane, whose articles "A Method of Shop Accounting to Determine Shop Costs and Minimum Selling Price" and "A Method of Determining Selling Price" were published in the Transactions of the American Society of Mechanical Engineers. At

Wheeling, engineers had no part in devising the system, for cost accounting appeared well before the professional engineers arrived. While the precise origin of cost accounting in Wheeling remains a mystery, it is clear from company records that one firm, namely, LaBelle, the first of the firms to operate blast furnaces, began the use of cost accounting sometime prior to 1866, and the practice spread to others very quickly.[42]

LaBelle was also the first to institute a system of measuring and recording various classes of expenses. As early as 1867, the minute book of the directors' meetings contained reports that break production cost of each keg down into several categories--"pig metal" (showing separate costs in produced and purchased metal), "wages," "expenses" (overhead), "kegs," "coal," "iron ore," "taxes," "brick," "clay," and several other categories. During the early 1870s other firms followed LaBelle's lead and instituted a similar system of recording costs. In 1872, for example, the directors of the Benwood Iron Works ordered the furnace clerk to provide a monthly statement of the "workings of the blast furnace," showing production, amount of stock used, and the purchase price of such stock.[43]

Table 1

The Expense of Making a Keg of Nails for the Year 1870
(Taken from the Minute Book
of the LaBelle Nail Works, Page 23)

Expense	$ .266
Pig metal	1.830
Oil and tallow	.026
Iron ore	.132
Steel and iron	.024
Coal	.155
Wages	1.338
Brick and clay	.042
Kegs	.200
Taxes	.053
Total cost	$4.066
Average selling price	$4.251
Profit	$ .185

By the end of the decade every firm for which records have survived was keeping close cost records, some even more detailed than LaBelle. In 1879, for example, directors of Benwood Mill, recently reorganized after bankruptcy, began keeping separate books for the furnace and the nail mill. Pig metal, labor, kegs, and other costs were recorded for the nail factory and puddling operations. The books, however, had still other entries that showed the cost of coke, ore, limestone, and cinders, and wages, expenses, and interest for each ton of pig iron manufactured.[44]

The cost accounting system has several important features that greatly aided in the management of the mills. First, and most important, it allowed the boards to evaluate and make decisions about operations without acquiring the technical expertise of the old working partners, thus permitting separation of mechanical and management skills. Moreover, this system permitted a quantification of operations that allowed relationships to be drawn between various and diverse elements of the manufacturing process.

Second, the data generated by the cost accounting system was comparative. The cost of a keg of nails manufactured in July 1875 could be compared with the cost six months or two years earlier and the directors could immediately see how well present performance compared with past performance. Furthermore, the data provided opportunity for comparison with other firms. Although there is no evidence in minute books that such comparisons were made for the record, bookkeepers changed employers enough to assure that information was dispersed. Also, interlocking ownership patterns (the Laughlin family, for example, owned stock in three firms) probably facilitated the exchange of production and cost information.[45]

Third, the accounting system also had diagnostic capabilities. Production cost could be broken down into enough categories so that the board could easily spot areas where costs were rising or falling. In some areas, such as ore costs, market factors were the prime reasons for the change and consequently lay beyond the control of board action. Other entries, however, served to identify internal problems. For example, an increase in the cost of labor per ton at the blast furnace could suggest poor management of that area. In 1872, the Benwood directors spotted just such an increase, and after an investigation the furnace master resigned. A constant cost for pig metal accompanied by increasing per-keg costs could suggest problems in the puddling, rolling, or nail mills. Scott recounted an instance in which directors noted such a disparity and sent orders to the mill managers to reduce the amount of waste metal being produced in each of these areas.[46]

Fourth, the diagnostic capabilities of the accounting system were expanded during the early 1870s by collecting other data. Beginning in 1870, the LaBelle minute book carried an entry showing the number of kegs of nails obtained from each ton of metal produced. These figures show a steadily increasing yield from 1,870 pounds of nails per ton of metal in 1870 to 1,955 pounds of nails per ton in 1877. Later, LaBelle maintained similar types of records for the amounts of coal, iron ore, and coke used.[47]

Finally, the accounting system also became a planning tool. During the 1870s, one of the difficult problems for managers of multi-unit enterprises was the matching of output capabilities of one unit with the input capabilities of the other. Since the structure of the Wheeling firms was basically linear--that is, metal moved from blast furnace to puddling mill to rolling mill to nail mill--altering the capabilities of one had repercussions on all of the other units.

As furnace technology improved, and output increased, accompanying changes had to be made in nail factories. The pattern of increasing furnace production, followed by increased mill capacity, is present throughout the decade. Between 1872 and 1879, for example, the Riverside furnace production rose from an average of 1500 tons per month to more than 2100 tons per month, or by about 40 percent. A corresponding increase then occurred in the size of the nail mill.[48]

In a general way, the cost accounting system helped establish something tantamount to an operations philosophy. By the early 1870s, the directors came to the conclusion that lowering production costs was the key to success. At one level this philosophy translated into an emphasis on efficiency. Initially efficiency was though of simply as making the maximum use of materials. Very quickly, however, efficiency also became associated with plant organization. The previously cited example of the materials-handling system at the Riverside furnace was one of the earliest examples of the emphasis upon organizational efficiency. Another example was the new Benwood Mill erected in 1877 to replace the old one that had been destroyed by fire. A visitor to the plant described the new factory as follows:

> The new Benwood has been built upon the latest and most improved plans for saving any waste expense, it has so arranged the building and heating furnaces with respect to the rolls, and the nail factory with respect to the piling and shipping of nails, and the whole mill with respect to the receipt of ore and pig metal by river and rail, and the receipt and distribution of coal on an elevated railway, as to reduce distance, labor and expense to the lowest minimum, considerations which every man knows are of the highest importance in these times.[49]

At another level, efficiency came to be related to the volume of production. Costs were measured in terms of the keg as output unit and included both operating and fixed expenses. Therefore, the fewer kegs sold the higher the fixed expenses and, consequently, the cost per keg. Thus, the manufacturers constantly pushed for more production in order to keep the fixed costs low. This strategy had a notable impact on marketing, which will be examined later, and on labor relations. In the latter area, the Wheeling firms did everything possible to avoid strikes. From the 1860s on, they based their wage scales on the ones prevalent for similar work in Pittsburgh, plus a small addition that came to be known as the "Wheeling Bonus." When industry-wide labor problems arose, the Wheeling mills promised to settle for what the Pittsburgh workers received plus the bonus, and except for a brief work stoppage in 1875, the Wheeling plants avoided any major labor disturbance during the 1870s. One mill, Bellaire, even went so far as to make a separate pact with its employees that contained provisions for continued work even if the other Wheeling mills were on strike.[50]

Overstatement of the importance of the cost control system would be difficult. It touched every area of operations and was a significant factor in almost every decision made by the firms. Neither the emphasis on cost control nor the cost accounting system that evolved at Wheeling can be found in other segments of the industry during the 1870s. Records from the Burden Iron Works at Troy, New York, the Bridgewater Nail Works in Massachusetts, and the Parker mills in New York and Massachusetts showed no hint that such a system was being used in these areas.[51]

The Wheeling manufacturers linked two basic assumptions. First, they assumed a continuing market for nails, a basic product that was required by many other industries. Second, they assumed that if they produced nails at the cheapest possible price, a share of the market would be guaranteed. Although novel in the nail industry, these two assumptions were not unknown to American business. Andrew Carnegie, for example, seems to have held precisely the same views. "Show me your cost sheets," he said. "It is more interesting to know how well and how cheaply you have done...than how much money you have made because, one is a temporary result, due possibly to special conditions of the trade, but the other means a permanency." John D. Rockefeller also seems to have arrived at the same view of operations. In 1899 he told the Industrial Commission, "I ascribe the success of the Standard to its consistent policy to make the volume of its business large through the merits and cheapness of its products."[52]

Given this view, managers were left with the task of controlling internal operations, something that was considerably easier and more profitable than attempting to control the market in which their products were sold. This was particularly so for enterprises that had just begun to operate in far-ranging markets and had yet to develop sophisticated sales systems. Throughout the 1870s and into the 1880s, the Wheeling firms shied away from and opposed price fixing or a joint-marketing scheme. Even when their profits were jeopardized at the end of the decade, they continued to perceive profits in terms of cost, choosing to better rather than cooperate with competitors.

Management's attention to cost, and therefore internal matters, also had important consequences for day-to-day operations. Cost containment was a measurable objective that could be shared by every unit of the firm and could force coordination of the diverse activities. This was of a considerable importance to the newly integrated firms.

Joseph Litterer pointed out in an article on scientific management during the late nineteenth century the importance of cost accounting as a tool for informing "higher management" of business activities throughout the organization.

Wheeling exemplifies this use of cost accounting. It served as an important bridge between directors, men largely unschooled in the technological aspect of nailmaking, and the men who actually ran the mills. It was, in short, the major interface between business and technology.[53]

It is also obvious that cost accounting was a tool devised by management and forced upon the mills. Scott related that a mill manager who was taken to task for producing too much scrap "put his hands in his pockets, shrugged his shoulders, and replied, 'Well, you [the directors] get the scrap, don't you? The men don't carry it home with them!'" Obviously, the poor man did not get the point.[54]

Concurrent with the development of the accounting system, the structure of top level management changed. In 1870 all of the firms were operated by a board of directors elected by stockholders, or in the case of LaBelle, appointed by the partners. The number of people on the board varied from seven to fifteen, and occasionally the boards were expanded when new stock was issued. Typically, the boards had a president, a secretary, and a vice president, who acted as the executive officers of the company. The boards met frequently, sometimes as often as once a week, to take whatever actions were needed or to discuss the general nature of the business. The records of these weekly meetings, as well as the annual and semiannual reports to the stockholders, contain the bulk of the information now available on the mills.[55]

Generally the boards operated in one of two ways. At the LaBelle and the Bellaire firms, individual members of the board were supervisory employees. Both of these operations retained many operative craftsmen on their boards (until after 1875) and frequently acted on advice or information from single individuals. At the other end of the scale, the Wheeling Iron and Nail Works and Benwood Mill evolved the committee system. As noted above, the committees were created initially to study or oversee certain aspects of furnace construction and operation, but by 1873 both firms had appointed an "operating committee." In addition, Benwood had three standing committees--control, finance, and salaries--and several temporary committees to look into specific problems, such as furnace renovation. The type of organization seemed directly related to the degree of technical expertise of the board. The more technically competent the individual members, the less likely was the committee structure to evolve.[56]

All of the boards operated basically in the same way. The president of the board, as chief executive and operating officer, oversaw the day-to-day operations. He was the highest paid employee, with an annual salary of as much as $3,500 per year. Generally, strong presidents managed the mills during the 1870s. Alexander Laughlin at Benwood, C.D. Hubbard at the Wheeling Iron and Nail, and J. R. McCourtney at Bellaire Mill all stand out as examples. All were men with extensive business experience, and at least two of the presidents--Hubbard and McCourtney--were prominent political figures in the area. These men rose to their respective positions largely through their ability to raise money, and each was wealthy in his own right.[57]

Next to the presidents, the secretaries were the most influential board members. Like the presidents, they were paid employees. The role of the secretary became much more important as the mills moved beyond the capital expansion phase of the early 1870s. In fact, one of the most noticeable trends in board organization was the gradual but persistent increase in the power and responsibility of the secretary. This increase in power appears to have resulted from the secretary's role in collecting information and reporting data to the board and as a result of his position as the only individual in the firms who had frequent contact with all of the operating units within the organization. This role could be seen most clearly at Benwood Mill. In 1872 the board of directors began ordering the secretary, Alexander Loring, to "cause" reports on various subjects to be made and financial records to be kept. In 1873 the secretary was "authorized" to order materials and equipment. By the end of the decade the secretary was taking charge of labor negotiations and representing the company at the Western Nail Association meetings. The predominance of the secretary was completed by 1880. On January 29 of that year the Benwood directors passed a resolution stating that "the president-elect shall be released from discharging of the active duties incumbant upon him...in consideration whereof, he hereby agrees to release all claims for a salary...but shall preside at meetings of the board of directors and shall, as president thereof, discharge those duties that are usually performed by a director." With this motion, the secretary formally became the chief operating officer and general manager and the active participation of the president in the day-to-day affairs of the mills came to an end.[58]

Second-level management of the mills was in the hands of a group of men generally referred to as superintendents or managers. The system was similar at each mill. The management group consisted of a bookkeeper, a nail factory manager, a forge manager, a furnace manager, and, in the case of mills that had keg factories, a keg manager. In addition, clerks were employed at the mill and the furnace. Although he was seldom mentioned in the minutes, the companies also employed a coal bank boss. These unit managers employed skilled laborers--nailers, founders, puddlers, etc.--and a labor boss to supervise a wide variety of unskilled laborers. Some skilled workmen such as nailers had the responsibility of employing their own laborers and were free to contract with them at whatever wage they saw fit. By the mid-1870s wages had become standardized and both mill managers and the boards were beginning to influence pay scales for the inside contractors.[59]

The clerks and the bookkeepers were in critical positions during the 1870s. The clerks in effect became the eyes and ears of the boards, collecting information that was fed to the secretary and then to the directors. As the boards of directors grappled with the problems of managing the rapidly expanding mills, they relied more and more upon statistical data from which to fashion decisions. As a result, they were in a position to rise quickly to managerial levels. In fact, the bookkeepers and clerks of the 1870s became the secretaries of the 1880s and the 1890s and formed the basis of a professional management group similar to the one that Chandler discusses in The Visible Hand. Cecil A. Robinson, for instance, who served as both secretary and president of the LaBelle Company, began his career as a bookkeeper for the Etna Company in 1875. Likewise, H. M. Priest, another president of LaBelle, had served as an assistant bookkeeper in the LaBelle factory. And yet a third person, Clarence E. Irwin, who became secretary of LaBelle in 1887, had begun his career as a mill clerk.[60]

With an effective management structure supported by the accounting system, the Wheeling firms were in a position to survive and even prosper in the declining nail market of the 1870s. Prices fell rapidly during the immediate postwar period and continued to slide downward throughout the 1870s. In 1866, for example, nails sold at $6.97 per keg; by 1871 the price had declined to $4.52 per keg; and by 1879 the price was $2.69 per keg. The receding prices initially resulted from a cooling of wartime demand but later, after the panic of 1873, a slackening of construction, particularly in the railroad industry, drove prices further from the high levels of the 1860-1866 period.[61]

As prices fell, so too did production. Between 1870 and 1873, national production declined by almost 13 percent. While demand shrank nationally, the western market held relatively firm through 1875. This condition was reflected in the number of plants operating in various areas of the country. In 1860, for example, Massachusetts had forty nail factories. By 1876 the number had dwindled to eleven. During the same period the number of nail factories in New York declined from fifteen to three. Even in Pennsylvania manufacturers were suffering. The number of firms remained fairly constant, but the output per firm declined during the early 1870s.[62]

Contemporary observations confirmed the statistics of the trade. The editor of The Iron Age suggested that while most nail manufacturers were having difficulties, the Wheeling firms were remarkably successful. In 1875 the editor commented, "Wheeling...is doing the larger share of the work, but she cannot hold this supremacy long, as there are other manufacturers and a great additional amount of manufacturing power, which will not lie idle long, and which will not consent that Wheeling should take the largest proportion of nails."[63]

As changes at Wheeling allowed an increase in production, the nail companies there had expanded their distribution system and put even more pressure on competitors. By the mid-1870s, a host of agents and traveling salesmen were marketing Wheeling nails throughout the South and West. Benwood Company records reveal the most detail about the distribution systems. The company had two marketing structures. Between 1869 and 1872, it appointed agents in several cities--New Orleans, Chicago, Memphis, Nashville, Cincinnati, Pittsburgh, Nebraska City, Marshall (Wyoming), and Norfolk. The agents in larger cities maintained sizeable warehouses, while those in smaller areas ordered as demand required. The size of the agency's business can be gauged approximately from shipments. The St. Louis agent, Moore & Company, sold as many as 50,000 kegs of nails per year in the mid-1870s.[64]

In addition to the fixed agents, the companies also employed traveling salesmen. The number varied from time to time and from firm to firm and very little is known about their activities. In the late 1870s, men like J. A. Metcalf, traveling agent for the Belmont Company, concentrated on the Far West looking for boom towns such as Denver.[65]

The marketing effort was not only a sizeable one, stretching over the better portion of a continent, but it was also a cooperative venture in which several firms worked closely with each other. During the 1860s, the firms established a reputation for high-quality nails and had begun to cooperate in several areas, including marketing. By the early 1870s, market coordination was beginning to take an organized form. On February 20, 1872, for example, the president of the Benwood Nail Works reported that he had met with other nail manufacturers in the city and had agreed not to sell nails at a price lower than that which was received in the final week of February 1872. Furthermore, the Wheeling firms had begun to appoint agents jointly in the early 1870s. Moorehead & Company in St. Louis, for example, served as an agent for both Benwood and the Wheeling Iron and Nail Company. Finally, the firms occasionally loaned nails to each other to meet short-term needs.[66]

While there is no evidence to suggest that the Wheeling firms had established a formal organization for the coordination of marketing activities, they had by the early 1870s begun to work very closely in marketing matters. This close cooperation did not escape the attention of observers. By 1874, the editor of The Iron Age had begun to consider Wheeling companies as a single marketing entity that had to be dealt with as a unit rather than on a firm-by-firm basis.[67]

In 1865, major eastern and western nail manufacturers had organized the National Nail Association in an attempt to set prices. For reasons that are unclear, the Wheeling firms never took part in the association, even though in 1872 and 1873 the annual meetings were convened in Pittsburgh and every other major producer from both the East and West was represented. In fact, it was not until 1874 that the industry even took notice of the developments in Wheeling, and by that time Wheeling manufacturers were the largest producers in the country.[68]

The National Association disbanded in late 1874 or early 1875, a time when many manufacturers were going out of business. It was at this point that the effectiveness of the Wheeling firms was noticed. In April 1875, for example, the New York Times reported that "for the past four months, they [Wheeling mills] have been running night and day. The have placed hundreds of thousands of kegs of nails all over the country at $3.00 per keg cash and in some instances less"--at a time when other manufacturers were attempting to market nails at $3.40 per keg.[69]

Not only were the Wheeling manufacturers undercutting the market on a day-to-day basis, but they had begun, by 1875, to take future orders at set prices, provide substantial discounts to large coustomers, and actually attempt to "cut Pittsburgh out of the market." With this in mind, the editor of The Iron Age surveyed the nail industry in April 1875 and raised several questions.

> Suppose all of the nail manufacturers in the country kept their people at work at the same price that Wheeling manufacturers are paying? How long would it take to more than surplus the market? If Wheeling is making so many nails--the Top Mill alone producing 1,000 kegs per day by running 106 cutters--is it not a question of whether there are too many nail manufacturers in the country?[70]

Clearly, the other manufacturers had to take some action if they were to escape losing out to Wheeling altogether. Just as clearly, however, the other manufacturers did not understand the forces at work in Wheeling. Instead of organizing production to meet the lower cost that Wheeling was establishing, the western manufacturers outside of Wheeling organized to keep prices artificially high, first by fixing prices at a predetermined level and then by curtailing production.[71]

In early 1876, led by Pittsburgh manufacturers, the western nailers organized the Western Nail Association. The first hint that Wheeling nail men were considering joining the other western manufacturers came on March 27, 1876, when the directors of the Wheeling Iron and Nail Company approved a resolution authorizing the president and secretary to "enter into a formal agreement with the nail manufacturers west of the Allegheny Mountains for the purpose of regulating the production of nails, [and] fixing the price and terms of sales under penalties...as may be deemed best in their judgment." A month later, on April 24, 1876, J. P. Gilchrist, the company's secretary, reported that "the organization of the Western Nail Association has been completed," and the Wheeling Iron and Nail Company had paid an assessment of $2,650 to the forfeiture fund. Gilchrist further informed the board of directors that "there was prospect that the eastern manufacturers would form an association similar to that of the western manufacturers." No direct mention of the Association was made in the surviving minutes of the other factories except for the account book of the LaBelle Company in August 1876 which contained an entry under assets of the firm in the amount of $10,922, labeled "Western Nail Association." This entry was probably the company's contribution to the forfeiture fund.[72]

By the beginning of 1877, all of the Wheeling and Pittsburgh firms had joined the Association, and by the end of 1878 every major producer west of the Allegheny Mountains was a member. In January 1879 the Association had thirty-one members divided into four groups--Pittsburgh and the Mahoning Valley (12), Wheeling and the immediate vicinity (8), Indiana and Illinois (6), and southeastern Ohio and northern Kentucky (5). The Wheeling contingent represented the largest number numbers to exert great influence over the Western Nail Association and could, by calling on the mills in southern Ohio, which were closely aligned with Wheeling, control an absolute majority of the members.[73]

Since records of the Western Nail Association are not extant, much of the information about its activities must be gleaned from the minutes of the board meetings of its members, newspaper accounts, and information in The Iron Age. The latter is a particularly good source since the editor, J. D. Weeks, was until 1885 secretary of the Western Nail Association.[74]

As the resolution passed by the Wheeling Iron and Nail Company suggested, the objective of the association was to control the prices and production of its members. Other matters, such as wages and iron prices, remained the prerogative of the Western Iron Association, an organization that had members from all branches of the iron trade.[75]

When the representatives of the Western Nail Association met in March 1876, they set about adopting policies to implement their previously stated objectives. The organization adopted a new price list--or card, as it was called. The price of 10d nails was set at $2.85 per keg, with other sizes, as was the custom, pegged to this price. Furthermore, the Western Nail Association established common terms for payment. Orders of 200 kegs or more could be discounted up to 10 percent and manufacturers were bound to require payment in sixty days with the provision that no more than 2 percent could be discounted for cash.[76]

Conditions of the agreement regulating the terms of sale specifically addressed the problem of jobbers and large customers. In addition to shopping for the best prices, the jobbers and large customers also bargained for liberal payment terms. Even among the Wheeling manufacturers, terms of sale varied dramatically. Given the business climate of the times, mills could, and in fact did, suffer heavy losses from dealers who purchased large quantities of nails on extended terms and failed before final payment. Benwood, for example, had taken a considerable loss under these circumstances when Charles Mendenhall, a jobber in Cincinnati, failed in 1873.[77]

A forfeiture provision was also adopted to put force behind the Western Nail Association's policies. Any manufacturer violating the policies was subject to a fine of $100 per machine, and each manufacturer was required to place with the Western Nail Association a cash deposit equal to $100 for each machine in its mill. Compliance with this provision was irregular. While LaBelle complied, the Wheeling Iron and Nail Company never deposited more than a fourth of the amount that was required under this provision.[78]

This agreement had very little chance of succeeding as long as the demand for nails was tight. Wheeling firms were notorious for and, it might be added, quite successful in violating the price guidelines. In 1877, for example, the Wheeling Iron and Nail Company produced nails at an average cost of $2.59 and sold them for an average price of $2.73, twelve cents under the established price guidelines. The LaBelle records show production costs of $2.67 per keg and a similar undercutting of the Association's price. Enforcement was so difficult, however, that only one of the Wheeling firms, LaBelle, appears to actually have paid any fine to the Western Nail Association during the 1870s.[79]

To prevent undercutting of the price guidelines, the Association attempted to control production by forcing plant shutdowns for periods sufficiently long to bring supply into balance with demand. While this tactic was grudgingly supported by the Wheeling firms during the 1870s and early 1880s, it did cause problems. First, it was not easy for an integrated firm to close. Blast furnaces, for example, were far more difficult to discontinue and restart than was a simple nail factory. Consequently, the Wheeling manufacturers, while closing nail works, continued producing metal throughout most of the shutdowns and used this stockpile to intensify production after operations commenced. Second, the cost accounting system had identified rather effectively fixed costs of operations and had distributed those costs over the units produced. Pricing, therefore, was in part at least related to volume and, since down time affected volume, the Wheeling firms were opposed to extended shutdowns. In effect, the accounting system by the middle and late 1870s had come to be a significant factor in marketing as well as production decisions. Wheeling firms came to accept and live by the proposition that lower unit costs were a function of volume and that a favorable market position depended not on the selling price alone but rather on the difference between selling price and production cost multiplied by volume. Given this view, improvements in profits could occur by manipulation of either of the three variables and did not depend on price alone.

What showed up in the relationship between the Wheeling firms and the Western Nail Association was a basic difference in management attitudes toward the market and toward the relationship between the market and production. Wheeling manufacturers, seeing cost, selling price, and volume as variables, began to press the Association to go beyond price matters and to take an active role in controlling other costs, such as labor prices.[80]

With Wheeling undercutting established prices and circumventing at least the spirit of shutdowns, the Western Nail Association attempted to place stricter controls on marketing. In 1878, the Western Nail Association proposed a pool for marketing all the nails produced by Association members. A board of six persons, two from Wheeling, two from Pittsburgh, and one each from the two other areas of the Association, would oversee the marketing of all nails so as to "remove all possibility of underselling the prices established." This board was to appoint agents who would act for the Association rather than individual firms and was to supply them with nails from the member firms in proportion to the productive capacity of the mills. Furthermore, the board of control was to have the power to "fix the number of kegs and nails to be made by each mill in each month."[81]

Although the plan was published in The Iron Age and discussed by at least two of the Wheeling firms, it was never implemented. The Wheeling manufacturers continued to be uncomfortable with a price-maintenance approach to the problem, desiring instead to have the Western Nail Association become active in labor cost controls. "We are being driven out of the markets in which we have heretofore sold our products," the directors of Benwood Iron Works claimed. "We find," they continued, "upon comparison of wages, we are compelled to pay thirty-three and one third percent to fifty percent more for various classes of skilled workmen than is paid at competitors in the East."[82]

In an uncharacteristic move, the Wheeling firms even closed down to support the Pittsburgh manufacturers in a dispute with the boilers in the summer of 1878. When the Pittsburgh negotiators acceded to the demands of the workmen, the Wheeling nail men were outraged. "The failure of the manufacturers of Pittsburgh to hold out in their opposition to the demands of the boilers," the president of the Wheeling Iron and Nail Company reported to his board, "has undercut all actions on the part of the Wheeling mills."[83]

The attitude of the Wheeling firms was not only consistent with policies that have prevailed for some time, but also appears to have been based upon a realistic assessment of changes in the industry during the years after 1874. As noted above, the efficiency of the Wheeling firms, and the general economic decline after 1873, forced many eastern firms out of business. Those manufacturers that continued adjusted to the new conditions by reducing wages.

Table 2

Wages Paid For Cutting Nails Per Keg (10d)[84]

	Wheeling	New England Mills
1875	$ .21	$ .168
1876	.21	.156
1878	.21	.146

Table 3

Wages Paid for Boiling (Per Ton)[84]

	The Wheeling Iron and Nail	Reading (Pa.) Iron Company	New York Mill	New Jersey Iron & Steel Co.
1874	$5.25	$4.00	$5.25	$5.00
1877	5.25	--	3.75	3.25
1878	5.25	3.00	3.25	3.25

By 1878, the lower wages of the eastern mills had begun to offset the advantages Wheeling realized as a result of efficiency, posing the possibility that eastern nails could compete in the West on a more or less equal footing. The Wheeling manufacturers perceived that an attempt to raise prices would invite the importation of eastern nails. To prevent this, they were even willing to sell at no profit or to take a loss. During the first six months of 1878, for example, the Wheeling Iron and Nail Company showed no profit for the first time in its history, and even the venerable LaBelle showed only minimal profits.[86]

In early 1879 when prices began what was to be a four-year rise, the Wheeling firms continued to favor low prices and volume production. In July, they resisted an increase approved by the Western Nail Association and for several months sold nails at 25 cents below the card rate. More importantly, the Wheeling manufacturers began considering the possibility of gaining control of the Western Nail Association and looking for methods to establish an even firmer grip on the industry. As in the early 1870s when blast furnaces were built, the manufacturers turned to technology to provide an advantage. In order to control labor costs, they increased mechanization, and in order to lower the cost of materials, they began to use steel. The full impact of this decision will be discussed in the next chapter.[87]

During the fifteen years after the Civil War, Wheeling manufacturers were confronted with two problems. First, the firms, if they were to prosper, had to meet the challenge of simultaneously falling nail prices and high pig metal costs. Concluding that pig metal could be made in Wheeling as cheaply as elsewhere, and looking to the example afforded by LaBelle Mill, the firms undertook the task of constructing blast furnaces. In arriving at this decision, the Wheeling manufacturers internalized a stage of the manufacturing process that theretofore had been separate and governed by the market. From the point of view of the manufacturers, the decision was an appropriate one since it allowed the management hierarchy to exert a considerable degree of control over the manufacturing process. Not only did the firms reap significant savings from the internal procurement of pig metal, improving their competitive position, but they also realized benefits from a long-range philosophy of operations that the new managers evolved. Unlike competitors who were at the mercy of fluctuating metal prices, the Wheeling firms by the late 1870s could more closely control costs and therefore nail prices, a situation that translated directly into a competitive advantage in the nail market.

The decision to internalize the blast furnace operations was not without consequence, however. The second major problem faced by the firms in the 1870s--exerting internal control over the manufacturing process--was a direct outgrowth of the decision to integrate blast furnace operations with those of nail and rolling mills. During the 1870s, the problem of internal control resolved itself into distinct but related needs. One of these needs was the coordination of the flow of material through various processes in such a way as to insure that waste and inefficiency did not negate the gains realized from internalization of the blast furnaces. By the early 1870s there was evidence of a production control system that measured kegs of nails per ton of metal. Likewise, accounts of mill superintendents' berating workmen for producing excess waste suggests that management understood and attended to the problems of coordination. As the manufacturing enterprises grew in size and as the relatively inexperienced directors who took control of the mills in the immediate postwar period came to power, there existed the danger of what Joseph Litterer called "organizational uncoupling." Records of the firms show that the directors expended considerable energies attempting to understand and provide coordination for the multidepartmental organizations and thereby to prevent uncoupling.[88]

In order to provide coordination and thwart the tendency toward disintegration, the board had to provide mechanisms that: (1) facilitated the collection and transmission of information for use in decision making and (2) allowed decisions to be transmitted to appropriate operational personnel. To ascertain the appropriate information, each of the firms devised a cost accounting system that relied upon a series of secretaries and bookkeepers to collect information and report it to the board of directors. The information was digested by board-level committees that relayed decisions and directions to lower-level personnel through the president and a series of mill superintendents.

By the mid 1870s all of these coordinating mechanisms were firmly enough fixed and sufficiently sophisticated to provide a powerful management tool. Secure in the belief that they could produce nails as cheaply as any competitor and with an understanding of the relationship between unit price, overhead, and volume production, the firms, unlike their competitors, formulated an aggressive production policy that sought maximum unit output instead of high unit profit margins.

This philosophy of operations determined not only the course of development of the Wheeling firms but also that of the competitors. Like the Wheeling manufacturers, those in the East affected cost reductions, but through wage controls instead of vertical integration and operating efficiencies. By the end of the decade, they were not only once again in a competitive position but were, in fact, forcing the Wheeling manufacturers to consider additional adjustments. The other western manufacturers eschewed cost controls, attempting instead to regulate demand and price. They never understood the reasons for Wheeling's success and, in fact, were confounded by Wheeling's consistent lack of interest in schemes to control prices and regulate competition.

Most significantly, by the late 1870s, the Wheeling manufacturers were using management mechanisms they had developed as diagnostic and planning tools to identify changes and fashion responses. The Wheeling firms not only quickly spotted the discrepancy in labor cost between the eastern and western manufacturers, but also had the capability of identifying points where the substitution of mechanical processes for manual labor could correct the imbalance. As a result, the Wheeling firms began to search for and evaluate substitutes for puddling and wrought iron in the late 1870s.

Notes

1. The Iron Age, April 15, 1875, p. 11.

2. Glenn Porter, The Rise of Big Business 1860-1910 (Arlington Heights, Ill: AHM Publishing Corp., 1973), pp. 27-31; Douglass C. North, Growth and Welfare in the American Past (Englewood Cliffs, N.J.: Prentice-Hall, Inc., 1966), p. 149.

3. Oliver E. Williamson, Markets and Hierarchies Analysis and Antitrust Implications (London: Collier MacMillan Publishers, 1975).

4. Alfred D. Chandler, Jr., The Visible Hand: The Managerial Revolution in American Business (Cambridge, Mass.: The Belknap Press, 1977), pp. 6-12.

5. Figures on employment during the 1850s were taken from the Directory of the City of Wheeling and Ohio County (Wheeling, Va.: The Daily Gazette, 1851), p. 11. Additional figures on employment in the 1860s and early 1870s are contained in a series of articles in The Wheeling Intelligencer between February 2 and March 4, 1874. Also see The Wheeling Intelligencer, April 30, 1875, and December 30, 1879.

6. The Wheeling Intelligencer, February 23, 1872; Wheeling Iron and Nail Co., "Minutes of the Stockholders' and Directors' Meetings from July 15, 1869 to July 22, 1892," p. 30, MS in possession of the Wheeling-Pittsburgh Steel Corporation, Wheeling, West Virginia.

7. The Iron Age, April 15, 1875, p. 11.

8. The success of Wheeling's nail industry puzzled everyone, just as its failure did. Henry D. Scott's book, Iron and Steel in Wheeling, repeatedly comes back to both questions.

9. Committee on Historical Statistics of the Social Research Council, The Statistical History of the United States from Colonial Times to the Present (Stamford, Conn.: Fairfield Publishers, Inc., 1965), p. 123; Woodward, Bailey & Co., "Minutes of the Meetings of the Board of Directors and Stockholders of the LaBelle Iron Works from January 28, 1868-September 20, 1873," p. 1. It should be noted that the title of this volume is misleading. Entries begin on January 1, 1867, for the preceding year and continue through 1895. MS in possession of the Wheeling-Pittsburgh Steel Corporation, Wheeling, West Virginia; Henry D. Scott, Iron and Steel in Wheeling (Toledo, Ohio: The Caslon Co., 1929), pp. 37, 45.

10. LaBelle, "Records," p. 1.

11. Wheeling Iron and Nail, "Records," p. 30; The Wheeling Intelligencer, February 23, 1872, January 10, 1874, February 5, 1874, and March 17, 1874. Scott has a good account of the business dealings that took place during and after the War. See pages 32-51 of his book, Iron & Steel in Wheeling.

12. LaBelle, "Records," p. 40; The Wheeling Intelligencer, February 5 and 7, 1874.

13. The Wheeling Intelligencer, February 23, 1872; Williamson, Markets and Hierarchies, pp. 9-11, 83-85. Glenn Porter, The Rise of Big Business, p. 53, also observed that "big business also grew in response to shortcomings in the system for supplying raw materials."

14. The Wheeling Intelligencer, February 23, 1872, January 10, 1874, and February 18, 1874.

15. Ibid., February 23, 1872, January 10, 1874, and December 30, 1879; American Iron and Steel Association, Directory to the Iron and Steel Works of the United States (Philadelphia: American Iron and Steel Association, 1882), pp. 52-53, 65-66.

16. The Wheeling Intelligencer, January 10, 1874; Wheeling Iron and Nail, "Records," p. 33.

17. History of the Upper Ohio Valley (2 vols., Madison, Wisc.: Bront and Fuller Co., 1890), I, pp. 330-332, 325, 471. This volume has no listed authors. It is primarily a collection of biographies of residents of the Upper Ohio Valley. Scott, Iron & Steel, pp. 40-52; John N. Ingham, The Iron Barons: A Social Analysis of an American Elite, 1874-1965 (Westport, Conn.: Greenwood Press, 1978), pp. 70-78.

18. Scott, Iron & Steel, p. 47.

19. While there is no solid evidence to show that the merchant background of the new owners was crucial, the knowledge of marketing, bookkeeping, and unit profit seems likely to have been transferred to manufacturing.

20. The Wheeling Intelligencer, January 6, 8, and 31, 1872.

21. Benwood Iron Works, "Minutes of Stockholders' and Directors' Meetings from June 29, 1864 to January 21, 1880," pp. 61, 146, MS in possession of the Wheeling-Pittsburgh Steel Corporation, Wheeling, West Virginia; Wheeling Iron and Nail, "Records," p. 30; The Wheeling Intelligencer, February 5 and March 7, 1874.

22. Ibid., January 31 and February 5, 1874.

23. Benwood Iron Works, "Records," pp. 101, 102, 103; Wheeling Iron and Nail, "Records," p. 33.

24. The Wheeling Intelligencer, February 23, 1872, and January 10, 1874.

25. Williamson, Markets and Hierarchies, pp. 96-100.

26. The Wheeling Intelligencer, January 10, 1874, and December 30, 1879.

27. Benwood Iron Works, "Records," pp. 104, 166, 189; The Wheeling Intelligencer, January 10, 1874.

28. The Wheeling Intelligencer, March 7, 1874, May 25 and 28, 1875.

29. Ibid., August 16 and September 10, 1875.

30. The Iron Age, April 6, 1876, p. 15; The Wheeling Intelligencer, March 7, 1874; Bureau of Statistics of U.S. Treasury Department, Statistical Abstract of the United States, 1878 (Washington: Government Printing Office, 1879), pp. 40-41; Francis A. Walker, The Statistics of the Wealth and Industry of the United States from the Original Returns of the Ninth Census (Washington: Government Printing Office, 1872), pp. 446, 617.

31. Committee, Historical Statistics, p. 123; LaBelle, "Records," p. 42; "Records of the Tremont Nail Company," vol. A-3, p. 588, MS in possession of the Baker Library of Harvard University; "Products of Industry in the Township of Boonton, in the County of Morris, State of New Jersey, during the Year Ending June 1, 1870," MS in possession of the New Jersey Historical Society.

32. American Iron and Steel Association, Directory 1882, pp. 97, 115-126; Ronald L. Michael, "Cut Nail Manufacture: Southwestern Pennsylvania," The Association for Preservation Technology, Bulletin VI (1974), pp. 106-109.

33. Bureau of the Census, The Statistics of the Wealth and Industry of the United States, 1870 III (Washington: Government Printing Office, 1872), p. 446.

34. The American Iron and Steel Association, Directory 1882, pp. 17, 31-32, 116, 123, 125.

35. "Products of Industry in Boonton, New Jersey"; Michael, "Cut Nail Manufacture," pp. 106-109; The Iron Age, April 6, 1876, p. 15.

36. "Products of Industry in Boonton, New Jersey"; The Iron Age, April 6, 1876, p. 15.

37. "Products of Industry in Boonton, New Jersey"; LaBelle, "Records," pp. 23, 36, 38, 50; "Products of Industry in the Township of Pequannac, in the County of Morris, State of New Jersey, during the Year Ending June 1, 1860," p. 1, MS in the possession of the New Jersey Historical Society.

38. The Wheeling Intelligencer, April 9, 1856.

39. Michael Chatfield, A History of Accounting Thought (Hinsdale, Ill.: The Dryden Press, 1974), p. 105; Marc Jay Epstein, The Effect of Scientific Management on the Development of the Standard Cost System (New York: Arno Press), p. 45; A. C. Littleton, Accounting Evolution to 1900 (New York: American Institute Publishing Company, 1933), p. 358; David Solomons, Studies in Cost Analysis (Homewood, Ill.: Richard D. Irwin, Inc., 1968), p. 17.

40. Epstein, Effect of Scientific Management, pp. 15, 49, 50; H. Thomas Johnson, "Early Cost Accounting for Internal Management Control: Lyman Mills in the 1850s," Business History Review (Winter 1972), p. 467; S. Paul Garner and Marilynn Hughes (eds.), Readings on Accounting Development (New York: Arno Press, 1978), pp. 523, 524.

41. Johnson, "Early Cost Accounting," pp. 466-474; Garner and Hughes, Readings, pp. 209-217; H. Thomas Johnson, "Management in an Early Integrated Industrial: E. I. du Pont de Nemours Powder Company, 1903-1912," Business History Review (Summer 1975), pp. 184-203.

42. Epstein, Effect of Scientific Management, pp. 51-57. Perhaps it should be noted also that Taylor published in the American Society of Mechanical Engineers Transactions. Other works that generally relate to cost accounting include Richard P. Brief, "The Origin and Evolution of Nineteenth-Century Asset Accounting," Business History Review (Spring 1966), pp. 1-24; David F. Hawkins, "The Development of Modern Financial Reporting Practices among American Manufacturing Corporations," Business History Review (Spring/Summer 1963), pp. 135-168; Michael Chatfield (ed.), Contemporary Studies in

the Evolution of Accounting Thought (Belmont, Calif.: Dickenson Publishing Company, Inc., 1968), pp. 222-236; S. Paul Garner, Evolution of Cost Accounting to 1925 (Tuscaloosa, Ala.: The University of Alabama Press, 1976), pp. 27-91.

43. LaBelle, "Records," pp. 1, 10, 22; Benwood Iron Works, "Records," p. 106; Wheeling Iron and Nail, "Records," p. 39.

44. Belmont Nail Company, "Minutes of the Stockholders' and Directors' Meetings of the Belmont Nail Company, July 11, 1879-January 28, 1890," pp. 40 and 44, MS in the possession of the Wheeling-Pittsburgh Steel Corporation, Wheeling, West Virginia.

45. At least twenty individuals held stock in more than one firm.

46. Benwood Iron Works, "Records," pp. 106, 128, 129; Scott, Iron & Steel, p. 67.

47. LaBelle, "Records," pp. 10, 36, 38, 50.

48. The Wheeling Intelligencer, February 23, 1872, and December 3, 1879; Iron and Steel Association, Directory 1882, pp. 52-53.

49. Scott, Iron & Steel, p. 76.

50. The Wheeling Intelligencer, April 26, 1875, and September 21, 1882; Scott, Iron & Steel, p. 95.

51. Burden Iron Company, "The Burden Iron Company Papers 1860-1900," n.p., MS in the possession of the New York Historical Society. See "Records of the Tremont Nail Company," vols. A-3, A-4, and B-2; "Parker Mills Trial Balance," 1870; "Parker Mills Trial Balance," 1875; "Parker Mills Trial Balance," 1879-1880. All documents are in the Tremont Nail Company papers collections at the Baker Library, Harvard University.

52. Harold C. Livesay, Andrew Carnegie and the Rise of Big Business (New York: Little, Brown & Co., 1975), p. 112; Thomas G. Manning (ed.), The Standard Oil Company, the Rise of a National Monopoly (New York: Holt, Rinehart & Winston, 1960), p. 19.

53. Joseph A. Litterer, "Systematic Management: Design for Organizational Recoupling in American Manufacturing Firms," Business History Review (Spring/Summer 1963), p. 380.

54. Scott, Iron and Steel, p. 67.

55. Benwood Iron Works, "Records," pp. 8, 19; Wheeling Iron and Nail, "Records," pp. 2, 7; Scott, Iron & Steel, pp. 47, 59, 82.

56. Benwood Iron Works, "Records," pp. 117, 118; The Steubenville Daily Herald, July 27, 1885.

57. Wheeling Iron and Nail, "Records," pp. 21, 56; Benwood Iron Works, "Records," pp. 56, 57, 97, 112; Scott, Iron & Steel, pp. 45-49.

58. Benwood Iron Works, "Records," pp. 106, 169; Benwood Iron Works, "Minute Book, January 27, 1880-August 4, 1892," p. 4, MS in the possession of the Wheeling-Pittsburgh Steel Corporation, Wheeling, West Virginia.

59. Benwood Iron Works, "Records," p. 112; Wheeling Iron and Nail, "Records," p. 16; Belmont Nail Company, "Records," p. 9; The Wheeling Intelligencer, April 26, 1875.

60. History of the Upper Ohio Valley, I, pp. 309, 310, 417, 418, 490; Chandler, The Visible Hand, pp. 8-10, 464-465.

61. Committee, Historical Statistics, pp. 123-124; The Iron Age, February 12, 1874, pp. 19-20.

62. The Iron Age, February 12, 1874, p. 19, April 6, 1876, p. 15; Bureau of the Census, Manufacturers of the United States in 1860 Compiled from the Original Returns of the Eighth Census (Washington: Government Printing Office, 1865), pp. cxciv-cxcv.

63. The Iron Age, April 15, 1875, p. 11.

64. Benwood Iron Works, "Records," pp. 77, 140, 175.

65. Wheeling Iron and Nail, "Records," p. 85, Benwood Iron Works, "Records," pp. 143, 148.

66. Benwood Iron Works, "Records," p. 164; Wheeling Iron and Nail, "Records," p. 52.

67. The Iron Age, April 15, 1875, p. 11, June 29, 1876, p. 11.

68. Ibid., January 16, 1873, p. 17, February 12, 1874, pp. 19-20; The Wheeling Intelligencer, March 7, 1874.

69. Quoted in The Wheeling Intelligencer, April 28, 1875.

70. The Iron Age, April 15, 1875, p. 11.

71. Ibid., April 13, 1876, p. 16.

72. Wheeling Iron and Nail, "Records," pp. 56-57; LaBelle, "Records," p. 46.

73. The Iron Age, April 6, 1876, p. 15. For a general discussion of the conditions in the hardware trade, see William H. Becker, "American Wholesale Hardware Trade Association, 1870-1900," Business History Review (Summer 1971), pp. 179-199.

74. A thorough search was made for records of the Western Nail Association. Their loss is regrettable because they would be very valuable, particularly insofar as they may deal with the "forfeiture fund."

75. Wheeling Iron and Nail, "Records," p. 56. The exact nature of the relationship between the Western Nail Association and the Western Iron Association is unclear. The two organizations were separate, although Wheeling firms participated in both. At times the company records are unclear in reference to the two groups. From the mid-1870s, the Wheeling manufacturers pressed the Western Nail Association to take over the wage-establishing functions and in the 1880s succeeded in their quest.

76. The Iron Age, April 6, 1876, p. 15, April 13, 1876, p. 15, December 28, 1878, p. 20.

77. Benwood Iron Works, "Records," pp. 152, 201.

78. The Iron Age, April 13, 1876, p. 15; LaBelle, "Records," p. 46; Wheeling Iron and Nail, "Records," p. 57.

79. LaBelle, "Records," pp. 46, 50; Wheeling Iron and Nail, "Records," p. 75.

80. Benwood Iron Works, "Records," pp. 365, 379; Benwood Iron Works, "Minute Book," p. 19; Wheeling Iron and Nail, "Records," p. 75.

81. Benwood Iron Works, "Records," p. 365; The Iron Age, December 28, 1878, pp. 20-21.

82. Benwood Iron Works, "Records," p. 365.

83. Ibid., p. 365; Wheeling Iron and Nail, "Records," p. 109.

84. J. D. Weeks, "Report of the Statistics of Wages in the Manufacturing Industries," Tenth Census of the United States, 1880 (Washington: Government Printing Office, 1886), p. 203.

85. Ibid, pp. 211, 212, 213.

86. Wheeling Iron and Nail, "Records," p. 105.

87. The Iron Age, July 24, 1879, p. 18.

88. Joseph A. Litterer, "Systematic Management," pp. 374-376.

4
The Steel Nail 1880-1886

> So far as Wheeling is concerned, it would have been better if the Englishman [Bessemer] had died before he discovered this process.
>
> The Wheeling Intelligencer
> October 23, 1884

As prosperity returned to the nail industry in the late 1870s many, if not all, of the Wheeling manufacturers looked to the coming decade expecting an era of prosperity. Confident in their ability to lead the industry, the nail men spoke of new plants, pressed forward with improvements to the management structure, and even began to expand their operations to other cities. Their ability to survive and even prosper during the 1870s had won them the respect and recognition of the rest of the industry. "The growth of Wheeling," the Chicago Tribune commented in 1880, "during the last ten years, considering the unprecedented depression in the iron business, is remarkable indeed." And The Iron Age, noting that the dividends from the Wheeling mills in 1881 had amounted to $712,000, commented that so much "money in a single year... from one industry alone is exceedingly flattering to this section of the country."[1]

While the prosperity and strength of the industry was quite real and Wheeling's place of leadership unquestionable, the 1880s were not to be an extension of the previous decade. Indeed, before the 1880s were half spent, the great nail factories of Wheeling would be on the brink of disaster. Those who looked back from the end of the decade would see even the halcyon days of 1880 and 1881 as prelude to a series of climactic events that pitted the cut nail against the wire nail. This hindsight suggests to many an inevitability that was not, nor could have been, perceived by the participants. For by the time the momentum of events was discernable, the cut nail was being driven from the market, leaving those who had operated the plants to place the blame for the disaster and direct their energies toward charting a new direction for the industry.

When the nail market revived in 1878, prices and profits increased to the highest level since the 1860s. As the money filled the coffers of the industry, existing nail manufacturers expanded their factories. They, along with many new firms organized to take advantage of high prices, swelled production and quickly drove down the price of nails. When the market began to cool in late 1883, competition became fierce and the entire industry eventually fell on hard times. The threat to profits not only prompted the Wheeling manufacturers to resume their search for new ways to reduce costs but also encouraged them to attempt to subdue competitors.

The response of the Wheeling manufacturers after 1883 was initially much like their response to the postwar crises. In the late 1860s, when the threat was from unfavorable iron prices, the Wheeling firms responded by internalizing pig iron production. Beginning in the late 1870s and throughout the first half of the 1880s, the manufacturers believed that high wages threatened profits. To counter this threat, the Wheeling firms undertook two major changes aimed at extending management's control of the labor market. One was the creation of an industry-wide bargaining agent to offset the strength of the Amalgamated Association of Iron and Steel Workers. The second thrust was aimed at mechanizing a portion of the manufacturing process so as to eliminate certain classes of high-paid employees.

Controlling wages required the cooperation of all western manufacturers, something that was difficult to achieve. The Wheeling manufacturers were successful only after they brought the force of their numbers and manufacturing efficiency to bear on the Western Nail Association and figuratively bludgeoned the other manufacturers into taking a stand. Mechanization, most clearly symbolized in the construction of the steel plants, required less industry-wide cooperation, but it did draw the Wheeling firms closer together, creating the conditions for the first horizontal integration.

The remainder of this chapter will examine these two solutions to the labor problem and the impact their pursuit had on the Wheeling firms and the industry as a whole. Particularly close attention will be paid to the decision-making process and to the way managment used a cost accounting system to arrive at conclusions about labor relations and technological change.

Because labor disputes were a constant and significant factor during the 1880s, a more detailed examination of the organization of work in the mills may be useful before proceeding with an examination of the events referred to above. During the 1870s and the early 1880s, the nail-manufacturing enterprises in Wheeling were organized into several departments. Processing of materials began at the blast furnace and was under the direction of an iron master or a furnace manager who was in charge of all of the blast furnace operations. Besides an assistant manager, a clerk, and an assortment of skilled workers who serviced and operated the machinery, the furnace departments employed mostly unskilled workmen who loaded raw materials into the furnaces, worked in the casting house, and performed the other labor required. The firms' records contained little information about the numbers, rates of pay, or other methods of calculating pay for furnace personnel aside from the furnace manager and clerk.

The intermediate stage in the nail-manufacturing process was the puddling (after 1870, boiling was the term most frequently used) and rolling mills. Pig iron was transported from the blast furnace to the boiling departments where it was remelted in the presence of mill cinder and converted into wrought iron. Each nail manufacturer had a number of boiling furnaces operated by "boilers" who, with the aid of several helpers, loaded, charged, and "worked" the boiling furnace until the metal had attained the proper degree of refinement. At the appropriate time, the hot metal, which had a pasty consistency, was removed from the furnace and transported to the squeezer, a machine that forced excess slag from the metal and shaped the bloom, a long cylindrical piece of iron.[2]

From the boiling departments the metal moved to the rolling mill, where the blooms were reheated and passed between a succession of rolls to attain the desired thickness and width. Here several classes of workers labored. A "roller" supervised and directed the operation of each "train" (set) of rolls with the aid of "shove-unders" who fed the metal into the rollers,"drag-outs" who retrieved the plate when it emerged, and "cutters" who cut the plates of metal into proper widths and lengths. Other workmen in the rolling mills pickled the metal and ran it through a lime slurry that added a lubricant to the plate that facilitated cutting when automatic feeders were used.[3]

Once cut into proper lengths and widths, the plates were delivered to the nail mill where "helpers" distributed them to the feeders who forced the plates into the nail cutters. A feeder operated each manually fed machine under the supervision of a nailer who had responsibility for a minimum of four machines. The nailer's main tasks were to adjust the machine, sharpen the blades, and oversee the quality of the nails produced.[4]

In addition to the major departments noted above, each mill had a shipping and warehouse department that loaded the nails into kegs, transported the kegs to the shipping point, and maintained inventories. Although no two mills were organized precisely the same, several had separate stables, repair shops, keg production shops, water works, and gas and coal houses that employed skilled and unskilled workmen.[5]

Each of the separate units had a superintendent or manager, although in some of the mills during some periods, service areas, such as stables, were attached to one of the larger subdivisions of the plant. The mill superintendents were salaried employes whose rate of compensation was established by the board of directors. With few exceptions, the superintendents were nailers, boilers, or rollers who had risen to the managerial levels from the ranks. The skilled workers--boilers, rollers, nailers, etc.--also worked directly for the company. Their wages were pegged either to the market value of nails or to an agreed-upon rate per pound. The nail machine feeders, and certain classes of workmen in the boiling and rolling mills, were contractors who worked for and were paid by the nailers, boilers, and rollers. The rates for these inside contractors, like those of skilled laborers, were tied to either the prevailing price for nails or the negotiated piecework rate for boiling and rolling.[6]

This division of labor was rooted in tradition and had existed relatively unchanged since the 1840s. Until almost the end of the 1870s, both management and labor respected the system and even delighted in the privilege and favorable economic position of the three basic crafts--nailers, boilers, and rollers. During the 1880s this respect disappeared in the face of management's attempt to reshape the nail-manufacturing process by eliminating one group of workmen--the boilers.[7] Management's motives and means of accomplishing this objective are interesting for the purposes of this study, because they provide some insight into the ways in which accounting data was used for decision making. Equally interesting is the managers' perception of technology, in this instance the Bessemer converter, as a mechanism to achieve cost reduction through employee replacement.

The first suggestion that management was considering changes came in 1878 just at the time the nail market hit its lowest point. The hard times prompted the Wheeling manufacturers to question the assumption that they could make nails cheaper at Wheeling than elsewhere. In the course of evaluating their competition, the manufacturers took a close look at wages and concluded that the eastern firms were paying one-third less for skilled labor. In May 1879 a circular of the Western Nail Association called for a wage reduction. "We ask," the printed request read, "the skilled operatives in our factories to consent to a reduction in wages to the prices paid in Eastern mills." Concurrently, the manufacturers began to look for alternate sources of materials from which to manufacture nails, seeking, through substitution, to reduce the cost of manufacturing wrought iron. LaBelle Company, along with the Bellefont Iron Works of Illinois, experimented with rerolling used rails into nail plates. And all of the Wheeling manufacturers briefly looked at using steel instead of wrought iron as the basic material for nails. By 1879, then, the managers had identified high wages, particularly in the boiling mills, as a key problem and had identified rerolled rails and steel as ways to dispense with the boilers.[8]

During late 1879, when demand for nails increased, manufacturers abandoned plans for steel plants and rail reprocessing mills. The same editor who had earlier predicted doom reported that "the consumption of nails, owing to the impetus given by the building of western cities, towns, mining camps and agricultural sections, has proven enormous, and prices, which were very low in the early part of the year subsequently advanced very materially." With the increase in prices efforts to reduce wages by technological changes were abandoned; however, the plans were not entirely forgotten and, as the strike of 1882 showed, even the flush times did not totally deflect the manufacturers' concern for the high cost of labor.[9]

Two basic conditions combined to inject new vitality into the nail industry. As the editor observed, building construction picked up. Local sources laid the resurrection of the industry to western construction. "New cities like Leadville, unknown a few years ago," a writer in The Wheeling Intelligencer reported, "have laid heavy requirements upon our jobbers, and these sales added to the sales to old customers, make the total an exceedingly liberal one." Statistics not available at the time confirm that the revival of construction was indeed the cause, or at least one of the causes, for the revival of the nail industry. Indexes compiled by Riggleman and Newcomb show that the dollar value of construction almost doubled between 1878 and 1881. This increase, coupled with an upsurge in railroad construction, dramatically increased the demand for nails and other building materials.[10]

Concurrent with the revival of construction, raw material prices began a downward slide. Ore costs, for example, dropped from $13.03 per ton in 1880 to $8.10 per ton in 1884. As a result of these cost reductions in the manufacture of pig iron, the cost of nails also fell. The Belmont Company records show that in the last six months of 1879 metal costs in a keg of nails were $1.28 per keg. For the corresponding period in 1883, metal costs were 92 cents for the same keg, a 28-percent decline.[11]

The growing market and the declining cost of metal brought profits, the likes of which had not been seen since the immediate postwar period. During the first six months of 1880, the Belmont Company averaged $1.10 profit per keg of nails; in 1882, 63 cents profit per keg; and in 1883, 47 cents profit per keg. These high profits provided the six Wheeling district mills with the highest dividends in their history in 1880 and 1881. Taking note of the $712,000 paid in dividends in 1881, a writer for the Bellaire Independent proclaimed that the industry had regained its full strength.[12]

With profits such as these to be had, the natural tendency was toward expansion of production facilities. The increase was minimal during 1880 and early 1881, probably because the strength of the revival was suspect and many manufacturers lacked the capital to finance major building programs. By 1882, however, suspicions were allayed, and as profit levels shown above suggest, capital had accumulated in sufficient amounts to fund expansion. Moreover, the price of pig iron continued to slip--a condition that encouraged firms previously not participating in nail manufacturing to add machines.

J. D. Weeks, secretary of the Western Nail Association, took note of the tendency to expand in 1883 and worried at the impact it would have. "The satisfying condition of the nail trade," he said, "cannot be permanently maintained." His prediction was of course correct. Between 1882 and 1885, the number of nail machines in operation in the United States increased from 3,995 to 5,695, or almost 43 percent. This dramatic increase in production capacity began to affect prices by early 1883, when capacity first outstripped demand and forced prices down.[13]

The new production capacity came in three areas. The largest increase was in existing plants. Seven of the nine Wheeling factories added new machines, increasing the total capacity of all Wheeling mills by almost 20 percent. Other factories in the Western Nail Association territory also added new machines and related equipment. Since the Western Nail Association had abandoned all effort to enforce the the production quotas that had been in effect in the late 1870s, the door was open for uncontrolled expansion.[14]

Competition also arose from new factories along the fringes of the Western Nail Association territory. During the 1880-1885 period new factories in Omaha, Nebraska, Pueblo, Colorado, Oakland, California, Woodward, Alabama, and Chicago, Illinois, went into production. It was these factories that J. D. Weeks referred to when he observed in 1885 that the recent "mania" for building new works was placing great pressure on the nail market.[15]

Several of these new factories were actually financed by Wheeling capital. A factory in San Pedro, California, for example, was organized at Steubenville by workmen of the Jefferson Iron Works. And the Woodward, Alabama, works was the brainchild of S. H. Woodward, a major stockholder of LaBelle Company and son of one of the founders.[16]

The new western factories were joined by other nail works operated by established firms in other branches of the iron industry. Between 1880 and 1884, fifteen rolling mills that had not previously operated nail mills added plants. The North Chicago Rolling Mill Company, for example, added a 100-machine nail mill to its rolling mill in 1883. With profits so high, companies that operated rolling mills could add nail machines at a minimal cost (about $30,000 could outfit a nail factory with between thirty and forty machines) and recoup the investment within a year's operation.[17]

Developments in the East paralleled those in the West. Several new factories and considerable expansion of existing plants increased the production capabilities of factories located in eastern and central Pennsylvania, for example. Between 1882 and 1884 manufacturers in this region added 318 new machines, increasing their productive capacity by almost 25 percent. The Williamsport (Pennsylvania) Iron and Nail Works, for example, added fifty-five machines to its rolling mill, and the Pottstown (Pennsylvania) Iron Company expanded an existing nail factory by sixteen machines. With the great demand for nails, and the sparkling new plants, the eastern firms began to encroach on the territory that had traditionally been claimed by western nail makers.[18]

The great expansion soon began to create a hugh oversupply of nails. J. D. Weeks observed in The Iron Age that the production capacity of the nation's nailworks had risen to nearly 10 million kegs in 1884 while consumption, including exports, was no more than 7 million kegs per year. In short, by 1885 capacity stood about 30 percent above demand.[19]

While the major impetus for the expansion was the higher prices, reduction in transportation costs also had some impact. Throughout the 1860s and 1870s, transportation costs for both raw materials and finished products had given the Wheeling firms an advantage. These transportation costs offset higher wages and stood as a barrier that excluded eastern firms from the lucrative western markets. In the 1880s this changed. Iron ore from Lake Superior could be shipped east by the lake route at far lower cost than previously had been the case, and railroad rebates and other practices familiar to students of American history made it possible to ship finished nails west at reasonable prices. One Pittsburgh manufacturer, for example, claimed that eastern Pennsylvania nail manufacturers could ship their products to Chicago at exactly the same rate as producers in Pittsburgh.[20]

The reduction of transportation costs was a particularly important element in the destruction of the regional markets. By 1882 the dividing lines between east and west had been severely blurred. While demand was high, this change did not present a real problem for the western manufacturers. In fact, it appears that the Wheeling manufacturers welcomed the opportunity to break out of the old western territorial confines and move into the urban markets of the Northeast. As early as 1881, for example, Wheeling manufacturers had agents in Baltimore and New York City.[21]

When the price slide began in 1883, the western manufacturers faced problems. They had lost a substantial part of their western and southern markets to the new mills, and cheap transportation and low labor costs made eastern nails very competitive. Moreover, as had been observed earlier, the production costs in the two sections had become very comparable--with the Wheeling mills having cheaper supplies and an edge on efficiency and the eastern mills having cheaper labor costs. It was this new set of conditions that set afoot many changes in the Wheeling manufacturing community.

Even though the market was strong and all of the firms were showing sizeable profits during the 1880-1882 period, the Wheeling management was concerned about the relatively lower eastern production costs. In 1882, when the Amalgamated scale was to be renegotiated, the Wheeling manufacturers organized to resist the increase that the union asked for and, in fact, attempted to obtain a reduction in wages. As in 1878, they attempted to enlist the support of the Pittsburgh manufacturers, but after finding no sympathy for the reduction, decided to hold out alone. A strike ensued and the Wheeling mills were closed for almost six weeks.[22]

This strike, the longest one in Wheeling to that time, was a turning point. Prior to 1882 the Wheeling firms, while frequently disagreeing with the other members of the Western Nail Association, had been content to limit their objections to vocal complaints, occasional subversion of pricing argeements, and, in the late 1870s, exploring cheaper technology. After the strike, the Wheeling manufacturers moved aggressively to impose their views on the other manufacturers and to gain competitive advantages that would force competitors from the market.

Not only did the other western manufacturers refuse to support Wheeling in holding out for wage reductions, they expanded production and marketing efforts in an attempt to win Wheeling markets. Moreover, other manufacturers even recruited the striking Wheeling workmen to staff their expanding mills. On September 27, 1882, <u>The Wheeling Intelligencer</u> reported that a "Mr. Timberlake" from Chicago had set up a recruitment office for the Chicago Nail Works and took note of the following scene:

> The office [Mr. Timberlake's] and the pavement in front presented an animated scene. About a hundred iron workers were there, all discussing the probable outcome of the manufacturers meeting that was in progress in the Riverside office. Every once in a while a delegation would go up the alley to Main Street and gaze at the windows of the office, but no news or consolation was to be obtained. About 1:00 o'clock someone cried out, "Well, boys, we better be getting to the depot," and the crowd began to move. At the B & O depot the scene was simply indescribable. The big waiting room and platforms were packed with nailers, feeders, boilers, helpers, and in fact, men from every department of the mills.
>
> At about 2:00 o'clock, vice president Thompson [vice president of the Amalgamated Association of Iron & Steel Workers] was seen hurrying along South Main Street. His approach was eagerly awaited, and as he entered the main waiting room, the crowd poured pell-mell after him. He mounted a bench and said, "Gentlemen. The manufacturers have sent word to me asking for a conference at 7:00 p.m. which I have agreed to call. I advised you yesterday to stay until today. Today I do not want you to be influenced at all by what I say. If you have made up your minds to go--go!"
>
> As Mr. Thompson stepped down, the crowd yelled "Go" and with a hurrah started for the doors when the voice of Mr. Timberlake was heard. Standing on a trunk, he said, "The train starts in fifteen minutes. What I want now is for those of you who are going with me to hold up your hands and pledge yourselves to remain two weeks."[23]

While there are no accounts of the manufacturers' reaction to this scene, its ramifications were inescapable. For the first time competitors were attempting, with some success, to lure workers away, thus opening a new arena of competition unfamiliar to the Wheeling firms who had theretofore been the recruiters. The Wheeling manufacturers were faced with a problem that, in the abstract at least, was not unlike the one their predecessors had faced in the 1860s. Just as the market for pig iron had put the Wheeling mills at a disadvantage, so it appeared in 1882 that the going price for labor was excessive and, potentially at least, threatened the existence of the business enterprises at Wheeling. The Wheeling manufacturers responded characteristically, with a series of actions that were aimed at circumventing the market as the determinant of cost and supply. Although there were several intermediate stages (which will be discussed below), management's objective after 1882 was to create conditions that would allow it to develop alternatives to specific classes of labor and determine who and how many people would be trained as skilled workmen. In pressing these objectives, management assaulted the most fundamental assumptions of two crafts--boilers and nailers--and, because of their central role in the industry, had to alter its basic structure.

Before moving to an examination of the Wheeling firms' efforts to control labor costs, a review of the operations of Belmont Mill may provide a good summary of the problems being faced by the Wheeling manufacturers. Belmont was rather typical--not the best, the largest, or the oldest of the firms. The firm had been reorganized in 1878 (after bankruptcy) under the leadership of some of the outstanding men in the business. The reorganizers included Samuel Laughlin, formerly of the Benwood and Laughlin Nail Company, J. M. Todd of the LaBelle Company, and A. W. Wilson of the Benwood Works. Records of the Belmont Company are complete enough to show with some accuracy what was happening to prices and costs during the first five years of the 1880s. The following table contains information from the minute book of the Belmont Company.[24]

TABLE 4

Cost, Selling Price, and Profits at the Belmont Mill

Year	Cost per Keg	Selling Price	Profit	Kegs Produced
1879*	$2.79	$3.30	$ .51	--
1880 (1st half)	3.31	4.42	1.11	78,442
1880 (2nd half)	2.75	2.97	.22	130,087
1881 (1st half)	2.62	2.97	.35	120,397
1881 (2nd half)	2.69	--	--	143,450
1882 (1st half)	2.80	3.43	.63	--
1882 (2nd half)	2.80	3.66	.86	75,940
1883 (1st half)	2.68	3.36	.68	134,317
1883 (2nd half)	--	--	--	--
1884 (1st half)	2.42	2.66	.24	126,396
1884 (2nd half)	2.38	2.31	-.07	95,897

*1879 statistics were for the full year.

The figures show that costs held relatively steady, fluctuating by only 93 cents per keg between the high in 1880 and the low in 1884. Prices, on the other hand, varied greatly with a difference of $2.11 between the high and low year.[25]

Two changes appeared in the cost of various items that went into nailmaking. The cost of iron dropped from 48 percent of the manufacturing cost in 1880 to 38 percent in 1884. At the same time, the cost of labor increased from 35.6 percent to 42.6 percent of the manufacturing cost. With metal costs going down for all manufacturers, with eastern competitors already having a cost advantage perceived to offset the efficiency that Wheeling enjoyed, and with other manufacturers thwarting their efforts to bring down wages, the

Wheeling men saw the increasing proportional cost of labor as most ominous.[26]

The Wheeling manufacturers alone recognized the potential problem, and as the events surrounding the strike of 1882 showed, they found no support in addressing it. Other producers, with a typical short-term view of operations, simply did not want to jeopardize the income that the lucrative markets of the early 1880s offered. The times were so good that the Western Nail Association's role was greatly diminished. The manufacturers met only infrequently, and at least the published accounts of the meetings give no indication that anything of significance occurred. These published reports generally contained no more than a listing of those in attendance and comments on the general affairs of the trade. The only matters of substance discussed between 1880 and 1884 were an occasional increase in the price of nails or a determination of the date for the annual summer "shopping," or shutdown for repairs.[27]

Under the stimulus of changing market and labor conditions, the Association began to revive in 1883. At first the members of the Association resorted to their old tactic of price fixing. Even when it became clear that overproduction was the problem, the manufacturers tried to hold prices high. With the new western mills in operation and the incursion of eastern mills, this course of action failed miserably. The Association then turned to another familiar ploy--controlling the rate of production. By extending the annual summer repair period in 1883 and 1884, the manufacturers cut their production by the equivalent of 1 million kegs per year. This "lay off" was successful, at least to a limited extent. J. D. Weeks, editor of The Iron Age, reported, "Since the Western manufacturers have been pressing a restricted policy, the price of nails had held much more steady." By 1884, however, neither the pricing nor the production control policies were effective. Mills outside the Association continued in the market, effectively defeating any plan and continuously pushing production higher and dropping prices lower.[28]

While the Western Nail Association was attempting to set prices and limit supply, the Wheeling manufacturers were pressing forward with their own methods, and these addressed costs rather than price. Foremost in the minds of the Wheeling manufacturers was the conversion to steel nail plate and the organization of an industrial bargaining agent.

Although conversion to steel had been considered as early as 1878, it presented certain technical problems and these, coupled with the heavy capital investment it required, prevented application of this solution. Effecting wage reduction proved equally difficult because it required concerted action of all mills. This sort of action was difficult to organize because of basic differences in the way the problem was viewed. The Wheeling manufacturers, as noted in the preceeding chapter, related profits to low cost and high volume, whereas the other manufacturers saw profits in terms of high margins and pushed for a controlled volume. After the revival of the trade in 1879 brought high margins, getting cooperation on this matter was difficult in not impossible.

Moreover, the organization of the industry and unions also mitigated against cooperative action on the part of the nail manufacturers. Prior to the formation of the Amalgamated Association of Iron and Steel Workers in 1875, wages were negotiated independently by each area or factory, and Wheeling always followed the lead of Pittsburgh in setting pay for laborers and skilled craftsmen (except nailers). Generally, Wheeling mills paid 25 cents more per ton for puddling and boiling than did Pittsburgh mills. When wage disputes resulted in strikes, Wheeling men stayed on the job and waited for the Pittsburgh settlement that set their wages. Several observers, depending upon their perspective, commented on this arrangement, alternately complaining of the effect that this arrangement had on Pittsburgh and lauding the stabilizing influence it had on Wheeling. In nonwage matters, and in dealing with unskilled labor or related enterprises such as coal mining and keg manufacturing, each manufacturer dealt with his own workmen.[29]

After the Amalgamated Association of Iron and Steel Workers was formed in 1875, the Western Iron Producers Association became the manufacturers' bargaining agent. Made up of representatives of producers from all segments--furnaces, rolling mills, etc.--the Western Iron Producers Association was largely controlled by Pittsburgh iron manufacturers. Although Wheeling had representatives, and the Western Nail Association took an active interest, the nail producers had no real influence on the Association's policy. They accepted the prevailing rates--or cards--as negotiated and implemented them in their mills.[30]

It was in 1879 that the Western Nail Association showed some interest in determining wages and, largely at the request of the Wheeling firms, published a request asking workmen to accept reduction in their pay. The request, quoted previously, claimed that the eastern nail workers were being paid one-third less than those in western mills. But, as noted above, after the upswing in 1879 and 1880 the Western Nail Association withdrew this request and, moreover, deferred to the Western Iron Producers Association in the contract negotiations of 1880.[31]

Negotiations in 1881 resulted in an increase in wages for boilers, puddlers, and their helpers. During the negotiations, Andrew Jarrett, vice president of the Amalgamated Association, promised the manufacturers that should a raise be forthcoming for the boilers, no adjustment would be sought the following year. The Wheeling manufacturers were not happy with this settlement and in fact were reported to be particularly bitter against signing the scale. When the boilers asked for an increase the following year, the Wheeling firms broke rank for the first time and negotiated directly with their own workmen. To conduct the negotiations, the manufacturers at Wheeling formed a local association made up entirely of Wheeling members of the Western Nail Association plus George Whitaker of Crescent Mill. The local association did thwart the wage increase but was unable to eliminate the "Wheeling bonus" or to roll back wages. In fact, before the negotiations were completed, the Wheeling firms had fallen to fighting among themselves, and Alexander Laughlin had pulled the Laughlin Nail Company out of the group. Primarily because mills in the rest of the Western Nail Association were at work and threatened to attract Wheeling workmen, the manufacturers gave up in late September. This attempt at local negotiations showed the Wheeling manufacturers that it was impossible to deal with workmen on a plant-by-plant or city-by-city basis.[32]

The 1882 strike was a turning point primarily because it pointed out emphatically to the Wheeling men that the wage question could not be dealt with outside of the Western Nail Association. Convinced that the Western Nail Association was the vehicle if control could be wrested from Pittsburgh manufacturers, the Wheeling men began asserting their presence in the Association's council more vocally and, it may be said, more ruthlessly than ever before. Led by J. N. Vance, an engineer who was president of the Riverside Works, the Wheeling contingent began holding strategy meetings prior to the monthly Western Nail Association meetings. By 1884, policy for the entire Western Nail Association was being made in the Wheeling district meetings and was given a perfunctury stamp of approval by the entire body.[33]

From the founding of the organization, the Western Nail Association had been closely associated with Pittsburgh. Weeks, The Iron Age editor, also served as its secretary and maintained an office for the Association in Pittsburgh. This arragement worked well during the first few years. Although Pittsburgh was on the eastern edge of the Western Nail Association, it had the second largest group of mills and was accessible to the majority of the manufacturers. Furthermore, Pittsburgh was a supply point and, as one of the owners of an Illinois mill noted, it was therefore a logical meeting place since the owners had to visit Pittsburgh frequently on buying trips.[34]

From the late 1870s on, the Wheeling manufacturers openly disagreed on the course of action to be taken in wage negotiations and pressed consistently for lower prices. Until 1883, however, the Wheeling representatives stopped short of open confrontation, choosing not to force a showdown. In 1883 and again in 1885, the Wheeling firms, after sharp debates, forced price readjustment over the objections of the Pittsburgh manufacturers. The friction between the two nail-making centers finally led to an open break in March 1885. The issue was pricing policy. In this instance, however, Wheeling representatives wanted higher prices for wrought iron nails because of their impending conversion to steel nails. At the February 12, 1885, meeting, Wheeling manufacturers had pressed for a price of $2.25 per keg for 10d common nails while Pittsburgh and Mahoning Valley representatives preferred $2.15 per keg.[35]

On March 21, 1885, the Pittsburgh Commercial Gazette reported that "an effort is being made to have the offices of the Western Nail Association moved from Pittsburgh in a very short time." The reporter interviewed several people, including Weeks, secretary of the Western Nail Association, and Ray F. Keating, president of Zug & Company, one of the largest nail manufacturers in Pittsburgh, and vice president of the

Western Nail Association. Both men agreed that the "report was absolutely without foundation." When the Western Nail Association met for its regular meeting on April 9, the delegates considered little business and adjourned to meet in Wheeling twelve days later. Plans laid by the Wheeling nail men came to fruition when the manufacturers reconvened. Headquarters of the Association were moved to Wheeling and Weeks was replaced by George Wise, an employee and stockholder of Belmont Mill. In addition, Vance of Riverside Mill was elected president of the Western Nail Association. Furthermore, the Wheeling men formally changed the Association's policy so that "hereafter the Western Nail Association will... treat with these unions [nailers, rollers, heaters, and feeders] and with other organizations whose branches of labor are employed in the bar, sheet, and iron mills." Finally, the Association went on record favoring a price differential between iron and steel nails.[36]

Except for two minor concessions--retaining General Fitzhughes, a Pittsburgh manufacturer, as vice president and promising to move the meetings from city to city--the Wheeling manufacturers carried the day completely. During the following decade and a half, Wheeling manufacturers never lost control of the Western Nail Association. They set prices, rolled back wages, and generally took a very hard line. Nevertheless, the Western Nail Association did not succeed. When the organization disbanded in 1898, the cut nail was all but an anachronism, largely supplanted by the wire nail.[37]

The Association's approval of the price differential for steel nails at the April meeting was perhaps the truest measure of Wheeling's success in capturing the policy-making function. The Wheeling manufacturers proposed in April 1885 that the Western Nail Association approve a separate price scale for steel nails, giving them a price advantage of about 10 cents per keg over wrought iron nails. This was an obvious move to gain a significant marketing advantage for the Wheeling mills, which had commenced the shift to steel as the basic material for nailmaking.[38]

With this move, the Wheeling manufacturers had gone well beyond simply trying to stabilize the industry through standard prices and equalization of wages and were mounting a campaign to destroy competition. As has been noted above, the Wheeling manufacturers first considered the use of steel instead of wrought iron toward the end of the 1870s as a means of eliminating the costly boiling operations. The discussions in 1878-1879 and after 1882 were frequently linked to the wages of boilers and helpers who, at Wheeling, were paid higher wages than in eastern mills. In 1880, for example, the average wage paid to Wheeling boilers was $5.25 per ton, while boilers at eastern mills averaged between $3.00 and $3.60 per ton. More importantly, from the vantage point of the Wheeling manufacturers, the efficiency of boiling departments was not improving. Unlike the blast furnaces and nail mills, where the output per unit of labor had shown a steady increase, the boiling department's production had remained steady and, after the Amalgamated negotiated reduction in the number of heats per turn in 1878, had actually shown a slight decline. Although the mill records do not make explicit reference to the production patterns, the figures were sufficiently clear to leave little doubt that the condition noted above was evident to the manufacturers. Moreover, J. D. Weeks took note of this condition in his comments on "Rolling-Mills and Nail Factories" in the 1880 census. "At most works, even within the past ten years, improved machinery and methods have greatly increased the output in most departments," he wrote. "This statement does not apply to the puddlers," he continued, "there having been little or no increase in the output of puddling furnaces in these years."[39]

Between 1879 and 1882, Wheeling's interest in steel nails found little support. Manufacturers who supported the use of steel were opposed by carpenters and most of the other manufacturers in the nail industry who claimed that steel was too hard and brittle for nails. Writing of the Wheeling interest in steel nails in 1884, a reporter for The Iron Age had implied that steel nails would not sell. "A great many attempts have been made to introduce the use of steel as a material for nails," the reporter wrote. He went on to say that all had failed "for various reasons."[40]

Although the early discussion of steel nails by the Wheeling manufacturers was not immediately followed by action, it was not forgotten. The matter came up again in 1880, for example. On June 17, the board of directors of the Benwood Iron Works requested the secretary to get information "in relation to the making of nails from Bessemer steel instead of iron" and to report on the comparative costs of manufacture. No record of the secretary's report can be found in the company's minutes but Scott, who was intimately involved with the industry at the time, claimed that steel plate was located, tests were run, and a few kegs of steel nails were actually produced. The events that followed indicated that the test must have been favorable.[41]

By mid-1882, writers for The Iron Age and The Wheeling Intelligencer were showing an interest in steel nails. Belmont Mill, the Benwood Iron Works, the Wheeling Iron and Nail Company, the Bellaire Nail Works, and the Riverside Nail Company were also displaying an intense interest in the nails. During the fall of 1882, J. N. Vance, president of the Riverside works, led an effort to erect a "union steel works" that would be jointly owned by all the Wheeling mills. A company, the Wheeling Steel Company, was incorporated with an authorized capital stock of $1 million to erect a Bessemer works. The corporation had a short life. On December 14, 1882, the stockholders of the Wheeling Iron and Nail Company refused to approve their board of directors' request to issue additional capital stock to raise the money for Wheeling Iron and Nail's purchase of one-seventh of the stock in the new corporation. A month later, the Benwood works also withdrew from the combination and its board was authorized to erect a separate steel plant. Following these defections, the proposed corporation was abandoned.[42]

The Wheeling Steel Company episode was notable for several reasons. First, the scheme was hatched during the six-week strike of 1882 when the boilers were demanding a sizeable pay increase. Interest waned quickly after the strike ended without the increase in pay. This suggests, once again, that the manufacturers saw a direct relationship between the introduction of steel and the cost associated with boiling. Second, the "union steel mill" was the first effort at horizontal integration within the Wheeling nail community. Although the attempt failed, the effort, coming as it did concurrently with the organization of a negotiating association, marked the beginning of a move toward combination of facility and resources that eventually culminated in the Wheeling Steel Corporation. Moreover, the episode suggested that a gap was developing between management and ownership. The management, particularly the secretaries and presidents of all of the firms, supported the steel mill. It was the stockholders of three firms--the Wheeling Iron and Nail Works, the Bellaire Nail Works, and the Benwood Iron Works--who vetoed the plan. Just why the stockholders rejected the joint venture is unclear. At the time, it was widely believed that workmen who owned stock in the companies influenced the vote. Stock-holding workmen could have affected the Bellaire works; however, by the 1880s, workmen in other mills owned very little stock. Some stockholders may have been frightened by an article that appeared in The Iron Age in which a writer asserted flatly that the cost of steel nails would prevent their widespread use. Since this article appeared when it did and in a publication edited by the secretary of the Western Nail Association, who was closely allied with the Pittsburgh manufacturers, it must have been viewed by those in Wheeling who favored the steel works as an attempt to prevent manufacture of steel nails. Vance, who had led the formation of the corporation to build the steel plant, later coordinated the Wheeling takeover of the Western Nail Association. After assuming the presidency of the Western Nail Association, Vance's first act, as noted above, was to replace Weeks.[43]

The defeat of the "union steel plant" was only the first of several disagreements between management and owners. By 1885, the separation so frequently noted by scholars who have studied this subject had occurred. On May 12, 1885, for example, a writer for The Wheeling Intelligencer quoted "a prominent Wheeling manufacturer" as being opposed to having the Western Nail Association meetings at Wheeling. "A few weeks ago," the manufacturer said, "all the directors and stockholders who cared to be were present. When the meeting was over a good deal of information that should have been kept very quiet was given to those who had no right to know it." Clearly, this attitude suggests that management had come to regard participation in the decision-making process as solely its prerogative. It may be also pointed out that the meeting the anonymous commentator referred to was the one at which the Western Nail Association decided to become the industrial bargaining agent and to give steel nails a price advantage. Both were major decisions that affected (and were perceived by those present as affecting) the basic welfare of the corporations and workmen.[44]

The management of the Wheeling nail firms had, by 1882, perceived the acquisition of steel works to be so important that the failure of the "Union Nail Works" had only a marginal impact on the resolve of the Wheeling mills to shift to steel. The Riverside and Bellaire nail works began making plans in early 1883 for their own steel plants and both firms had completed Bessemers by late spring of 1884. The Benwood Company proceeded at a slower pace and was eventually joined by the Wheeling Iron and Nail Works and the Belmont Company in the construction of a joint bessemer plant. The LaBelle built its own steel plant, using the Clapp-Griffiths patent, in Steubenville; and the Laughlin Nail Mill constructed a bessemer furnace at Mingo Junction in concert with the Junction Iron Company. By 1886, all of the Wheeling firms were in the steel business.[45]

At some point in 1883, the western nail manufacturers began to take Wheeling's move toward steel seriously. Steel nails could be made less expensively and therefore provided an opportunity for undercutting prices. Since the Wheeling manufacturers were the only ones pushing ahead aggressively with steel works, this realization was sobering to all of the manufacturers--most particularly to the smaller ones, who had no prospects of raising the capital required for Bessemer converters. The prospect of facing competition from steel nails left many, much like a "Massachusetts mill owner," to wonder how they could stay in business without access to steel.[46]

Publicly the Wheeling firms argued that the conversion to steel was nothing more than a move to prevent competition with the eastern nail makers. Privately they had different motives. As the pricing differential approved by the Western Nail Association showed, their intention was to control, if not subdue, competition through a pricing structure that rested heavily upon the firm's ability to raise capital. Although the new pricing arrangement would have affected the Pittsburgh and Mohoning Valley mills, the availability of steel in both areas would have permitted manufacturers to convert at least partially to steel. The smaller mills down the Ohio River and further west had no such opportunity. Their closest supplier of steel would be Wheeling, and by controlling the sale of steel nail plates the Wheeling firms could have a marked impact on the production capabilities of these mills. From late 1884 through 1887, the Wheeling firms did exert pressure in just this manner. Moreover, they refused to sell steel to new mills organized by workmen during the Great Strike of 1886 and used steel supply as a means of forcing compliance with the Cincinnati wage scale.[47].

The steel mills did lower the cost of nailmaking dramatically. During 1884, the last full year the Belmont Company used wrought iron, labor costs averaged $1.03 per keg. Two years later, after the switch to steel was complete, labor costs dropped to 56 cents per keg.[48]

By 1883, Wheeling was alive with rumors of impending change. Profits from 1880, 1881, and 1882 filled the coffers of the several mills and, judging from the dividend records, the pockets of a large number of stockholders. Local and foreign investors were anxious and the city fathers were ecstatic about the future. The newspapers spoke freely of plans to "boom the town" and regularly spread forth the praises of the social, economic, and political climate the city had to offer. The city was billed as "progressive" with frequent notations of the abundance of coal and natural gas and the excellent rail and water connections the city offered. During late 1883 and early 1884, delegations of businessmen from other cities were regularly brought to Wheeling as part of a campaign to attract new industry.[49]

All was not well, however. The nail industry, although profitable, was careening toward a disastrous showdown. An opening skirmish between the owners and workmen resulted in the six-week strike mentioned above and a settlement that, on the surface, maintained the status quo. As the foregoing discussion has pointed out, the 1882 strike was actually a turning point; one that in fact set the stage for the catastrophic confrontation between labor and management during 1885 and 1886. The "Great Nail Strike," as it was frequently called, resulted from a wage dispute between the Western Nail Association and the United Nailers. While this event was viewed by contemporary and later observers as the most significant in the industry's history, it was only the final chapter of a long struggle, the roots of which stretched back into the 1870s.[50]

Tracing the course of events that led to the Great Strike of 1885 necessitates recounting certain labor/management and internal labor relationships that began to evolve in the early 1870s. These relationships affected the decision to introduce steel, management's perception of labor's strength, management's perception of its ability to manipulate various classes of workers, and management's interpretation of conflicts between various classes of workmen.[51]

The Wheeling mills were built around two groups of workers--the boilers who worked the wrought iron and the nailers who manned the nail machines. In the prewar period, the owners of nail mills came largely from these two classes of workmen and, even as late as the 1880s, some continued to own stock in the hopes of moving into the ranks of management. By the standards of the day, both groups of workmen were well paid. Alexander Glass, who went to work in the nail factories in 1873 at the age of 14, noted in his reminiscenses that in the 1877-1879 period he consistently earned between $12 and $20 a day after paying his helpers. Glass' claims were substantiated by others. The boilers were paid equally well.[52]

Although the boilers and nailers were the two most important groups of workmen, they were by no means the largest group. Wheeling firms probably never employed more than 350 nailers at any given time. The precise number of boilers is much more difficult to determine but, based on the number of furnaces, Wheeling firms probably never exceeded more than 900 workers in this category. The largest number of workmen were semiskilled (helpers, feeders, rollers, etc.) and laborers such as "drag-outs," "shove-unders," and the like. All of the craftsmen (nailers, boilers, blacksmiths, etc.) and laborers, as well as some semiskilled workmen, were employed by the firms. A few groups of semiskilled employees, such as nail plate feeders, were inside contractors who worked for and were paid by individual craftsmen. Except at the blast furnaces, this system had prevailed from the earliest days of the Wheeling mills and continued well into the twentieth century.[53]

The skilled craftsmen were all piecework employees with pay determined by either the market value of nails or an agreed-upon rate per ton. Generally, management either directly or (after 1874) through a third party negotiated a rate with each group of workmen. For example, when 10d common nails sold for between $2.00 and $3.00 per keg, nailers were paid $.21, boilers $5.75 a ton for wrought iron, and coal miners $.03 a bushel. If prices rose to $5.00 per keg, nailers received $.30 per keg, boilers $9.55 per ton, etc. During negotiations, the central question always turned out to be adjustments to the scale. Such adjustments could take many forms, ranging from actually changing the rate to limiting or expanding the range within which a particular rate was paid.[54]

Throughout the period from 1875 to 1885, the rate for nailers remained constant. The 21-cent scale, as it was called, held firm with neither party showing much interest in changing the base rate. The boilers, on the other hand, constantly agitated for change. They demanded and received adjustments in prices or working hours in 1879 and in 1881, and asked but failed to get an adjustment in 1882 and 1884. The manufacturers were particularly concerned over adjustment in the boiler's rate because of the productivity problem and the growing discrepancy between wages in the eastern and western nail mills. Moreover, the wage rates of the semiskilled employees were tied to the craftsmen's pay scale. For example, muckrollers received one-eight of the rate for boiling. Consequently, any change in the boiling rates affected several other classifications.[55]

Given these considerations, manufacturers were not favorably disposed toward the boilers' request for pay increases and, in fact, came to regard them as a troublesome lot by the early 1880s because of their frequent demands. The manufacturers, in fact, made no secret of their dislike for the boilers. For example, "a well-known iron man" was quoted in The Wheeling Intelligencer as saying, "steel makers are rolling out steel nails at less cost than they can produce muck bar." "Now you want to know why," he continued. "Simply because we have to pay such a high price for puddling."[56]

The nailers presented a dramatic contrast to the boilers: During the ten-year period between 1874 and 1884, the nailers' output increased constantly, they were content with the fixed rate, and they were not responsible for a single work stoppage. The only problems in the nail mills resulted from constant conflict between the nailers and the feeders that began in 1872 when "bad blood" developed between the two groups of workers. The difference was centered around the issues of money and apprenticeships. In 1875, the feeders went on strike, demanding that nailers increase their rates from two-fifths to one-half of the money earned by the nail machine that the feeder operated. The nailers retaliated by introducing automatic feeders and broke the strike. While the automatic feeder had been available from the very early days of the industry, it had been ineffective because it produced a large number of irregular nails. After the Civil War, several new feeders that reduced waste became available, but because craftsmen, rather than the firms, were expected to purchase the machines, the automatic feeder was slow to find wide aceptance. Improvements, particularly the perfection of the "flip-plate feeder," greatly improved the machines and served notice to everyone interested enough to pay attention that a completely satisfactory feeder was not far away.[57]

After the strike of 1875, most of the feeders returned to their old jobs, working alongside the automatic feeders that had been installed during the strike. In some cases, the nailers who had purchased the machines actually removed them, preferring to have hand-fed nails. Nonetheless, the automatic feeders were a threat to the feeders, who correctly blamed the nailers for their introduction. The bitterness that resulted may aptly be guaged from comments made by J. Elmer Bell, a feeder at Benwood Mill. Speaking for the feeders' union in April 1875, he said:

> Once more we are called upon and assembled here for the purpose of taking steps to remove from our necks the tyrannical yoke of oppression...that unprincipled men have placed us in....
>
> Behold the nailer as he appears before the eyes of the world living in one of the finest residences in the city, of which he is owner and landlord; his wife and children clad in the finest garments the city can produce; and when you encounter him upon the highway you will quickly observe the air of independence that he exhibits, which tends to show his superiority over the poor and almost despised feeder, whom he robs of his just dues.[58]

The bad feeling between the feeders and the nailers carried over into the organized labor movement, when the Amalgamated Association of Iron and Steel Workers was formed in 1875. For almost five years, the nailers exerted pressure to keep the feeders out of the union so they could retain a free hand in dealing with them on wage and working condition questions.[59]

For a time, the factory managers refused to become involved in the differences between the feeders and the nailers. In the early 1880s this changed when the manufacturers, who correctly perceived that the automatic feeder had been sufficiently developed to offer some economies, purchased the existing machines from the nailers and took responsibility for adding new ones. From this point forward, the owners used the automatic feeders to manipulate both the nailers and the feeders. When the feeders complained, threatened to strike, or demanded improvements in conditions, the owners simply added a few new automatic feeders and brought the men back into line. When the nailers spoke, as they did in 1883, of a scale adjustment, the manufacturers let it be known that they favored either an increase in the feeders' pay or an adjustment downward in scale when automatic feeders were employed. The threat worked effectively for the manufacturers and ensured relatively smooth operation in the nail departments of the factories.[60]

Until 1884 the "baiting" was confined to the nail departments. When the boilers resisted the introduction of steel nails, the manufacturers turned to this tactic to control the Amalgamated Association and to reduce the resistance of the boilers. When and by whom the strategy was formulated is unknown.

After it became apparent that the Wheeling manufacturers were intent upon converting to steel nail plate, the boilers conceived a strategy that offered some hope for stalling, if not blocking, the move. At the Wheeling district Amalgamated Association meeting in March 1884, the boilers proposed and the Association accepted a resolution asking the National Amalgamated Convention to demand a 10-percent increase in nail rates when steel was used. The rationale was that steel was harder, caused more breakages in machines (for which the nailer had to pay), and made the job of the feeder more difficult. The resolution had the support of the nailers, who brought it before the convention where it was approved and written into the 1884 Scale Agreement. Just how the manufacturers reacted is unknown. Since only the Wheeling manufacturers were converting to steel it would have been clearly in the interest of the Pittsburgh, Mahoning Valley, and Ironton manufacturers to have the provision included. With no knowledge of the manufacturers' reaction, one can only speculate that the Wheeling representatives to the Western Iron Association were overruled on any objections that they may have made. If this were in fact what happened, it would have been another contributing factor in the Wheeling men's desire to take over the Western Nail Association and turn it into the industrial bargaining agent.[61]

The provision appeared to have the desired result. As early as January 1884, the nailers let it be known in an interview published in <u>The Wheeling Intelligencer</u> that they would ask for the increase. Even after the Bellaire Nail Works and the Riverside works put Bessemer converters into operation in April and May 1884, boilers were kept on the payroll. LaBelle, through its secretary, announced that the company intended to continue making iron nails and even went so far as to install a new gas boiling furnace. The most widely held opinion was that the companies would continue to manufacture iron nails along with steel nails and that the loss of jobs among boilers would be minimal. To compensate for jobs that would be lost, a group of businessmen, including some of the nail manufacturers, even organized a bridge factory expressly to utilize the boilers thrown out of work by the steel nail.[62]

Just when the Amalgamated Association seemed to have hammered out a process for saving some of the boilers' jobs, the nail feeder controversy surfaced again. At the August 7, 1884, meeting of the Amalgamated Association of Iron and

Steel Workers, feeders requested that their wages be increased from two-fifths to one-half of the income earned by each machine, thus reducing the nailers' income from three-fifths to one-half. Although unsuccessful, this request received considerable support from various groups of workmen, including boilers. "In the opinion of many mill men," an anonymous delegate said, " the feeders are pretty near right in their demand for more wages." Before the convention ended, the nailers had begun to rethink their position on the steel nail question. "If steel could be made having a carbon content as low as .9 of a percent," reasoned one nailer, "the steel nail might be a success."[63]

Less than a day after the wage question came before the Amalgamated convention, the manufacturers struck with a vengeance. LaBelle, the company that only three months earlier had built new boiling furnaces, posted notices discharging all of its boilers. In reporting the action, a Wheeling Intelligencer reporter commented:

> Such a notice without warning came with the force of a blow....
>
> A feeling of uneasiness took possession of all the mill men. It was regarded as a break which would be followed by all the other mills in due time. Of course it could have but one meaning, that the use of iron for nail making was to be abandoned and steel is to be substituted.[64]

Every bit of information points to manipulation. There is no doubt that the Bellaire and Riverside owners struck a deal in which they promised not to support the feeders' demand for an increase if the nailers dropped the extra charge for cutting steel nails. The workmen in other departments of the mills regarded the actions of the nailers with suspicion and passed on rumors of a party at which the nailers and owners had met to hammer out their agreement. What is unknown is whether or not the manufacturers had any hand in encouraging the feeders to make their demands for higher wages.[65]

After the August meeting, the nailers openly defied the Amalgamated Association by refusing to request the additional 10 percent for cutting steel nails. The Amalgamated leadership requested, demanded, and begged the nailers to comply with the agreement, but to no avail. As the firms closed the boiling departments, the boilers became progressively more hostile toward the nailers and the Amalgamated. In October 1884 the boilers at Belmont Mill, feeling that the Amalgamated was not pursuing the issue with enough resolve, broke with the union in protest. After hearings on the matter, convened in Wheeling by the president and the secretary of the Amalgamated Association, preparations were made to expel the nailers at the Bellaire Nail Works (the Hershey Lodge). Before the Amalgamated could act, the Hershey Lodge voluntarily gave up its charter, and John K. Weir, the president, began laying the groundwork for a new union--the United Nailers. In short order, the other nail lodges of the Amalgamated Association also surrendered their charters and joined the Hershey Lodge. During the early months of 1885 the nailers organized the new union and convinced the heaters and rollers to join them.[66]

By January 1885 the Amalgamated forces in the Wheeling area were in total disarray. As the approaching wage negotiations came nearer, the Amalgamated Association not only backed away from its insistence on retaining the boilers' jobs but also abandoned its insistence on retaining wages at the 1884 level. Willingness to sacrifice the boilers and willingness to take a 10-percent cut in other wages cost the Amalgamated Association even more members.[67]

With the boilers in check, the manufacturers turned their attention to the nailers. As the 1885 scale talks opened, the nailers asked that wages be continued at their old levels (21-cent scale) and that the manufacturers pay for the cost of repairing broken machines. Meeting at Cincinnati on May 27, 1885, the manufacturers drew up a plan that called for the reduction of nail rates from 21 cents to 17 cents per keg for 10d nails, plus an additional reduction of one-fourth when automatic feeders were employed, and for the nailers to continue paying for breakages. The nailers, except those at Bellaire Mill, refused to sign the manufacturers' scale and called a strike.[68]

Publicly the manufacturers defended their reduction of the nail scale by pointing to lower wages paid by the eastern competitors and rising transportation costs. This defense was not entirely inaccurate. At the end of 1884 the Parker Mill, a Massachusetts firm, was selling at $2.77 per keg while the Wheeling Iron and Nail Company was selling for $2.67 and Belmont was selling for $2.31 per keg. The Wheeling firms were not making a profit. Volume had dropped off greatly in 1884 and early 1885, leaving large inventories of unsold nails. The Wheeling Iron and Nail Company, for example, ended 1884 with fully 20 percent of the year's run unsold. Since the market was falling, the nails stacked in the company's warehouses would eventually become a loss. The Belmont Nail Company was caught in this position in 1885 when it sold 9,000 kegs of 1884 nails that cost $2.42 to manufacture for $2.31 per keg.[69]

The steel nail offered hope in the long term, but when the manufacturers began the wage negotiations in 1885, only three firms had operating steel plants. The other three were still under construction, scheduled for completion in the fall of 1885. Moreover, the large inventory of iron nails still had to be sold even after the Bessemers did begin producing nail plate, and the prospect for large short-term losses probably frightened the manufacturers.

Having been successful in curbing other unions, the manufacturers undoubtedly felt that the time was right to gain the upper hand with the nailers. Several manufacturers had come to believe that the nailers were not indispensable and that any reasonably skilled person could learn to adjust the machines, sharpen the blades, and perform other tasks that the nailers had claimed required special skills. Events would prove the manufacturers correct.[70]

While the manufacturers looked to the ledger books to justify their actions, the nailers dismissed the strike in a half-humorous way. "It's a bluff," one nailer was quoted as saying in The Wheeling Intelligencer. Others claimed that the Western Nail Association's motive was to drive the eastern nail makers from the market.[71]

Within two weeks after the strike commenced, the controversy between the nailers and the feeders revived. The immediate cause of the difficulty was apprenticeships. During 1884 and early 1885, the manufacturers had introduced more automatic feeders, and it was clear to many people that the days of the manual feeder were limited. Shortly before the strike began, the nailers had "decided to cut off all apprenticeships" of feeders. When the feeders learned of this, they went before each lodge of nailers and asked for a reversal of the decision, demanding that 3 percent of the feeders in each mill be taught the nailers' craft each year. The feeders also appealed to the manufacturers for support in this matter and received assurances from them that "if they [the feeders] would maintain their demand, the mill owners would do all they could to see that the feeders had justice done in this matter."[72]

The manufacturers moved quickly to take advantage of the controversy. On July 8, 1885, in a meeting of the Western Nail Association at Cincinnati, the delegates passed a resolution giving the nailers until July 11 to accept the "Cincinnati Scale." If the nailers refused, "the mills connected with the Western Nail Association will be opened and the machines given to nail feeders or any competent person or persons who would agree to cut nails at the price in said scale."[73]

Though the threat was meant to be serious, the nailers treated it with a laugh and assumed that "no man who has not served a regular apprenticeship as a nailer can do a nailer's work." "Talk about circuses," one nailer said, "that would beat any three-ring show Barnum ever dreamed of." The nailers refused to give even the courtesy of a reply to the manufacturers' demand. At a meeting convened in Wheeling on July 15, the nailers formally organized a new union, the United Nailers, Heaters and Rollers, and drew up bylaws. They reaffirmed their position on wages, demanding the 21-cent scale, reasserted their position that the manufacturers should pay for broken machines, and went on record favoring the fifty-hour work week.[74]

Shortly after the nailers adjourned their meeting, the area feeders met and agreed to accept the manufacturers' offer to take control of the nail machines. On July 26, the first feeders began operating machines at Benwood Mill. During the following weeks, every mill trained feeders to operate machines and, by early fall, had resumed production. By January 1886, it was apparent that the feeders could easily become skilled nailers. At that time, approximately two-thirds of the machines in the Western Nail Association were in operation.[75]

The nailers' contention that they possessed irreplaceable talents was debunked. The feeders who took over the machines quickly picked up the critical skills of grinding (sharpening) the blades of the nail machines, the aspect of the nailers' job that had been assumed to be the part requiring the most experience and training. Many observers had suspected for a long time that the real secret of the nailers' trade was that there was no secret at all. "Any man who had worked about a nail machine for a long time," one mill owner said at the beginning of the strike, "if he had average intelligence ought to soon give acceptable service as a nailer." This in fact proved to be a correct assumption.[76]

As the nail strike dragged on, the nailers were finally and completely separated from the management of the mills. This class of workmen, who had built the industry, was finally torn away from any role in determining its direction. Although the nailers had not been part of management for many years, the strike pointed out the realities that many had refused to recognize. Those nailers who had become superintendents, such as Jacob Altmeyer of Benwood and John Morrison of the Wheeling Iron and Nail Company, were faced with a dilemma. While the boards ordered them to teach the feeders to operate the machines, their sense of loyalty to their craft demanded that they refrain from imparting such skills. Both men, and several more who were put in similar positions, resigned their posts and left Wheeling for mills in other states.[77]

The nailers at first held firm in the faith that the manufacturers would fail. When it became apparent that they would not, the strikers turned in desperation to violence. Several minor machine-breaking incidents occurred in August. These were followed by attacks on "scab" labor, particularly the few nailers who refused to leave the mills and those imported from outside Wheeling to teach the feeders. Violence reached a climax in late September when about forty striking workmen attacked and laid siege to the Laughlin Nail Works at Martins Ferry. After a two-hour gun battle, the attackers were driven away without doing any real damage.[78]

All the nailers' efforts to disrupt the manufacturers failed or had only limited impact. The manufacturers moved cautiously, bringing more and more machines on the line as men became available either from the internal training programs or from other factories outside the Western Nail Association. In November the manufacturers, who were by this time satisfied that the new men were capable, responded to an overture to negotiate by declaring that "our obligation to these new nailers is such that we could not entertain any proposition that would interfere with these obligations." Individually, the mill owners reinforced this attitude by running ads promising feeders "a chance to learn nailing" with the attached provision that "places are guaranteed to those who accept this offer."[79]

By the end of November 1885, strikers and manufacturers settled into a stand-off, neither offering to compromise. Each month the Western Nail Association released figures showing that the number of machines in operation was rising, but it steadfastly refused to discuss output or sales figures. Nailers responded with an information campaign claiming that a nail shortage was imminent and with testimonials criticizing the quality of nails being turned out.[80]

In an effort to bring pressure on the manufacturers, the nailers organized a boycott. "Will the United Nailers, after opposing the feeders, as they have done for years, after sacrificing the boilers as they did, after deserting the Amalgamated Association as they did, explain by what right they assume to say that scab nails will bury in paupers' graves those that produce them" asked one critic of the boycott.[81]

As the months passed, the nailers saw their occupations surely and steadily slipping away from them. Some reacted by seeking employment in eastern factories. Others moved west to work in the California plants. A few returned to the Wheeling factories. At least two groups formed cooperative factories. By the spring of 1886, it was clear that the manufacturers had won the contest. Even the Bellaire Works which had operated throughout the strike served notice on April 15, saying that, in keeping with its policy of paying prevailing wages, it would reduce the nailers' rates from 21 cents to 17 cents per keg for 10d common and would conform to the Western Nail Association's Cincinnati scale on all other sizes.[82]

The disheartened nailers, numbers steadily dwindling, conceded defeat in May. They turned back to the Amalgamated Association, asking for readmission to the union that they so recently had left. On June 1, four days shy of one year after the strike began, the nailers not only voted to ask for readmission to the Amalgamated Association but also requested that the Association take up their cause with the manufacturers. On June 26, the Amalgamated Association settled for the 17-cent scale with adjustments upward in the lower size ranges. The manufacturers were obligated to take the nailers back only if they had machines available, the feeders who had taken over machines were to be considered as nailers, and a newly employed feeder was to be paid one-half to three-fifths of the income from the machine he worked. In July and early August the nailers who had remained at Wheeling gradually found machines. In order to stretch the limited work available, the old nailers worked split shifts, sharing their machines and incomes with each other.[83]

The manufacturers had won. They had succeeded in destroying both the nailers and the boilers and reducing the wages of all workmen. Cost data contained in the minute books of Belmont Mill show the impact that the events of 1885 and 1886 had on the cost of producing nails. In 1884, while wrought iron was still being used and the 21-cent scale was in effect, labor costs were $1.03, or about 39 percent of the cost of a keg of nails. Three years later, after steel had replaced wrought iron and the 17-cent scale was accepted, labor costs had declined to 42 cents or about 21 percent of the cost of a keg of nails. Spotty information from other mills in the Wheeling area confirms that this pattern prevailed everywhere.[84]

When the nailers agreed to the 17-cent scale in July 1886, the manufacturers had apparently solved what they had defined as their most pressing problem--high wages. With eastern and western wages roughly equal and with the advantage that steel offered, it appeared that the manufacturers at Wheeling had regained the competitive advantage that they had enjoyed in the 1870s. As the next chapter will show, this was not to be.

The period between 1880 and 1886 was a time of change for the nail industry in general and the Wheeling firms in particular. Even so, there was considerable continuity in the Wheeling personnel as well as in the basic philosophy. In this sense, the 1880s may be seen as an extension of the 1870s. Specifically, the continued use and perfection of analytical tools, most particularly cost accounting, developed in the 1870s to diagnose and gauge management decisions, links the two decades.

It is particularly important to note that after 1878 the Wheeling manufacturers were applying their accounting system to competitors and were determining at what points relative strengths and weaknesses existed. In some instances data was being gathered through personal relationships between Wheeling employees and those in other mills. Particularly in the West, former Wheeling employees were to be found in almost every mill. J. D. Weeks was, however, the most important conduit of information from the eastern mills. Weeks, who prepared the 1880 census report on rolling mills and nail factories, used the Wheeling cost format in tabulating the cost of manufacturing in several of the eastern mills. The use of the Wheeling format is notable since it required much work and probably a considerable amount of personal contact to extract the information from the records of the twenty eastern firms used in the report, none of which had adopted the Wheeling system. Weeks' figures not only allowed instant comparison of the costs in 1879, but provided the historic data which clearly showed that the eastern manufacturers had systematically offset Wheeling's efficiency through wage reductions.[85]

Just when the Wheeling manufacturers gained access to Weeks' information is uncertain; that they had at least parts of it by the early 1880s (well before publication in 1885) is unquestionable. Their attempt in 1882 (when the prices and profits were high) to force wages down suggests that they were quite aware of the eastern developments. While other sources, such as personal connections, undoubtedly provided some insight into competitors' operations, the extreme interest in the eastern firms, which Weeks emphasized in his report, and the complete exclusion of reference to operations of the Pittsburgh firms suggest that it was Weeks' data that they were acting on. Weeks, who had very close ties to Pittsburgh, all but ignored the western Pennsylvania manufacturers in his study, an oversight that can hardly be regarded as an accident.[86]

Although not apparent to anyone outside of Wheeling, the analytical elements of the Wheeling management system were, during the early 1880s, being extended to the entire industry. The Wheeling manufacturers clearly understood that the regional marketing system that had prevailed since the late 1860s was disappearing and that in the future competition would be on a national scale. Consequently, they sought to adjust their manufacturing operations to accommodate the new conditions, looking to meet and better the lowest cost in the industry.[87]

The central problem was that while the product market was becoming a national one, the Wheeling firms were purchasing labor in a market that was still regional. Just as the pig iron market of the early 1860s discriminated against the Wheeling manufacturers, so they perceived the labor market in the 1880s as discriminating against the western branch of the industry. This realization was first evident in the late 1870s, it was confirmed by Weeks' study, and the magnitude of the problem was driven home with the force of a blow during the strike of 1882. Between 1878 and 1882 the Wheeling manufacturers had defined the problem almost totally in internal terms, concluding that either a negotiated wage reduction among Wheeling employees or the conversion to steel (which was in effect a forced reduction in wages) was the solution. During this period, however, they had failed to understand the true nature of the regional labor situation. In their assessment of the demand for wage increases in 1882, they reacted characteristically, attempting to solve the problem as if it were purely local. A scene at the railroad station, with Mr. Timberlake standing atop a trunk bidding for the services of workmen, sent the message that the Wheeling manufacturers would have to deal with the problem in conjunction with other western firms.[88]

Indeed, what distinguished the post-1878 period from the earlier decade is the necessity, imposed by the very nature of the solutions, for the management of the Wheeling firms to look outwardly and to abandon their heavy reliance upon increased efficiency. There was, in short, no escaping the need for concerted action in dealing with the Amalgamated Association of Iron and Steel Workers, and in the cases of at least four of the firms that built Bessemers, joint action was, if not necessary, at least useful in raising the money for the steel plants.

Essentially, then, the Wheeling manufacturers were forced to take action to alter the conditions that governed the acquisition and control of labor. Altering this transaction would have had far-reaching consequences under any circumstances, but particularly in the Wheeling mills, where many patterns were based on old traditions and reinforced by a belief in the indispensable nature and prerogatives of the skilled crafts.

As Oliver Williamson suggested in his study of markets and business organizations, changes in basic transactions have an inevitable impact upon the structure. While the changes were not as visible as those in the 1870s, they were no less significant, for what resulted was a new definition of management/labor relations as well as management/owner relations.[89]

As observed in the preceding chapter, the top-level managers in the mills after the mid-1870s were drawn almost exclusively from the ranks of the clerks. During the late 1870s a noticeable distance between management and workman was beginning to emerge. This continued into the 1880s and was, it may be argued, a basic condition that had to occur before the labor problem could be dealt with. Likewise, a growing distance between management and ownership was becoming apparent by the early 1880s. By the end of the 1870s the secretaries had become the chief officers of the firms, and the boards had all but abandoned any effort to involve themselves in daily operations. Moreover, stock was increasingly being dispersed, so the stockholders as a group were far less powerful.

The professional manager who had considerable expertise in operating the mills and who had unquestioned faith in Wheeling's statistically based system of management had assumed control by 1880. He had little sympathy for or belief in the long-standing assumptions that certain classes of labor or a traditional relationship between classes was sacred. As a consequence, it was possible to question and change conditions that even in the mid-1870s were beyond the authority of management.

The earliest evidence that management was redefining certain internal relationships between workmen was the purchase of the automatic nail feeders. Although hardly noticeable at the time, this was the first of many decisions by which management more-or-less systematically destroyed the internal contracting system and gained direct control over all classes of workmen.

While many of management's actions may be viewed as attempts to alter relationships between classes of workmen, they were also clearly aimed at redefining the skilled workman's relationship to his craft. One important point of contention in the 1885 strike, for example, was apprenticeships. Management was asserting its right to say who would be admitted to the craft and was therefore attacking a basic prerogative of the nailer. Management went further after the strike began and even assumed the right to determine who had the skill, and then to bestow upon them the title, completely ignoring the old craft system.

By the time the strike ended in 1886, management had almost complete control over a host of intricate craft relationships that had formerly been the prerogative of the workmen. While the elimination of the boilers and the subduing of the nailers were widely viewed as a defeat of the union, it was no less a defeat for the craft system. With victory, management in effect gained control over all the internal transactions within the mills.

In addition to transforming the relationship between craftsmen, the actions of the Wheeling manufacturers also wrought noticeable changes in the relationship between middle-level (middle superintendents) management and the craftsmen. The manufacturers, for example, forced the superintendents, many of whom had been craftsmen, to choose between loyalty to their craft and loyalty to managment. After management opened the mills to the nailers, the superintendents were given the choice of training the new men or leaving. Several chose to leave and those who remained were forever separated from the men who worked the machines. This choice was rather significant since it firmly bound the mills superintendents to management and destroyed the widely held assumption that the superintendent was simply the most mastered of the craftsmen.

Management's pursuit of cost reduction also led to changes in its relationship to stockholders. Two instances of conflict between the groups--the union steel plant and the attendance at Western Nail Association meetings--were discussed earlier. Although noteworthy, neither was as important or as illustrative of management's desire to exclude the stockholders from decision making as was the organization of the Wheeling Iron and Steel Company. This firm was organized as a separate corporation in 1883 with a board of directors made up of secretaries of the three existing firms. The new corporation purchased iron from the parent firms, manufactured steel, and then sold it either to the parent firms or to other consumers. While owned, at least in theory, by the stockholders of the parent firms, the Wheeling Iron and Steel Company was, practically speaking, independent and came quite quickly to control many important elements of the parent firms' operations. By varying the prices paid for pig iron and charged for steel and by manipulating the dividends, the Wheeling Iron and Steel Company was in a position to exercise much influence over the operation of the old companies. This was particularly so during the late 1880s when, after the nail market declined, profits from the sale of steel made up an increasingly larger part of the profits of the parent firms.[90]

Clearly, the "visible hand" Alfred Chandler speaks of in his study of professional management was being felt in the Wheeling firms during the 1880s. By brute force and by guile, the managers of the Wheeling mills had assumed the responsibility for coordinating and controlling almost all aspects and conditions of operations. Having gained the upper hand in the Western Nail Association and having acquired control over wages, the Wheeling managers seemed to be in an unassailable position. Yet, within five years they would be struggling to keep their factories operating. They had overlooked one critical market--the marketplace of ideas--and were caught completely unaware of a major technological advance that revolutionized the cut nail industry.[91]

Notes

1. The Iron Age, February 23, 1882, p. 17; quoted in The Wheeling Intelligencer, June 30, 1880.

2. Frederick Overman, A Treatise on Metallurgy (New York: D. Appleton & Co., 1873), pp. 567-573, 603; Henry Dickerson Scott, Iron and Steel in Wheeling (Toledo, Ohio: Caslon Co., 1929), pp. 65-67.

3. Scott, Iron & Steel, pp. 66-68; F. H. Kindl, The Rolling Mill Industry (Cleveland, Ohio: Penton Publishing Co., 1913), pp. 21-36.

4. Scott, Iron & Steel, pp. 67-68.

5. Benwood Iron Works, "Minutes of Stockholders' and Directors' Meetings from June 29, 1864 to January 21, 1880," p. 123, MS in the possession of the Wheeling-Pittsburgh Steel Corporation, Wheeling, West Virginia; Belmont Nail Company, "Minutes of the Stockholders' and Diretors' Meetings of the Belmont Nail Company, July 11, 1879 to January 28, 1890," pp. 19, 46-48, MS in the possession of the Wheeling-Pittsburgh Steel Corporation, Wheeling, West Virginia; Woodward, Bailey & Co., "Minutes of the Meetings of the Board of Directors and Stockholders of the LaBelle Iron Works from January 28, 1868-September 20, 1873," p. 46, MS in the possession of the Wheeling-Pittsburgh Steel Corporation, Wheeling, West Virginia.

6. The Steubenville Daily Herald, November 19, 1885; The Wheeling Intelligencer, September 21, 1882, and April 22, 1885.

7. The Wheeling Intelligencer, April 16 and June 30, 1879; Wheeling Iron and Nail Works, "Minutes of the Stockholders' and Directors' Meetings from July 15, 1869 to July 22, 1892," p. 108, MS in the possession of the Wheeling-Pittsburgh Steel Corporation, Wheeling, West Virginia.

8. Benwood Iron Works, "Records," p. 365; The Wheeling Intelligencer, April 16, 1879; The Iron Age, September 13, 1877, p. 15.

9. The Wheeling Intelligencer, December 29, 1879; The Iron Age, April 28, 1881, p. 5.

10. Committee on Historical Statistics of the Social Research Council, The Statistical History of the United States from Colonial Times to the Present (Stamford, Conn.: Fairfield Publishers, Inc., 1965), p. 383; The Wheeling Intelligencer, December 29, 1879.

11. Belmont Nail Company, "Records," pp. 42, 67, 166, 177.

12. Ibid., pp. 42, 129, 166; The Iron Age, February 23, 1882, p. 17.

13. The Iron Age, October 18, 1883, p. 14, April 2, 1885, p. 14.

14. The number of machines added by the firms has been determined from reports published in American Iron and Steel Association, Directory to the Iron and Steel Works of the United States (Philadelphia: American Iron and Steel Association, 1882), pp. 85-155; Iron and Steel Association, Directory, 1884, pp. 131-145.

15. The Iron Age, April 2, 1885, p. 26; H. Lee Scamehorn, Pioneer Steelmakers in the West: The Colorado Fuel and Iron Company 1872-1903 (Boulder, Colo.: Pruett Publishing Co., 1976), pp. 48-49.

16. The Wheeling Intelligencer, February 21, 1884; The Steubenville Daily Herald, July 27, 1885.

17. The Iron Age, October 16, 1883, p. 14, April 2, 1885, p. 26; American Iron and Steel Association, Directory, 1882, p. 149; Directory, 1884, p. 165.

18. Iron and Steel Association, Directory, 1882, pp. 99-122, Directory, 1884, pp. iv, 162-164.

19. The Iron Age, April 2, 1885, p. 26.

20. The Steubenville Daily Herald, September 4, 1885; The Wheeling Intelligencer, May 27, July 9, July 27, and August 28, 1885.

21. Belmont Nail Company, "Records," pp. 35, 49.

22. The Wheeling Intelligencer, June 9, August 17, and September 21, 1882.

23. Ibid., September 29, 1882.

24. Ibid., June 30, 1879.

25. Belmont Nail Company, "Records," pp. 1, 34-194. The statistics for the Belmont Nail Company were taken from semiannual statements contained in the minutes of the firm. Less complete records of the other firms show a similar picture.

26. The Wheeling Intelligencer, September 18, 1884; also see J. D. Weeks, "Report of the Statistics of Wages in the Manufacturing Industries," Tenth Census of the United States, 1880 (Washington: Government Printing Office, 1886), pp. 197-233. The section on "Rolling-mills and Nail Factories" was written by J. D. Weeks. It contains a review of the costs of several mills.

27. The Wheeling Intelligencer, March 18 and July 8, 1880.

28. The Iron Age, October 18, 1883, p. 14.

29. The Wheeling Intelligencer, December 29, 1853, May 31 and August 18, 1882; Benwood Iron Works, "Records," p. 369.

30. The Wheeling Intelligencer, May 31 and June 9, 1882. Various examples could be cited to show that the Wheeling manufacturers followed the lead of the Pittsburgh manufacturers until 1882. For example, see Wheeling Iron and Nail Company, "Records," p. 108; William T. Hogan, Economic History of the Iron and Steel Industry in the United States, I (Lexington, Mass.: D. C. Heath and Company, 1971), pp. 85-90.

31. Benwood Iron Works, "Records," p. 365; Benwood Iron Works, "Minute Book January 27, 1880 to August 4, 1892," p. 9, MS in possession of the Wheeling-Pittsburgh Steel Corporation, Wheeling, West Virginia; The Wheeling Intelligencer, June 9, 1882.

32. The Wheeling Intelligencer, August 17, 18, September 21, 29, 1882.

33. The Iron Age, January 29, 1885, p. 14. Although Vance's role is clouded, his leadership in the move to steel, his election as president of the Western Nail Association after the "Wheeling Coup" in 1885, his central role in the manufacturers' association during the 1882 strike, and his leadership in breaking the United Nailers Union in 1886 are evidence of his leadership position.

34. The Wheeling Intelligencer, April 22, 23 and May 12, 1885.

35. Ibid., February 13 and April 23, 1885; The Iron Age, January 29, 1885, p. 14.

36. The Wheeling Intelligencer, March 21 and April 23, 1885.

37. Ibid., April 23, 1885; LaBelle Iron Works Stockholders, "Minutes September 13, 1887 - March 25, 1902,"

April 22 and May 13, 1889, and May 25, 1895 meetings (unnumbered pages).

38. The Wheeling Intelligencer, April 9, 1885.

39. Benwood Iron Works, "Minute Book, January 27, 1880 to August 4, 1892," p. 19, MS in the possession of the Wheeling-Pittsburgh Steel Corporation, Wheeling, West Virginia; Weeks, "Report of the Statistics of Wages," pp. 197, 205-236.

40. Benwood Iron Works, "Minute Book," pp. 4, 330; Iron Age, November 30, 1882, p. 26; The Wheeling Intelligencer, October 23, 1884.

41. Benwood Iron Works, "Minute Book," p. 19; Scott, Iron & Steel, p. 89.

42. The Iron Age, November 30, 1882, p. 26; Wheeling Iron and Nail, "Records," pp. 168, 169, 173; Benwood Iron Works, "Minute Book," pp. 80, 82, 101, 105.

43. Wheeling Iron and Nail, "Records," p. 173; The Iron Age, August 23, 1883, p. 30.

44. The Wheeling Intelligencer, April 25 and May 12, 1885.

45. Scott, Iron & Steel, p. 92.

46. The Wheeling Intelligencer, August 16, 1886. The quote from the Boston Herald reads, "It is a serious question with the majority of nail manufacturers in New England today as to whether to put in a Bessemer plant or go out of business. Go out they must if the attempt is made to compete with steel nails."

47. The Wheeling Intelligencer, November 20, December 25, and December 31, 1885, January 4, January 5, and March 1, 1886.

48. Ibid., April 29, 1884; Benwood Iron Works, "Minute Book," p. 178; Wheeling Iron and Nail, "Records," pp. 193-194; Belmont Nail Company, "Records," pp. 176, 177, 227.

49. The Wheeling Intelligencer, June 30, 1880, and January 5, 1884.

50. Ibid., September 21, 1882, and May 29, 1885.

51. At least some observers at the time saw that the strike was the outgrowth of events of the preceding years. "This strike commenced some five or six years ago," wrote the "Quiet Observer" in The Steubenville Daily Herald, October 29, 1885.

52. Robert L. Plummer (ed.), Sixty-Five Years of Iron and Steel in Wheeling (n.p., n.d.), pp. 9-14, contains the reminiscences of Alexander Glass, a nailer who later became bookkeeper for the LaBelle Company and eventually chairman of the board of Wheeling Steel; James E. Reeves, The Physical and Medical Topography of the City of Wheeling (Wheeling: The Wheeling Daily Register, 1870), pp. 23-24.

53. The Steubenville Daily Herald, September 4, 1885, has a list of employee classes in the mills; The Wheeling Intelligencer, April 26 and April 28, 1875. The current manager of the LaBelle Nail Works has in his office a check written in 1942 by a nailer that is clearly marked as wages for feeding.

54. The Wheeling Intelligencer, May 25, 1882; The Steubenville Daily Herald, November 14, 1885.

55. Wheeling Iron and Nail, "Records," pp. 108, 109, 157, 165; The Wheeling Intelligencer, January 6, 1875, May 25, August 17, and September 30, 1882.

56. The Wheeling Intelligencer, September 18, 1884.

57. Ibid., February 28, 1872, April 24 and 26, and May 11, 1875. Company records do not show which particular models of feeders the workmen purchased. See The Iron Age, March 12, 1874, p. 3, and December 30, 1875, p. 5, for discussion of the state of automatic self-feeders. Also see Chapter 1 of this book for discussion of self-feeders in more detail.

58. The Wheeling Intelligencer, April 26, 1875.

59. Ibid., August 8, 1884.

60. LaBelle Nail Company, "Records," p. 72; Benwood Iron Works, "Minute Book," p. 111; Belmont Nail Company, "Records," p. 98; The Steubenville Daily Herald, July 9 and 27, 1885; The Wheeling Intelligencer, June 12, 1885.

61. The Wheeling Intelligencer, April 22, 1884 and May 10, 1886.

62. Ibid., January 16, April 29, May 10 and 16, 1884.

63. Ibid., August 8 and 12, 1884; The Iron Age, April 23, 1885, p. 17.

64. The Wheeling Intelligencer, August 9, 1884.

65. Ibid., September 20, 1884; The Steubenville Daily Herald, November 19, 1885.

66. The Wheeling Intelligencer, September 15, 1884, January 19 and March 27, 1885; The Steubenville Daily Herald, July 15, 1885.

67. The Wheeling Intelligencer, May 23, 1885.

68. Ibid., May 29 and June 2, 1885.

69. Parker Mills, "Parker Mills Journal 1878-1886," Vol. A-4, May 30, 1885, MS in the possession of the Baker Library of Harvard University; Wheeling Iron and Nail Company, "Minutes of the Stockholders' and Directors' Meetings from July 15, 1869 to July 22, 1892," pp. 194, 200, MS in possession of the Wheeling-Pittsburgh Steel Corporation, Wheeling, West Virginia; Belmont Nail Company, "Records," pp. 173, 184; The Wheeling Intelligencer, July 10, 1885.

70. The Wheeling Intelligencer, July 10, 1885.

71. Ibid., July 10 and August 24, 1885.

72. Ibid., June 12, 1885; The Steubenville Daily Herald, July 7, 1885.

73. The Steubenville Daily Herald, July 9, 1885.

74. The Wheeling Intelligencer, July 10, 1885; The Steubenville Daily Herald, July 17, 1885.

75. The Steubenville Daily Herald, July 27, 1885; The Wheeling Intelligencer, January 6, 1886. On January 13, 1886, 1,157 machines were producing under the Cincinnati scale and 606 were producing under the Nailers' scale.

76. The Wheeling Intelligencer, July 10, 1885.

77. Wheeling Iron and Nail, "Records," p. 207; Benwood Iron Works, "Minute Book," p. 190; The Wheeling Intelligencer, January 20 and August 13, 1886.

78. The Steubenville Daily Herald, September 28, 1885.

79. Ibid., November 11 and 12, 1885.

80. The Wheeling Intelligencer, November 6 and December 5, 1885; The Steubenville Daily Herald, October 30 and November 4, 1885.

81. The Wheeling Intelligencer, April 14, 1886.

82. Ibid., April 22, 1886.

83. Ibid., June 1 and June 26, 1886.

84. Belmont Nail Company, "Records," pp. 173, 294.

85. Weeks, "Report on the Statistics of Wages," pp. 197-223.

86. Ibid.

87. Insofar as can be determined, Weeks' report for the 1880 census was the first publication that addressed the basic accounting assumptions of the Wheeling system. Since the "Cost of Making Nails at a Mill in the Wheeling District" table (page 206) matches the LaBelle records exactly, and since he identifies the Jefferson Iron Works (page 228) and the Aetna Iron and Nail Company (page 217), he clearly had access to the books of these and probably other firms. Weeks, "Report of Statistics of Wages," pp. 206, 217, 228; LaBelle Nail Company, "Records," pp. 42, 50.

88. The Wheeling Intelligencer, September 29, 1882.

89. Oliver E. Williamson, Markets and Hierarchies Analysis and Antitrust Implications (London: Collier Mac-Millan Publishers, 1975), p. 2.

90. Scott, Iron & Steel, p. 90.

91. Alfred D. Chandler, Jr., The Visible Hand: The Managerial Revolution in American Business (Cambridge, Mass.: The Belknap Press, 1977).

5
Competition from the Wire Nail

> The wire nail appeals to certain characteristic national traits. It is cheap, easy to handle, can be driven by any creature that can lift a hammer, and can be readily pulled out again. In an age of shoddy materials and shoddy mechanics, it is inevitable that the cheap, facile wire nail should hold sway.
>
> Henry Dickerson Scott
> Iron and Steel in Wheeling, 1929

Scarcely half a year after the Great Strike was concluded, The Wheeling Intelligencer published a special sixteen-page edition celebrating the arrival of natural gas at Wheeling. In this edition the editor commented extensively on the future of Wheeling, citing "splendid facilities," "solid men of means," "established industries," "health," "low taxation," and a host of other advantages. The editor concluded by proclaiming that "Wheeling stands on the threshold of a new era. It is on this foundation [of established industries] that the superstructure of a new and greater Wheeling is to be built."

The observation and optimistic prediction of the editor proved to be at once true and false. Within a few years the marvelous new fuel the paper heralded had vanished, at least temporarily, and the coal bins that had been ceremoniously whitewashed were again pressed into service. Moreover, the great nail factories, like the natural gas, vanished. The blast furnaces, the bessemers, and the rolling mills, all built to provide nail plate, had to be turned to other products. Herein lies the final chapter in the history of Wheeling's nail industry. It is the story of a tenacious adherence to the cut nail that had put Wheeling on the map and the frustrating search for a new product to replace the cut nail.

From the standpoint of those who were proponents of the cut nail, the decade and a half after the Great Nail Strike was a difficult period. Wheeling manufacturers could not cope with the wire nail, and for a time they seemed unable to withdraw from their old enterprises. After the initial shock of wire nail competition had passed, the manufacturers did regroup and turn their facilities to other products. After successive waves of reorganization and after almost forty years, the Wheeling firms ended up merged into a major steel corporation.

The origin of the wire nail, a nail with a round shank of constant diameter, is uncertain. Small nails that fit this description appeared in the early eighteenth century and were used by cabinet makers to attach decorations to furniture. Any similarity between these nails and the wire nails of the late nineteenth century is little more than coincidental, however. Peter Priess, one of the few researchers to consider the origin of the wire nail, suggested that it originated in France sometime around 1820. His evidence rests largely on several French patents for machines to manufacture wire nails and the common name--"French nails" or "pointes de Paris"--used to identify nails with round shanks during the nineteenth century.[1]

Throughout the first half of the nineteenth century the manufacture of wire nails appears to have occurred only in Europe. The nails were limited to smaller sizes, used primarily for upholstering, picture frames, and similar types of construction. Although several sources give 1877 as the date of the first American patent for wire nail machines, one New York manufacturer, T. C. Richards & Company, advertised "Richards Patent Porcelain-Headed Picture Nails" as early as 1873. A drawing of the Richards nail which appeared in The Iron Age shows clearly that it was a wire nail. The Richards advertisement also contained reference to imported nails and specifically mentioned "wire nails."[2]

After the initial notation of wire nails in the Richards advertisement, The Iron Age, which served also as a trade journal for the hardware industry, contained frequent references to the wire nail. In 1878, for example, the Dunbar, Hobart & Whidden Tack Company of South Abington, Massachusetts, advertised "Any kind of wire nails...made to order from description or samples," and the ad included an illustration showing wire nails up to two and a half inches in length. Two years later, in 1880, The Iron Age carried the first description of wire nail manufacturing, describing a German wire nail machine in a lead article. These references and several others in The Iron Age continued to suggest that the wire nail was not comparable to the cut nail. The wire nails advertised were for use in furnishings, boxes, saddles, decorative work, picture frames, and the like and not as an element in buildings or other types of heavy construction. As such, the wire nail offered no competition for the American cut nail manufacturers during the 1870s.[3]

During the early 1880s, larger size wire nails, potentially suited for construction purposes, appeared. The availability of cheap steel wire seems to have been of importance for the wire nails. Iron wire simply did not have sufficient strength to serve as a material for the relatively small shanks of the wire nail. But as domestic steel production increased during the late 1870s and steel wire became more readily available, three American wire nail manufacturers appeared. The first, the American Wire Nail Company of Covington, Kentucky, began operations sometime around 1880. This company was joined by the H. P. Nail Company of Cleveland, Ohio, in 1882. By 1885, the latter company had a full range of wire nails on the market, including "wire spikes for track, bridge, and dock work." A third wire nail manufacturing firm, the Salem Wire Nail Company of Salem, Ohio, joined the two older firms in 1886. Like the H. P. Nail Company, the Salem firm produced large as well as small wire nails.[4]

All three of the wire nail manufacturers grew up in the Western Nail Association territory, and the Salem Wire Nail Company was literally in Wheeling's back yard. Yet there is no indication that the cut nail manufacturers took any note of the presence of these firms. During the early 1880s, when the market for nails was rapidly expanding, the cut nail manufacturers would have had little reason to be concerned. As the market began to contract in 1883, the Wheeling manufacturers turned their attention to acquiring steel facilities and placed their faith in the development of a superior, cheap steel nail. Even if they did take note of the presence of the wire nail, they were most likely of the opinion that the steel cut nail would be of superior quality and was sufficiently inexpensive to compete with the wire nail.[5]

Proponents of the cut nail also assumed that the "holding power" of the cut nail was superior to that of the wire nail. Swank noted in 1892, "Deep rooted prejudices of all kinds had to be overcome before the wire nail could be accepted." The first step toward overcoming the prejudices was taken in 1884 when the wire nail manufacturers convinced the Watertown Arsenal to run tests on the holding power of the wire nail. Results of the tests showed that the wire nail, particularly in the smaller and intermediate sizes, had holding power comparable to that of the cut nail. The Salem Wire Nail Company took note of these tests in its advertisement by showing the wire nail and the cut nail side by side driven through a board. The advertisement pointed out that wire nails did less damage to the wood, a particularly important point for carpenters who did interior trim work.[6]

Without question, however, the most important factor in the initial acceptance of the wire nail was the Great Nail Strike of 1885 and 1886. By early 1886 hardware jobbers and dealers had exhausted nail stocks. The eastern mills that continued in operation simply could not fill the orders coming in from the West. In January of 1886, the editor of The Iron Age took note of the opportunity the strike was offering for wire nail manufacturers.

> Another factor, of course, which cannot be overrated is the wire nail. The strike offered a splendid opportunity for its introduction....There can be no doubt that a very large number of important customers have learned...to appreciate the economy of wire nails [and]...have been taught to value them for many points of excellence they possess for specialty work. The wire nail has conquered territory which in the future it may claim as its own. The loss to the cut nail is greater than even has appeared on the surface.[7]

The loss was great, indeed far greater than anyone at the time, including that editor, imagined that it might be. Cut nail production peaked in 1886 at 8,160,973 kegs and began a rapid decline thereafter. A decade later, in 1897, cut nail production had declined to 2,100,000 kegs. During the same period of time wire nail production had risen from about 500,000 kegs to just slightly more than 9 million kegs. By 1912, the wire nail accounted for 92 percent of the total nail production in the United States and had effectively replaced the cut nail.[8]

During the disruption in supply created by the Great Nail Strike, several superior qualities of the wire nail quickly became apparent. Most notably, the wire nail was cheaper; less metal was required to make the nail, and the technology was more automated. A spool of wire replaced the nail plate, and an attendant who either fed the machine by hand or filled the automatic feeder was no longer needed. Furthermore, the wire fed continuously into the machine, which eliminated the necessity of flipping plate and therefore increased the rate of production. The wire nail was also easier to use. It did, as advertised, less damage to the wood and could be straightened if bent and even removed if necessary.[9]

In December 1885, some members of the Wheeling manufacturing community began to talk about the dangers presented by the wire nail. A writer in The Wheeling Intelligencer sounded the alarm on December 1 in an article titled, "A New Nail Competing." The newspaper reported that "the short production of the nail mills throughout the West has introduced a new and dangerous nail for the trade--the wire nail." Little more than a month later, on January 5, 1886, the directors of the Belmont Mill discussed the wire nail and appointed a committee to purchase shop rights for the Bradford wire nail machines. Throughout the spring and early summer both the Intelligencer and The Steubenville Daily Herald contained several articles on the wire nail, and at least one other mill, Benwood, appointed a committee to investigate the "workings of the wire nail machine."[10]

One of the more interesting commentaries on the new nail appeared in February 1886, when The Steubenville Daily Herald carried an account of a meeting of wire nail manufacturers held at Pittsburgh. William Taylor, a wire nail manufacturer from Albany, Pennsylvania, summarized what seemed to be the prevailing attitude of his colleagues. Taylor commented, "The constantly recurring difficulties in the nail trade have led inventors to work on various plans...to dispense with manual labor." "The wire nail," he continued, "is destined to drive the cut nail out of the market, as it answers all the purposes fully as well, and does not require so much skilled labor." Obviously, the wire nail manufacturers had gained some insight into the problems of their colleagues in the cut nail field and had, moreover, identified as crucial for their industry the same factor that the cut nail manufacturers had emphasized--labor costs.[11]

Aside from the two companies that appointed committees to investigate the wire nail, there is little to suggest that the cut nail manufacturers took any direct action to counter the potential threat of the wire nail in the years immediately after its introduction. The attitude that David Spaulding, secretary of the LaBelle Nail Works, took toward the steel nail also prevailed in the wire nail matter. "Why is it the American people want everything new? It is one of those fantasies which I think will wear out."[12]

In the short term, the manufacturers could easily have concluded that the fantasy had worn out. Sales rebounded after the strike and reached an all-time high in 1886. Furthermore, sales remained brisk during early 1887. The skilled-labor problem had been taken care of with the demise of the puddlers and the demoralization of the nailers. Moreover, the western factories appeared to be in a position to eliminate eastern competitors who publicly lamented that they could not compete unless they added Bessemers.[13]

Beginning in late 1887, however, cut nail prices began to slide, and by 1890 the Wheeling companies were selling for less than it cost to manufacture nails. In July 1888, for example, the Belmont records showed that the cost of manufacturing a keg of nails was $2.04 per keg and the selling price was $2.07 per keg. Six months later, Belmont's manufacturing costs was $2.05 per keg and the selling price no more than $1.93. The Wheeling Iron and Nail Company had a similar experience. By 1890, the firm was losing 33 cents on each keg of nails it sold. Even the operators of the venerable LaBelle found conditions intolerable. In 1889, the directors finally, "after general review of the conditions of the business," considered the purchase of wire nail machines.[14]

Insofar as can be determined, no Wheeling manufacturer ever actually switched to wire nail production. Several writers, most notably Scott, have puzzled over why the wire nail was so universally rejected in the Wheeling manufacturing community. He theorized that the strong prejudices in favor of the cut nail refused to yield and allow the manufacture of what many in the industry regarded as an inferior product. This theory contains a grain of truth, but it must be seen in conjunction with other explanations.[15]

There can be no question that, in the first few months after the wire nail threat became apparent, the Wheeling manufacturers displayed an aloof attitude. The euphoria from the victory over the puddlers and nailers, from new Bessemer plants, and from the profitable market seemed to suggest that the cut nail could become even more profitable than it had been in the early 1880s. When the profits disappeared in 1887, 1888, and 1889, the manufacturers assumed that the problem was a matter of overproduction, as it had been in 1883 and 1884. Their initial response was to attempt to control production and thereby drive prices up. To control prices and production, the Wheeling manufacturers attempted to form a corporation to control the mills. While the specifics of the proposed organization and the events surrounding it are unclear, the organization seems to have been very similar to that which had existed in the tack industry. Individual firms and stockholders were to surrender their stock in exchange for stock in a corporation that controlled all of the mills. The effort failed miserably. In 1889, the LaBelle Corporation not only withdrew from this venture but also dropped out of the Western Nail Association.[16]

Actually, the market was substantially changed from what had existed in the late 1870s and early 1880s. The cut nail manufacturers had lost control. With every attempt to limit production, the wire nail simply gained new customers. That the cut nail manufacturers did not understand this is almost beyond comprehension in the light of hindsight; at the time, however, such a misreading of the situation was not only plausible but quite possible. The assumption about the quality of the two products, the lack of accurate sales information (the wire nail manufacturers were never a part of the Western Nail Association, so the cut nail manufacturers could not obtain production figures), and the prevailing opinion expressed by The Iron Age that overproduction was solely responsible for the price decline made an accurate assessment of events almost impossible.[17]

Once the manufacturers did conclude that the wire nail was competing for traditional markets, they had insurmountable problems. The technology of the two products, while appearing at first glance to be similar, was actually very different. Here, technology, rather than business, became the dominant influence. The cut nail was a product of the rolling mill. Wrought iron (and later steel) was rolled into slabs and then into plate. Wire nails were the end product of an entirely different process. The steel ingots were converted first to blooms, then to billets, and then into bars from which the wire rod was formed. Consequently, to convert to the wire nail, manufacturers would have had to retool not only the nail factories but also the rolling mills.[18]

Under the most favorable conditions, this conversion would have been expensive; for Wheeling manufacturers, it was all but impossible. Their heavy investment in Bessemer converters in the mid-1880s had consumed the capital that had accumulated from the flush period between 1880 and 1883. Furthermore, the Great Nail Strike had kept income down during the mid-1880s. In the final analysis, cut nail manufacturers simply did not have the resources available for retooling their nail factories and rolling mills.[19]

Finally, the Wheeling manufacturers and the rest of the cut nail industry in general faced competition from a vigorous new industry that quickly became organized and developed rapidly. By 1889 there were thirty-seven wire nail works in the United States. Four years later, in 1892, the number of firms had increased to forty-nine, and this trend continued through the end of the century. By 1901 there were fifty-eight manufacturers of wire nails producing the 9.8 million kegs turned out that year.[20]

Not only was the number of producers growing but the wire nail manufacturers were becoming increasingly well organized. In 1897, John H. Parks, a seasoned industrial promoter from Indiana, undertook a combination of wire nail mills. A year later he was joined by John W. Gates, a fellow Indianian, who was attempting to consolidate barbed wire manufacturers. The two combined their efforts and in 1898 formed the American Steel and Wire Nail Corporation, a company that brought most of the nation's wire producers under its control. By the turn of the century, when United States Steel purchased the American Steel and Wire Nail Corporation, the firm owned eleven blast furnaces, fifteen steel works, thirteen wire rod plants, twenty-three wire drawing plants, sixteen nail mills, eight iron mines, almost 12,000 acres of coal land, 1,800 coke ovens, and a fleet of lake steamers. Furthermore, the marketing system developed by the American Steel and Wire Nail Corporation reached to every corner of the United States, to most of the western European countries, and to the larger cities in the Near East.[21]

Cut nail manufacturers simply could not compete with this well-organized industry. Many cut nail manufacturers outside of the Wheeling district switched partially to wire nails, by purchasing wire, and managed to retain a portion of the local market. At Wheeling, all of the cut nail manufacturers clung to the old product, but by the early 1890s most firms ceased to hold any hope of a revival of the market and instead had begun the search for alternative products.[22]

Between 1890 and 1900, three of the Wheeling nail mills discontinued operations completely. The first to go was Benwood Mill, followed by Bellaire Mill and later the Junction Nail Works. Additionally, those mills remaining showed a steady decline in production. "The nail factory was entirely idle during the months of January and February," the secretary reported to the directors of Belmont Mill, "because the price at which nails was selling was too low." Scott commented that the Laughlin factory, "once the pride of the Ohio Valley, was little better than a junk heap" by 1900. By 1914 only LaBelle Mill at Wheeling remained in operation. All of the others had been disassembled or sat idle.[23]

The Wheeling firms finally turned to other products. The Riverside was the first to diversify. In 1887 the firm opened a tube works, becoming the first mill in the country to produce butt and lap-weld Bessemer steel tubing. This venture proved very successful. The Riverside pipe found a lucrative market in West Virginia and Ohio oil fields. The Wheeling Iron and Nail Company switched to the production of sheet in 1888, and, along with the Whitaker Iron Company, gained a sizeable share of the roofing and metal utensil market. Belmont and Benwood both attempted to shift a portion of their nail works to tack production, although never very successfully. The two latter firms also went into the production of sheet, converting much of it into shovel plate.[24]

Salvation for the faltering mills did not finally arrive until the mid-1890s when the full effects of the McKinley Tariff on foreign tinplate stimulated domestic tinplate production. Two small firms, the Etna-Standard Works of Martin's Ferry and the Wheeling Corrugating Company (neither had been nail producers), added tin mills in 1893 and 1894. The following year the Laughlin Nail Works and LaBelle both followed suit. For about five years these firms prospered. The LaBelle tin mill, for example, showed almost $60,000 profit in the first full year of operation.[25]

Just as the Wheeling firms' tin mills were allowing the firms to recuperate from the loss of nail markets, they became caught up in a round of mergers. The first merger, a local one, came in 1892, when the Wheeling Iron and Nail Company, the Belmont Iron Works, the Benwood Nail Works, and the Wheeling Steel Works combined to form the Wheeling Steel and Iron Corporation. This new firm, with an authorized capital stock of $5 million, became the largest and most stable of the Wheeling firms during the 1890s and the first decade of the twentieth century. The new company built a substantial trade in semifinished products--muck bar, steel billets, steel slabs, and sheet production. Additionally, the Wheeling Steel and Iron Corporation built a tube works and sporadically operated the old nail mills.[26]

Beginning in 1897, the firms (except for Wheeling Steel and Iron) that had developed finished product mills participated in a series of reorganizations that radically altered the manufacturing community in Wheeling. In late 1897 the Riverside sold its tube works to the National Tube Corporation. Initially only the tube works was sold, but by 1901 National Tube, which by that time had become part of the United States Steel Corporation, had controlling interest in the Riverside furnace, Bessemer, and abandoned nail mill. That pattern became a common one. LaBelle sold its tin mill to the National Tin Plate Corporation, as did Bellaire, the Laughlin Nail Company, and the Etna-Standard Company. By 1901, the only tin mill that remained under local control was the Wheeling Corrugating Company works. Like the Riverside Mill, Bellaire, Etna-Standard, and the Laughlin Company were eventually consumed by other, larger corporations in horizontal combinations.[27]

At the time of the reorganization not a single objection was heard. The "combinations" brought considerable profit to the firms and to the stockholders. Events that took place at the LaBelle Company may serve as a typical example of the impact that the combinations had on individual firms and stockholders. In September 1898, the directors held a special meeting to consider an offer to purchase the LaBelle tin mill. The minutes of the meeting record that "the meeting was called for the purpose of considering a proposition that had been made...by F. S. Wheeler, representing Judge Moore, et al., of Chicago, who are working to effect a consolidation of the full production capacity of tin, terene, and black plate in the United States." The directors agreed to recommend to the stockholders that Judge Moore be granted an option to purchase the company's tin plate works for not less than $500,000. On November 22, 1898, the National Tin Plate Corporation exercised this option, offering, instead of cash, $500,000 in preferred stock. LaBelle accepted the offer plus a $91,615 cash settlement for the inventories on hand. LaBelle made an immediate net profit of almost $300,000 on the sale; the real value, however, was boosted to almost $750,000 when American Tin Plate stock was exchanged for United States Steel stock in 1901.[28]

Insofar as can be determined, all of the deals were made along similar lines. Some, like the Riverside, took place in two stages, but the method was similar. In every instance the purchasing firm paid in stock, or exchanged its stock for that of the old firm. Everyone appeared to profit, particularly after the National Tin Plate Corporation and National Tube were absorbed by United States Steel.[29]

Of less concern to the stockholders, but of great significance to the companies, was the change in managerial leadership prompted by the sales. Frank Hearne left Riverside when the tube works was sold to become the vice president of National Tube. Cecil Robinson of LaBelle, W. T. Graham of Etna-Standard, and about two dozen other top managers also left to become officers or managers in the firms that had purchased the tin mills. In addition, a considerable number of engineers and middle-level managers took positions with the purchasing corporations. This talent drain severely hurt several of the firms and was at the time regarded as a key factor in the demise of the Etna-Standard and Bellaire Nail Works.[30]

After the flurry of buying and selling settled in late 1901, Wheeling was left with two firms intact (the Wheeling Steel and Iron and the Whitaker Iron Company) and four firms (LaBelle, Laughlin, Etna-Standard, and Wheeling Corrugating) that were partially dismembered. All of the firms, but particularly the ones that had engaged in the mergers, were wealthy from the sale, from capital gains, and from the dividends they received from United States Steel stock. Beginning in 1901 several of the firms expanded, attempting to fill the gaps left by the sales and mergers. LaBelle reinvested its profit from the tin mill sale in another tin mill after a four-year absence from the industry stipulated as part of the agreement with National Tin Plate. The Laughlin Company purchased, in concert with the Wheeling Corrugating Company and the Whitaker Iron Company, the Burgess Steel Corporation, an open-hearth works at Portsmouth, Ohio. In 1903 these three companies combined to form Whitaker Glessner Corporation, and the old Laughlin Company passed completely out of existence.[31]

By 1905, only three locally owned firms remained. LaBelle, with blast furnaces and a steel works at Steubenville and Mingo Junction, a tin mill at Mingo Junction, and a rolling mill at Wheeling, was the smallest. The Whitaker Glessner Corporation owned blast furnaces at Wheeling, Martins Ferry, and Portsmouth, Ohio, steel works at Portsmouth, and a sizeable rolling mill, tin works, and sheet mill at Wheeling. Wheeling Steel and Iron Corporation owned three blast furnaces, a steel works, three rolling mills, and a tube works, all at Wheeling. The three corporations and their component works, plus related mining and transportation facilities, formed the basis of what would become in 1920 the Wheeling Steel Corporation.[32]

The preceding pages have recorded the events that led to the decline of cut nail manufacturing in the Wheeling area. Because the firms had integrated structures, the loss of the nail market was not as disastrous to them as it might have been. As the price of nails declined, the firms turned to selling pig iron and steel, thus retaining solvency--at least until adjustments could be made in their operations.

Within a short period, each of the firms had begun to search for alternate finished products and in short order had integrated forward into other lines. This strategy suggests that the manufacturers, individually and as a group, perceived the market to be more lucrative in finished products than unfinished metal products. That manufacturers chose to search out and produce new finished products is also not surprising in light of the developmental patterns of the firms. Undoubtedly, forces that led firms to integrate forward after the Civil War exerted some influence. The manufacturers, nurtured in an environment in which production was viewed as a mine-to-market process, felt more comfortable with finished product sales. As observed in Chapter 3, the urge to exercise maximum control and thereby alleviate the uncertainties inherent in the intermediate products market had considerable influence upon the industry.[33]

The very practical matter of profitability was also an important factor. Data contained in the records of several firms show that while profits were realized from the sale of steel and pig iron, they did not approach the levels that had been previously associated with nails. Perceiving the price to be unsatisfactory, the manufacturers moved to circumvent the market by becoming, once again, the primary consumer of their own unfinished products.

The combination of these factors--low profitability of unfinished products and the experience with an integrated business structure--worked to favor rebuilding the old integrated structure with a new product in place of nails. During the late 1880s, the firms, except for the Wheeling Iron and Steel group, chose to retain their individual identity and separately select their own course of development. For a brief period they were successful, then the tin trust purchases and succeeding combinations reduced the firms to the status of unfinished product manufacturers again by 1900. Feeling no less uncomfortable with the condition in 1900 than they had in the 1880s, the individual firms set out to once again reestablish the mine-to-market structure. The agreements with the "trusts" that left some firms free to enter the tinplate or pipe production market, and prohibited others from such activities, and uneven growth patterns that had resulted in more modern furnaces and rolling mill equipment at various firms dictated a different approach after 1900. Instead of striking out as separate firms, they eventually decided to combine resources, integrate horizontally, and through a succession of combinations that circumvented the "trust" agreements form a single company--the Wheeling Steel Corporation. Just as vertical integration in the 1870s had been a response to market conditions and management's perception of the most advantageous method of controlling certain transactions, so, too, the decision to combine the firms under a single ownership after 1900 resulted, at least in part, from a desire to keep trnsactions internal.[34]

Notes

1. Peter Priess, "Wire Nails in North America," The Assocation for Preservation Technology _Bulletin_ V (1973), p. 87.

2. _The Iron Age_, January 2, 1873, p. 2; Priess, "Wire Nails," pp. 88-89.

3. _The Iron Age_, March 28, 1878, p. 25, July 15, 1880, p. 1. The first American-made wire nails were probably produced by tack manufacturers. Because tack and nail manufacturing were regarded as separate industries throughout the nineteenth century, this study has not looked carefully at manufacturers who specialized in tacks. The industry does deserve more study because, unlike the eastern nail manufacturers, the tack producers modernized, and by the mid-1870s, a trust had been formed. Every major manufacturer in the East and West surrendered stock to a controlling corporation in return for shares.

4. Priess, "Wire Nails," p. 89; _The Iron Age_, March 19, 1885, p. 34, April 16, 1885, p. 9; _The National Cyclopaedia of American Biography_ XV (New York: James T. White & Co., 1916), p. 306.

5. Just how much information the Wheeling manufacturers had about wire nail manufacturing is unclear. If they read _The Iron Age_, as they almost certainly did, they had to be aware of the new technology and the existence of the Salem Wire Nail Company.

6. James M. Swank, _History of the Manufacture of Iron and Particularly in the United States from Colonial Times to 1891_ (New York: Burt Franklin, 1892), pp. 450-451; _Report of the Tests of Metals and Other Materials for Industrial Purposes Made with the United States Testing Machine at Watertown Arsenal, Massachusetts_ (Washington: Government Printing Office, 1886), pp. 448-463. "Holding power" was an imprecise term used by nailers. It referred to the amount of force required to withdraw a nail from a piece of wood.

7. _The Iron Age_, January 7, 1886, p. 22.

8. F. H. Kindl, _The Rolling Mill Industry_ (Cleveland, Ohio: Penton Publishing Co., 1913), p. 41.

9. _The Wheeling Intelligencer_, December 1, 1885; Priess, "Wire Nails," p. 89; J. Bucknall Smith, _A Treatise upon Wire, Its Manufacture and Uses_ (New York: John Wiley & Sons, 1891), p. 335.

10. _The Wheeling Intelligencer_, December 1, 1885; Benwood Iron Works, "Minute Book, January 27, 1880-August 4, 1892," p. 215; Belmont Nail Company, "Minutes of the Stockholders' and Directors' Meetings of the Belmont Nail Company, July 11, 1879-January 28, 1890," p. 214. Both manuscripts are in the possession of the Wheeling-Pittsburgh Steel Corporation, Wheeling, West Virginia.

11. _The Steubenville Daily Herald_, February 1, 1886.

12. _Ibid._, March 25, 1886.

13. _The Wheeling Intelligencer_, August 16, 1886.

14. Belmont Nail Company, "Records," pp. 294, 304; Wheeling Iron and Nail Company, "Minutes of the Stockholders' and Directors' Meetings from July 15, 1869-July 22, 1892,"

pp. 253, 266, MS in the possession of the Wheeling-Pittsburgh Steel Corporation, Wheeling, West Virginia.

15. Henry Dickerson Scott, Iron and Steel in Wheeling (Toledo, Ohio: Caslon Company, 1929), pp. 99, 107.

16. Wheeling Iron and Nail, "Records," p. 253; LaBelle Iron Works, "Stockholders' Minutes, September 13, 1887-March 25, 1902," May 13, 1889 entry (unnumbered pages), MS in the possession of the Wheeling-Pittsburgh Steel Corporation, Wheeling, West Virginia.

17. The Iron Age, January 7, 1886, p. 22, June 30, 1886, p. 20.

18. Kindl, Rolling Mill Industry, pp. 20-23.

19. Scott, Iron & Steel, p. 91; The Steubenville Daily Herald, June 24, 1885.

20. American Iron and Steel Association, Directory to the Iron and Steel Works of the United States, 1892 (Philadelphia: The American Iron and Steel Association, 1892), p. xiii; Kindl, Rolling Mill Industry, p. 41.

21. American Iron and Steel Association, Directory, 1901, pp. 29-38; Joseph M. McFadden, "Monopoly in Barbed Wire: The Formation of the American Steel and Wire Company," The Business History Review (Winter 1978), pp. 472-474.

22. American Iron and Steel Association, Directory, 1901, pp. 381, 385; Scott, Iron & Steel, p. 99.

23. Belmont Nail Company, "Records," p. 250; Scott, Iron & Steel, pp. 147, 158, 159; American Iron and Steel Association, Directory, 1901, pp. 380-381.

24. Scott, Iron & Steel, pp. 110-112, 114; The Wheeling Intelligencer, July 12, 1886.

25. Scott, Iron & Steel, pp. 120-129.

26. Wheeling Iron and Nail, "Records," p. 274; Scott, Iron & Steel, p. 114; American Iron and Steel Association, Directory, 1901, p. 121.

27. Scott, Iron & Steel, pp. 137-141.

28. LaBelle Iron Works, "Minutes," September 16 and December 12, 1898 entries; Scott, Iron & Steel, p. 134.

29. Scott, Iron & Steel, p. 137; LaBelle Iron Works, "Annual Statement July 14, 1898-July 1, 1899."

30. Scott, Iron & Steel, pp. 112, 121; LaBelle Iron Works, "Minutes," January 12, 1899 entry.

31. Scott, Iron & Steel, p. 145.

32. American Iron and Steel Association, Directory, 1901, pp. 119-121; Scott, Iron & Steel, p. 158; Wheeling Steel Corporation, "Annual Report to the Stockholders, April 15, 1921."

33. Oliver E. Williamson, Markets and Hierarchies and Antitrust Implications (London: Collier MacMillan Publishers, 1975), pp. 83-99.

34. Scott, Iron & Steel, pp. 146-157.

Conclusion

In assessing the rise and decline of the cut nail industry, it has been necessary to consider the significance of technologies, markets, organizational structures, management styles, and a number of other factors that affected to a greater or lesser degree the evolution of the product and of the enterprise that manufactured it. Each of the enumerated factors has been considered individually and as a group by scholars who have studied business growth during the nineteenth century, and all have been identified as important elements in the changing configuration of enterprises during that era. This book has attempted to suggest just how various elements were related in one industry.

The history of the nail industry has offered particularly clear insight into the relationship between technologies, organizational structures, and management decisions--three factors that have fascinated scholars for some time. Williamson argued that technology, while important, was not a determinative element in establishing organizational format or management style. Others, such as Samuel Hayes and Thomas Cochran, suggested that technology was a major factor in the development or organizational format and management style. "The machine," Cochran wrote, "as an instrument of competition, tended always to become the mother of monopoly."

In the context of the nail industry, technology was neither the "mother of monopoly" nor a minor contributing factor to the organizational and management formats. It functioned complementarily with the market, and together the two created a set of conditions that always influenced and, at certain times, forcefully directed changes in both management and organizational structures. Clearly, the combination of extensive demand and high-output technology were responsible early in the century for the factory and a management system that relied heavily upon the mechanic and craftsman. Likewise, the changing demand--production patterns of mid-century --called forth the integrated structure and professional manager in the 1870s and 1880s.

But, as allusions to factories outside of Wheeling suggested, the mere changes in relationship between supply capability and demand was not alone sufficient for modernization of either structural or management technique. Indeed, even an understanding that integrated structures offered advantages was not a guarantee that management techniques capable of creating or operating integrated businesses would evolve.

Rather success was contingent upon the development of operative methods for controlling cost formerly mediated by the market and the effective linkage of separate units that had been combined within the organization. At Wheeling, both of these needs were answered by a system of cost accounting that adequately replaced the market as a cost determinor and served to relate the various units. Just why the management at Wheeling developed a cost accounting system and operative forms of efficiency monitoring so early remains unclear. The heavy involvement of merchants appears to have been in part responsible, but not totally so, since the system of accounting clearly developed at the LaBelle factory, the one firm where the involvement of the merchant was least felt. If the birth of the concept was hazy, its growth was clear. It spread from firm to firm, increasing all the while in both precision and sophistication. Eventually, the central concept of quantitative cost measure that allowed efficiency ratios to guide decisions became the controlling feature from which sprang the new breed of manager, a rather definitive set of assumptions about the competition, and revised perceptions of the relationships between technological components and labor.

Actually, cost control became a central feature of the entire industry after it became apparent that the strategies to fix prices and reduce production were not workable. The firms outside Wheeling, however, chose to reduce labor costs instead of transactional costs. Particularly during the 1870s and 1880s, the nail industry illustrates the relative merits of these alternative approaches to cost containment. Although many manufacturers who chose labor cost reductions were forced into bankruptcy, the approach did succeed well enough to provide a parity with the Wheeling firms by the late 1870s and, for a brief time, to restore competitive equality. From that point forward (until the strike of 1885), the differences between the two groups of manufacturers lay more in the potential for change than the two approaches held. And it was the capability of the Wheeling mills to identify problems, organize responses, raise capital, and formulate a concerted course of action that made them relatively more successful.

The emphasis on cost was not unique to the nail industry, if the remarks of such prominent industrialists as Carnegie and Rockfeller are taken at face value. Indeed, concern for cost control appears to have become increasingly widespread as the nation entered the last third of the nineteenth century. Certainly, the roles of regional and national areas were a factor for, in these larger market units, individual producers within the industries had to face competitive pressures not felt when sales were more locally concentrated. But technology also played an important role, permitting in many instances supply to approach demand as the rate of output in many industries increased.

The ways in which managers viewed costs, specifically their analysis of the components of cost, appear to have been a central feature in the rise of the multi-unit enterprise. Moreover, it was also most important for the evolution of the concept of operational efficiency. The nail industry suggested that, where management understood the characteristics of technology and where it emphasized transactional cost, modernization occurred. There is no suggestion that the approach taken by the Wheeling firms was the only, or even the most prominent, one. Indeed, the particulars certainly vary with almost every industry. Rockfeller, for example, responded to high prices in the chaotic oil supply market by horizontal integration of refining capacities and achieved both cost control and supply market regulation.

The significance of the alternative approaches to cost control found in the nail industry was apparent in two key areas of operations--labor relations and technological innovation. Initially, at least, the attention to transactional costs resulted in a more harmonious labor-management relationship. However, when transactional savings were fully realized, the favorable relations were disrupted, as management began to view the acquisition of labor as another transaction subject to the same scrutiny as that of materials. Just as management attempted to impose maximum control over the conditions relating to the purchase of pig iron in the 1860s, it asserted prerogatives over the inter- and intra-work group relationships in the 1880s, quite successfully internalizing what previously had been factors (inside contractors, worker training, pay scales, etc.) over which it had little or no control.

The parallel between supply and the labor market extends even further when the effects and results of the two attempts at management control are compared. Both involve the use of related (blast furnace and Bessemer converter), although by no means new, technologies, and both required capital increases that had an impact upon the existing structure of the industry. What was novel in the latter attempt was Wheeling's break with its long-standing emphasis of meeting competition and the emergence of a thoroughly premeditated attempt to extend management control over markets. Even here, the strategy was rooted in the desire to control labor costs modified by the belief (after 1882) that industry would write off action as the only chance of success.

The emphasis firms placed on cost, particularly capital costs, had severe implications for innovation that became clear only during the late 1880s. By relating cost to volume and distributing that cost forward, management had little reason to make major changes that would not be immediately reflected in cost reductions. The tendency was to incrementally improve the existing machines and processes rather than to experiment with or adopt completely new technologies. As a consequence, the nail manufacturers were not responsible for, nor did they adopt, the wire nail, an innovation that fully answered all of the labor cost problems that the firms faced during the mid-1880s.

Moreover, that the cut nail manufacturers were taken quite by surprise when the wire nail appeared and spread so rapidly indicates how narrowly focused their management system had become. In the fine tuning and honing of the quantitative indicators, the nail makers had created such a specialized system that a competitive product manufactured literally within their own backyard could not be taken into account until it had nosed aside the cut nail.

In the end, then, the management system was flawed. It took no account of the possibility of technological obsolescence and had no means of gauging the impact of any product or process other than that of the cut nail. During the early years of the twentieth century, when the cut nail was little more than a memory in Wheeling, those who had spent their youths in the mills frequently puzzled over the catastrophic events of the 80s, searching for some explanation as to why the Wheeling mills were so completely unprepared. Henry Scott, in particular, raised the question, and curiously enough in the proces resurrected the reputation of those men, such as the Norton brothers and Stephens, who had been forced aside and publicly criticized by the new management of the 1870s. The implication, buried deep within Scott's analysis, was that Norton and Stevenson would have envisioned the wire nail earlier and compensated more effectively.

Although speculative, Scott's feeling was probably correct, for the mechanics who established the industry were keenly concerned with the technology and with the product. Those who replaced them viewed both as a means to a more important end--long-term profits. The concept of industrial research, except as it related to specific cost problems, was never developed, in the context of either product improvement or unrelated innovation. Failure to recognize the need for, and the long-term profitability of, industrial research was the missing component in a management philosophy that was otherwise remarkably successful.

Bibliography

Primary Sources

Manuscripts

Belmont Nail Company. Minutes of the Stockholders' and Directors' Meetings July 11, 1879-January 28, 1880. Manuscript in the possession of the Wheeling-Pittsburgh Steel Corporation, Wheeling, West Virginia.

Benwood Iron Works. Minutes of the Stockholders' and Directors' Meetings from June 29, 1864-January 21, 1880. Manuscript in the possession of the Wheeling-Pittsburgh Steel Corporation, Wheeling, West Virginia.

_________. Minute Books, January 27, 1880-August 4, 1892. Manuscript in the possession of the Wheeling-Pittsburgh Steel Corporation, Wheeling, West Virginia.

Boonton, New Jersey. Products of Industry in the Township of Boonton, in the County of Morris, State of New Jersey (1860-1870). Manuscript in the collections of the New Jersey Historical Society.

Burden Iron Company. The Burden Iron Company Papers, 1860-1900. Manuscript in the possession of the New York Historical Society.

Johnston, John. Account Book of Gen. John Johnston, Indian Agent, Ft. Wayne, Indiana, 1802-1811. Manuscript copy. Library of the Ohio Historical Society, Columbus, Ohio.

LaBelle Iron Works. Minutes of the Meetings of the Board of Directors and Stockholders of the LaBelle Iron Works (Bailey, Woodward & Company) from January 28, 1868-September 20, 1893. Manuscript in the possession of the Wheeling-Pittsburgh Steel Corporation, Wheeling, West Virginia.

Litle, John. Accounts of Smiths and Nailers Work Received from January 19, 1778-October 1, 1779. Manuscript in the library of The American Philosophical Society, Philadelphia.

Papers of Thomas Worthington. "Bills for Repairs on House." Manuscript in the collections of the Ohio Historical Society, Columbus, Ohio.

Parker Mills. Parker Mills Journal, 1878-1886. Volume A-4. Manuscript in the collections of The Baker Library of Harvard University.

Tremont Nail Company. Records of the Tremont Nail Company. Manuscript in the collections of The Baker Library of Harvard University.

Trustees' Sale of Valuable Ironworks, Mineral Lands, and etc. Broadside in the collections of the West Virginia Historical Society, Charleston, West Virginia.

Wheeling Iron and Nail Company. Minutes of the Stockholders' and Directors' Meetings from July 15, 1869-July 22, 1892. Manuscript in the possession of the Wheeling-Pittsburgh Steel Corporation, Wheeling, West Virginia.

Government Documents

Annual Report of the Secretary of State to the Governor of the State of Ohio for the Year 1872. Columbus, 1873.

Hoadly, Charles J. (ed.). The Public Records of the Colony of Connecticut from May 1717 to October 1725. Hartford, 1872.

U.S. Army, Watertown Arsenal. Report of the Tests of Metals and Other Materials for Industrial Purposes Made with the United States Testing Machine at Watertown Arsenal, Massachusetts. Washington, 1886.

U.S. Census Bureau. Manufacturers of the United States in 1860 Compiled from the Original Returns of the Eighth Census. Washington, 1865.

________. Report of the Statistics of Wages in the Manufacturing Industries. Washington, 1886.

________. Twelfth Census of the United States Taken in the Year 1900. Vol. VII, pt. 1. Washington, 1902.

U.S. Census Office. Digest of Accounts of Manufacturing Establishments in the United States in 1823. Washington, 1823.

U.S. Commissioner of Patents. A List of Patents Granted by the United States from April 10, 1790 to December 31, 1836. Washington, 1872.

________. Report for 1856. Vol. I. Washington, 1857.

U.S. Treasury Department, Bureau of Statistics. Statistical Abstract of the United States, 1878. Washington, 1879.

Walker, Francis A. The Statistics of the Wealth and Industry of the United States from the Original Returns of the Ninth Census. Vol. III. Washington, 1872.

Serials

American Iron and Steel Association. Directory of the Iron and Steel Works of the United States. Philadelphia, 1880, 1882, 1901.

________. Statistics of the American and Foreign Iron Trades for 1899. Philadelphia, 1900.

DeBow's Commercial Review of the South and West, Vols. V and XVII.

Hunt's Merchant Magazine, Vols. I-XXIII.

The Iron Age, 1872-1890.

Scientific American Supplement, Vol. I, pp. 89-90.
The Steubenville Daily Herald, 1880-1886.
The Wheeling Intelligencer, 1852-1918.

Other

Abridgments of the Debates of Congress from 1789 to 1856, Vol. I. New York, 1857.
Bishop, J. Leander. A History of American Manufacturers from 1608 to 1860. 3 vols. Philadelphia, 1864.
Coxe, Tench. A Statement of the Arts and Manufactures of the United States of American for the Year 1810. Philadelphia, 1814.
French, B. F. History of the Rise and Progress of the Iron Trade of the United States from 1621 to 1857. New York, 1858.
Greeley, Horace, et al. The Great Industries of the United States. Hartford, Conn., 1872.
History of the Upper Ohio Valley. Madison, Wisc., 1890.
Overman, Frederick. A Treatise on Metallurgy. New York, 1873.
Plummer, Robert L. (ed.). Sixty-Five Years of Iron and Steel in Wheeling: Reminiscences of Alexander Glass. n.p., n.d.
Reeves, James E. The Physical and Medical Topography of the City of Wheeling. Wheeling, W. Va., 1872.
Scott, Henry Dickerson. Iron and Steel in Wheeling. Toledo, Ohio, 1929.
Smith, J. Bucknall. A Treatise upon Wire, Its Manufacture and Uses. New York, 1891.
Swank, James M. History of the Manufacture of Iron in All Ages and Particularly in the United States from Colonial Times to 1891. Philadelphia, 1892.
Taylor, Oliver I. Directory of Wheeling. Wheeling, Va., 1851.
Thwaites, Reuben Gold (ed.). Early Western Travels, 1748-1846, Vols. X and XI. Cleveland, 1907.

Secondary Sources

Abernathy, William J., and James M. Utterback. "Patterns of Industrial Innovation." Technology Review (June/July 1978), pp. 42-49.
Becker, William H. "American Wholesale Hardware Trade Associations, 1870-1900." Business History Review (Summer 1971), pp. 179-199.
Berry, Thomas S. Western Prices Before 1861. Cambridge, Mass., 1943.
Bolles, Albert S. Industrial History of the United States. Norwich, Conn., 1881.
Bond, Beverley W., Jr. The Foundations of Ohio. Columbus, Ohio, 1941.
Boorstin, Daniel J. The Americans: The National Experience. New York, 1966.

Bradlee, Francis B. C. "The Salem Iron Factory." Historical Collections of the Essex Institute (April 1918), pp. 103-107.

Brief, Richard P. "The Origin and Evolution of Nineteenth-Century Asset Accounting." Business History Review (Spring 1966), pp. 1-24.

Buggey, Susan. "Supplying Building Materials to the British Army in the Colonies: An Illustrated Document." The Association for Preservation Technology Bulletin VIII (1976), pp. 89-118.

Chandler, Alfred D., et al. The Changing Economic Order. New York, 1968.

________. The Visible Hand: The Managerial Revolution in American Business. Cambridge, Mass., 1977.

Chatfield, Michael. A History of Accounting Thought. Hinsdale, Ill., 1974.

Chatfield, Michael (ed.). Contemporary Studies in the Evolution of Accounting Thought. Belmont, Calif., 1968.

Clark, Victor S. History of Manufacturers in the United States 1607-1860. 2 vols. New York, 1949.

Cooke, Lawrence S. "Nail Rod and Some of Its By-Products." The Chronicle of the Early American Industries Association, (March 1961), pp. 6-7.

Crofut, Florence S. March. Guide to the History and Historic Sites of Connecticut. 2 vols. New Haven, Conn., 1937.

East, Robert A. Business Enterprise in the American Revolutionary Era. New York, 1938.

Epstein, Marc Jay. The Effect of Scientific Management on the Development of Standard Cost Systems. New York, 1978.

Everhart, J. F. History of Muskingum County, Ohio. Columbus, Ohio, 1882.

Ferguson, Eugene S. (ed.). "Early Engineering Reminiscences (1815-1840) of George Escol Sellers." United States National Museum Bulletin, 238, p. 125.

Field, Walker. "A Reexamination into the Invention of the Balloon Frame." Journal of the American Society of Architectural Historians II (1942), pp. 7-8.

Garner, Paul S. Evolution of Cost Accounting to 1925. No. 1., 1976.

Garner, Paul S., and Marilynn Hughes (eds.). Readings on Accounting Development. New York, 1978.

Giedion, Sigfried. Space, Time and Architecture: The Growth of a New Tradition. Cambridge, Mass., 1949.

Habakkuk, H. J. American and British Technology in the Nineteenth Century. Cambridge, Mass., 1962.

Hawkins, David F. "The Development of Modern Financial Reporting Practices among American Manufacturing Corporations." Business History Review (Spring/Summer 1963), pp. 135-168.

Hunter, Louis C. "Financial Problems of the Early Pittsburgh Iron Manufacturers." Journal of Economic and Business History II, pp. 521-523.

________. "Influence of the Market upon Technique in the Iron Industry of Western Pennsylvania up to 1860." Journal of Economic and Business History I (1928-1929), p. 245.

Hunter, W. H. "The Pathfinders of Jefferson County." The Ohio Archaeological and Historical Publication VI (1898), pp. 210-249.

Ingham, John N. The Iron Barons: A Social Analysis of an American Elite, 1874-1965. Westport, Conn., 1978.

Johnson, H. Thomas. "Early Cost Accounting for Internal Management Control: Lyman Mills in the 1850's." Business History Review (Winter 1972), p. 465.

________. "Management in an Early Integrated Industrial: E. I. duPont de Nemours Powder Company, 1903-1912." Business History Review (Summer 1975), pp. 187-196.

Kasson, John F. Civilizing the Machine, Technology and Republican Values in America 1776-1900. New York, 1976.

Kellar, Herbert Anthony (ed.). Solon Robinson: Pioneer and Agriculturist, Selected Writings I. Indianapolis, Ind., 1936.

Kindl, F. H. The Rolling Mill Industry. Cleveland, Ohio, 1913.

Kingsburg, Susan M. (ed.). The Records of The London Company of Virginia IV. Washington, 1936.

Lippincott, Isaac. A History of Manufacturers in the Ohio Valley to the Year 1860. New York, 1914.

Litterer, Joseph A. "Systematic Management: Design for Organizational Recoupling in American Manufacturing Firms." Business History Review (Spring/Summer 1963), pp. 369-391.

Littleton, A. C. Accounting Evolution to 1900. New York, 1933.

Livesay, Harold C. Andrew Carnegie and the Rise of Big Business. New York, 1975.

McFadden, Joseph M. "Monopoly in Barbed Wire: The Formation of the American Steel and Wire Company." Business History Review (Winter 1978), pp. 446-517.

McIlvaine, Mabel (ed.). Reminiscences of Chicago during the Forties and Fifties. Chicago, 1913.

Manning, Thomas G. (ed.). The Standard Oil Company, the Rise of a National Monopoly. New York, 1960.

May, Earl Chapin. Principio to Wheeling 1715-1945. New York, 1945.

Mercer, Henry C. Ancient Carpenters' Tools. Doylestown, Pa., 1929.

________. "Dating Old Houses." Old Time New England, (April 1924), pp. 171-195.

Michael, Ronald L. "Cut Nail Manufacture: Southwestern Pennsylvania." The Association for Preservation Technology Bulletin VI (1974), pp. 99-108.

"Nail Headers." The Chronicle of The Early American Industries Association (November 1965), p. 36.

National Cyclopaedia of American Biography XV. New York, 1916.

Nelson, Lee H. "A Nail Chronology." Technical Leaflet #48. Nashville, Tenn., 1968.

North, Douglass C. Growth and Welfare in the American Past. Englewood Cliffs, N.J., 1966.

Pettingell, Charles I. "Powow River Industries." The Essex Institute Historical Collections LXXXII (1946), pp. 322-338.

Porter, Glenn. The Rise of Big Business 1860-1910. Arlington Heights, Ill., 1973.

Pratt, Harry E. "Chicago in 1833 and 1834." Journal of the Illinois State Historical Society XXVIII (1935), pp. 10-11.

Priess, Peter. "Wire Nails in North America." The Association for Preservation Technology Bulletin V (1973), pp. 87-92.

Scamehorn, H. Lee. Pioneer Steelmakers in the West: The Colorado Fuel and Iron Company 1872-1903. Boulder, Colo., 1976.

Social Science Research Council, Committee on Historical Statistics. The Statistical History of the United States from Colonial Times to the Present. Stamford, Conn., 1965.

Solomons, David. Studies in Cost Analysis. Homewood, Ill., 1968.

Sutherland, Tucker. Ohio Almanac. Lorain, Ohio, 1967.

Taussig, F. W. The Tariff History of the United States. New York, 1923.

Taylor, George R. The Transportation Revolution 1815-1860. New York, 1968.

Temin, Peter. Iron and Steel in 19th Century America. Cambridge, Mass., 1964.

Uselding, Paul J. "Henry Burden and the Question of Anglo-American Technological Transfer in the Nineteenth Century." The Journal of Economic History XXX, pp. 312-337.

Utter, William T. The Frontier State. Columbus, Ohio, 1942.

Wade, Richard C. The Urban Frontier: Pioneer Life in Early Pittsburgh, Cincinnati, Lexington, Louisville, and St. Louis. Chicago, 1964.

Weisenburger, Frances P. The Passing Frontier 1825-1850. Columbus, Ohio, 1941.

Weslager, C. A. The Log Cabin in America. New Brunswick, N.J., 1969.

Williamson, Oliver E. Markets and Hierarchies: Analysis and Antitrust Implications. London, 1975.

Wilson, Kenneth M. "Nailers' Anvils at Old Sturbridge Village." The Chronicle of The Early American Industries Association (June 1960), p. 1.

Wingerter, Charles A. Greater Wheeling and Vicinity. Chicago, 1912.

Index

ABOUT THE AUTHOR

AMOS J. LOVEDAY JR. is Chief Curator of the Ohio Historical Society. He has published articles on the cut nail industry in the _Proceedings_ of the Business History Conference and the _Upper Ohio Valley Historical Review_.

9 780313 239182

Printed by Libri Plureos GmbH in Hamburg,
Germany